NATO

GARLAND REFERENCE LIBRARY
OF SOCIAL SCIENCE
VOL. 92

NATO
A Bibliography and Resource Guide

Augustus Richard Norton
Robert A. Friedlander
Martin H. Greenberg
Donald S. Rowe

GARLAND PUBLISHING, INC. • NEW YORK & LONDON
1985

© 1985 Augustus Richard Norton, Robert A. Friedlander,
Martin H. Greenberg, and Donald S. Rowe
All rights reserved

Library of Congress Cataloging in Publication Data
Main entry under title:

NATO, a bibliography and resource guide.

(Garland reference library of social science ;
v. 92)
   Includes index.
   1. North Atlantic Treaty Organization—Indexes.
I. Norton, Augustus R. II. Title: N.A.T.O., a
bibliography and resource guide. III. Series.
UA646.3.N224 1985   355'.031'091821   80-9038
ISBN 0-8240-9331-3 (alk. paper)

Printed on acid-free, 250-year-life paper
Manufactured in the United States of America

For Sally

CONTENTS

Foreword ix

Preface xi

Bibliography and Resource Guide

General Section
    1945–1949   3
    1950–1954   4
    1955–1959   8
    1960–1964   13
    1965–1969   23
    1970–1974   38
    1975–1979   60
    1980–1981   69

Member States
    Belgium   75
    Canada   75
    Denmark   79
    France   80
    Great Britain   87
    Greece   93
    Iceland   94
    Italy   96
    Netherlands   97
    Norway   98
    Portugal   99
    Spain   100
    Turkey   100
    West Germany   102

Issues in NATO
  Berlin   113
  Economics and Scientific Cooperation   115
  SALT   124
  General Disarmament and Force Reductions   128
  National Nuclear Strike Forces and Nuclear Spread in
     NATO   135

Doctrines, Strategies and Military Issues
  Military Doctrine   141
  Military Technologies   155
  Structure of the Alliance   164
     Air   172
     Land   175
     Sea   177
  Nuclear Tactics, Strategy and Doctrine   180

Alliance Politics
  Alliances in World Politics   193
  International Relations of NATO   194

Warsaw Pact
  General   201
  Military   217
  Nuclear   223

Index   227

FOREWORD

As a formal organization, NATO has existed for more than thirty years. Its continued existence and vitality are essential to the freedom and security of the great western democracies. However, momentous political, economic, and military changes have occurred in the past thirty years that affect both the missions and the viability of the organization.

An enormous literature on NATO and its functions has been generated during this period of time. It is no longer feasible for those writing on the topic of NATO to make an independent search of the literature. The present bibliography, therefore, will be of invaluable assistance to scholars, journalists, editorial writers, strategists, military historians, and students.

The editors have been diligent and industrious. As they point out, the categories they use necessarily overlap and some articles or books do not fall neatly into any particular category. Despite this, the topical organization of the bibliography will be of considerable assistance to the researcher. Every research library will require a copy of this bibliography and many individual scholars will find it an invaluable adjunct to their own library.

Morton A. Kaplan

PREFACE

More than three decades after the signing of the North Atlantic Treaty, NATO continues to provide the foundation for the western security system. However, the alliance's tenure has hardly been marked by tranquillity. Crises, both internal and external, have caused dissension, dissatisfaction, and even doubts as to the validity of NATO in a rapidly changing world.

Two members, France and Greece, have at different times withdrawn from NATO's Military Command as a result of keen disagreements concerning the proper role of the alliance. Yet, NATO has proven to be a remarkably resilient structure, frequently confounding pessimistic prognosticators. The organization has weathered the storms of numerous international crises, including: Hungary and Suez, 1956; Czechoslovakia, 1968; the 1973 October War and the subsequent oil embargoes and shortages; and, the Falklands crisis. While the divergent perspectives and interests of its member-states have often produced sharp disagreements concerning NATO's proper response to external crises, the alliance remains intact.

Thus, the study of NATO is not a mere exercise in diplomatic history. It is instead an exciting exploration of contending conceptions of states' interest, of great debates over the proper role of weapons of mass destruction in NATO war plans and competing perspectives on the appropriate character of member-states' relationships with the Soviet Union and its allies.

Given the rich and varied history of NATO, it is hardly surprising to find that the alliance has been the subject of literally thousands of articles and hundreds of books. Although the need for a comprehensive and up-to-date bibliography and resource guide is clear, we faced a number of decisions regarding the organization of the book, as well as establishing the criteria for inclusion and exclusion of materials. The latter matter proved easier to resolve than the former one. While our intent is to provide a comprehensive bibliography—useful for student and established scholar alike—we decided that absolute comprehensiveness would result in a book unwieldy in both size and price. Accordingly, we decided that we would serve our readers best by excluding *nearly all* references to popular magazines and newspapers. Not only are such materials readily accessible through standard library indexes but their perishability tends to be high. We believe that most users of this volume will agree that we made the right decision.

As to the organization of the book, after a very lengthy consideration we developed what we hope is a useful and efficient schema. As veteran bibliography compilers, we knew that categories usually suggest themselves over time based on such criteria as the number of references in a given topical area, the clarity of definition provided by a given category, and the long-term relevance of the categories. While we concede that there are other perfectly logical schemes by which our book might have been organized, we are confident that most users will accept our organization as the most beneficial approach.

Since many of the references are general in scope, or at least transcend several categories, the first section of the book is devoted to general entries. To facilitate the use of this section, the reader will find the entries segregated in chronological segments. None of the subsequent sections were long enough to justify this form of presentation.

The "Member-States" section is straightforward, presenting materials that treat a single state's participation in NATO. However, when seeking citations referring to a given state's role in an issue area, the user is advised to check both the Member-States section and the appropriate "Issues in NATO" subsection (e.g., Disarmament and Force Reductions). In other words, it is inevitable that there will be overlap between some sets of categories. We believe that a perusal of the table of contents will insure the most efficient use of this research guide.

While this book does not focus primarily either on alliances in general or the Warsaw Treaty Organization, we felt that the inclusion of materials on "Alliance Politics" and the "Warsaw Pact" would be helpful. We do not, however, make the same claim for comprehensiveness in respect to these final two sections as we make for the earlier ones.

We have a number of people to thank for their assistance and support during the five years that this book was in preparation. Helen Cox and Victoria H. Lilos provided able assistance. Skillful research help was provided by Brian Buckley, David Samuels, Robert Stewart and Kirk Warren. A very special note of thanks to our very competent typist,

Audrey Hanson, who suffered through corrections, additions, deletions, and changes with good humor and extraordinary efficiency. Audrey Hanson also prepared the index. We would also like to thank John Fairlamb for his assistance in identifying citations for Iceland and Nordic security. A warm note of gratitude must be added for Dr. Morton Kaplan of the University of Chicago, whose fertile mind and distinguished scholarship have been a constant source of inspiration and stimulation. Finally, we would like to thank our families who cheerfully survived the boxes of file cards and sundry other inconveniences that sometimes made this project seem more than a bit tedious.

NATO

GENERAL

1945-1949

Armstrong, Hamilton Fish. "Regional Pacts: Strong Points or Storm Cellars?" *Foreign Affairs* 27 (April 1949): 351-368.

Baldwin, Hanson W. "The Myth of Security." *Foreign Affairs* 26 (January 1948): 253-263.

Beloff, Max. "No Peace, No War." *Foreign Affairs* 27 (January 1949): 215-231.

Blackette, Patrick M. *Fear, War and the Bomb.* New York: Whittlesey House, 1949.

――――. *Studies of War: Nuclear and Conventional.* Westport, CT: Greenwood Press, reprint of 1962 edition, 1978.

Boyd, Andrew and Metson, William. *Atlantic Pact, Commonwealth and United Nations.* London: Hutchinson, 1949.

Bundy, McGeorge. "The Test of Yalta." *Foreign Affairs* 27 (July 1949): 618-629.

Butler, Sir Harold. "A New World Takes Shape." *Foreign Affairs* 26 (July 1948): 604-615.

Byrnes, James Francis. *Speaking Frankly.* Westport, CT: Greenwood Press, reprint of 1947 edition, 1974.

Challener, Richard D., ed. *The Vandenberg Resolution and the North Atlantic Treaty (May, June 1948; February, March, April and June 1949).* New York: Garland Publishing, Inc., 1979.

Dean, Vera M. *Europe and the United States.* Westport, CT: Greenwood Press, reprint of 1950 edition, 1976.

――――. *The United States and Russia.* Westport, CT: Greenwood Press, reprint of 1948 edition, 1972.

Eliot, George Fielding. *If Russia Strikes.* Indianapolis, IN: Bobbs-Merrill, 1949.

Hoskins, Halford L. *The Atlantic Pact.* Washington, D.C.: Public Affairs Press, 1949.

Ireland, Timothy P. *Creating the Entangling Alliance: The Origins of the North Atlantic Treaty Organization.* Westport, CT: Greenwood Press, 1981.

Kaplan, Lawrence S. for the United States Department of Defense, Office of the Secretary of Defense, Historical Office. *A Community of Interests: NATO and the Military Assistance Program, 1948-1951.* Washington, D.C.: Government Printing Office, 1980.

Kirk, Grayson. "The Atlantic Pact and International Security." *International Organisation* 3 (May 1949): 239-253.

Lippmann, Walter. *The Cold War: A Study in U.S. Foreign Policy.* New York: Harper, 1947.

Mason, Edwards. "American Security and Access to Raw Materials." *World Politics* 1 (1948-49): 147-160.

Murray, John Middleton. *The Free Society.* London: Dakers, 1948.

Vagts, Alfred. "The Balance of Power: Growth of an Idea." *World Politics* 1 (October 1948): 82-101.

Ward, Barbara. *The West at Bay.* New York: Norton, 1948.

White, Gilbert F. *The United States and the Soviet Union: Some Quaker Proposals for Peace.* New Haven: Yale University Press, 1949.

X. "The Sources of Soviet Conduct." *Foreign Affairs* 25 (July 1947): 566-582.

1950-1954

Armstrong, Hamilton Fish. "Eisenhower's Right Flank." *Foreign Affairs* 29 (July 1951): 651-663.

———. "The World Is Round." *Foreign Affairs* 31 (January 1953): 175-199.

———. "The Grand Alliance Hesitates." *Foreign Affairs* 32 (October 1953): 48-67.

———. "Postscript to E.D.C." *Foreign Affairs* 33 (October 1954): 17-27.

Aron, Raymond. *The Century of Total War.* Garden City, NY: Doubleday, 1954.

Baldwin, Hanson W. *Power and Politics: The Face of Security in an Atomic Age.* Claremont, CA: Castle Press, 1950.

———. "Strategy for Two Atomic Worlds." *Foreign Affairs* 28 (April 1950): 386-397.

Beckett, (Sir) Eric W. *The North Atlantic Treaty; The Brussels Treaty and the Charter of the United Nations.* London: Stevens, 1950.

Bernard, S. "Choice in the West." *World Politics* 5 (January 1953): 133-167.

Bundy, McGeorge, ed. *The Pattern of Responsibility; Policy Statements of Dean Acheson.* Fairfield, NJ: Kelley, reprint of 1952 edition, 1975.

Carleton, William Graves. *The Revolution in American Foreign Policy, 1945-1954.* New York: Doubleday, 1954.

Dean, Vera Micheles. *Europe and the United States.* New York: Knopf, 1950.

Defense in the Cold War: The Task for the Free World. London and New York: Royal Institute of International Affairs, 1950.

Dennett, Raymond. "Danger Spots in the Pattern of American Security." *World Politics* 4 (July 1952): 447-467.

Dulles, John Foster. "Policy for Security and Peace." *Foreign Affairs* 32 (April 1954): 353-364.

Earle, Edward Mead. "The American Stake in Europe: Retrospect and Prospect." *International Affairs* 27 (October 1951): 423-433.

East, W. Gordon. "The Mediterranean: Pivot of Peace and War." *Foreign Affairs* 31 (July 1953): 619-633.

Finletter, Thomas K. *Power and Policy: U.S. Foreign Policy and Military Power in the Hydrogen Age.* Westport, CT: Greenwood Press, reprint of 1954 edition, 1974.

Freedman, Max. "The Lisbon Conference." *International Journal* 7 (Spring 1952): 85-93.

Gaitskell, Hugh. "The Search for Anglo-American Policy." *Foreign Affairs* 32 (July 1954): 563-576.

Geiger, Theodore and Cleveland, H. van B. *Making Western Europe Defensible.* Washington, D.C.: National Planning Association, 1951.

Haas, Ernst B. "The Balance of Power: Prescription, Concept or Propaganda." *World Politics* 5 (July 1953): 442-447.

Harrod, Roy. "Hands and Fists Across the Sea." *Foreign Affairs* 30 (October 1951): 63-76.

Hayter, Sir William. "The Meaning of Co-Existence." *Survey* 50 (January 1954): 17-22.

Holborn, Hago. "American Foreign Policy and European Integration." *World Politics* III (October 1953): 1-30.

Ismay, Lord. "Atlantic Alliance." *International Journal* 9 (Spring 1954): 79-86.

———. *NATO--The First Five Years*. Paris: NATO, 1954.

Jones, Stephen B. "The Power Inventory and National Strategy." *World Politics* 6 (July 1954): 421-452.

Kaplan, Lawrence S. "NATO and Its Commentators: The First Five Years." *International Organisation* 8 (November 1954): 447-467.

Kaysen, Carl. "The Vulnerability of the United States to Enemy Attack." *World Politics* 6 (January 1954): 190-208.

Kennan, George F. "America and the Russian Future." *Foreign Affairs* 29 (April 1951): 351-370.

———. *Realities of American Foreign Policy*. Princeton, NJ: Princeton University Press, 1954.

Kruls, (General) H.J. "The Defense of Europe." *Foreign Affairs* 30 (January 1952): 265-276.

Liddell Hart, B.H. *Defense of the West*. New York: Morrow, 1950.

Makins, Sir Roger. "The World Since the War: The Third Phase." *Foreign Affairs* 33 (October 1954): 1-16.

Marshall, Charles Burton. *The Limits of American Foreign Policy*. New York: Henry Holt & Co., 1954.

Mayo, H.B. "The Western Alliance--Ideological or Defensive?" *International Journal* 9 (Spring 1954): 87-95.

McLachlan, Donald, ed. *Defense in the Cold War*. New York: Royal Institute for International Affairs, 1950.

Middleton, Drew. "NATO Changes Direction." *Foreign Affairs* 31 (April 1953): 427-440.

Millis, Walter and Duffield, E.S., eds. *The Forrestal Diaries*. New York: Viking, 1951.

Morgenthau, Hans J. *In Defense of the National Interest.* New York: Knopf, 1951.

Moyse, Robert. "No Star for the Wise Men: Some Fiscal Problems of NATO Countries." *International Journal* 7 (Winter 1951-52): 1-11.

Munro, Dana G. "The First Years of the Cold War." *World Politics* 4 (July 1952): 536-547.

NATO and the Peoples. London: British Society for International Understanding, 1952.

Osgood, Robert E. *Ideals and Self-Interest in America's Foreign Relations.* Chicago, IL: University of Chicago Press, 1953.

Reynaud, Paul. *Unite or Perish: A Dynamic Program for a United Europe.* New York: Simon and Schuster, 1951.

Roskill, S.W. *The War at Sea.* London: Her Majesty's Stationery Office, 1954.

Royal Institute of International Affairs and Chatham House Study Group. *Atlantic Alliance: NATO's Role in the Free World.* Westport, CT: Greenwood Press, reprint of 1952 edition, 1979.

Sandwell, B.K. "North Atlantic--Community or Treaty?" *International Journal* 7 (Summer 1952): 169-172.

Sapin, Burton M. and Snyder, Richard C. *The Role of the Military in American Foreign Policy.* New York: Doubleday, 1954.

Smith, Walter Bedell. *My Three Years in Moscow.* Philadelphia, PA: Lippincott, 1950.

Spofford, Charles M. "Toward Atlantic Security." *International Affairs* 27 (October 1951): 434-439.

---. "NATO's Growing Pains." *Foreign Affairs* 31 (October 1952): 95-105.

Stevenson, Adlai Ewing. *Call to Greatness.* London: Rupert Hart-Davis, 1954.

Turner, Arthur C. *Bulwark of the West: Implications and Problems of NATO.* Toronto, Canada: The Ryerson Press for C.I.I.A., 1953.

United States Department of State, Bureau of Public Affairs, Office of the Historian. *Foreign Relations of the United States, 1951, V. 3, European Security and the German Question.* Washington, D.C.: U.S. Government Printing Office, 1981.

Vandenberg, Arthur H., Jr., and Morris, Joe A. *The Private Papers of Senator Vandenberg*. Westport, CT: Greenwood Press, reprint of 1952 edition, 1975.

Ward, Barbara. *Policy for the West*. New York: Norton, 1951.

Warne, (Wing-Comm.) J.D. *Nato and Its Prospects*. New York: Praeger, 1954.

Williams, John H. "The Marshall Plan Halfway." *Foreign Affairs* 28 (April 1950): 463-476.

———. "End of the Marshall Plan." *Foreign Affairs* 30 (July 1952): 593-611.

Wright, Quincy. "American Policy Towards Russia." *World Politics* 2 (July 1950): 463-481.

1955-1959

Acheson, Dean. "The Illusion of Disengagement." *Foreign Affairs* 36 (April 1958): 371-382.

———. *Power and Diplomacy*. London: Oxford University Press, 1958.

———. "The Premises of American Policy." *Orbis* 3 (Fall 1959): 269-281.

Ball, M. Margaret. *NATO and the European Union Movement*. (Library of World Affairs, London, Institute of World Affairs). Westport, CT: Greenwood Press, reprint of 1959 ed.

Barkway, Michael. "Canada's Changing Role in NATO Defense." *International Journal* 14 (Spring, 1959): 99-110.

Beal, John Robinson. *John Foster Dulles: Eighteen Eighty-eight to Nineteen Fifty-nine*. Westport, CT: Greenwood Press, reprint of 1959 ed., 1974.

Bieri, Ernst. "An Atlantic Dialogue in Bruges." *Orbis* 1 (Winter 1958): 397-407.

Blackett, P.M.S. *Atomic Weapons and East-West Relations*. Cambridge, MA: Cambridge University Press, 1956.

Brown, George W. "The 'Atlantic Alliance' in Perspective." *International Journal* 12 (Spring 1957): 79-82.

Buchan, Alastair. *NATO Today*. Toronto: Canadian Institute of International Affairs, 1959.

Carleton, William G. "Brain-Trusters of American Foreign Policy." *World Politics* 7 (July 1955): 617-639.

Catlin, George. *The Atlantic Community.* London: Coram Publishers Ltd., 1959.

Challener, Richard D. "The Military and the Conduct of Foreign Policy." *World Politics* 9 (July 1957): 610-622.

Chamberlin, Waldo. "The North Atlantic Bloc in the U.N. General Assembly." *Orbis* 1 (Winter 1958): 459-473.

Crowther, Geoffrey. "Reconstruction of an Alliance." *Foreign Affairs* 35 (January 1957): 173-183.

Deutsch, Karl Wolfgang. *Political Community and the North Atlantic Area.* Princeton, NJ: Princeton University Press, 1957.

Donovan, Robert J. *Eisenhower: The Inside Story.* New York: Harper, 1956.

Dulles, John Foster. "Challenge and Response in United States Policy." *Foreign Affairs* 36 (October 1957): 25-43.

Eppstein, John. *NATO: Past, Present and Future.* London: British Society for International Understanding, 1959.

Farran, Charles d'Oliver. *Atlantic Democracy: A Comparison of the NATO Member States.* New York: Praeger, 1957.

Fosdick, Dorothy. *Common Sense and World Affairs.* New York: Harcourt, 1955.

Foster, William C. "Toward a Balanced Defense." *Orbis* 3 (Spring 1959): 26-37.

Friedmann, Wolfgang. "New Tasks for NATO?" *International Journal* 11 (Summer 1956): 157-164.

———. "Meeting of East and West?" *International Journal* 14 (Autumn 1959): 235-243.

Furniss, Edgar S., ed. *American Military Policy.* New York: Rinehart, 1957.

Gaitskell, Hugh. *The Challenge of Co-Existence.* Cambridge, Mass.: Harvard University Press; London: Methuen, 1957.

———. "Disengagement: Why? How?" *Foreign Affairs* 36 (July 1958): 539-556.

Goldman, Eric F. *The Crucial Decade and After: America, 1945-1960.* New York: Vintage Books, 1960.

Gordon, Lincoln. "NATO and European Integration." *World Politics* 10 (January 1958): 219-231.

———. "NATO in the Nuclear Age." *Survival* 1 (May/June 1959): 35-41.

Grosser, Alfred. "Suez, Hungary and European Integration." *International Organisation* 11 (Summer 1957): 470-480.

Haas, Ernst B. "Regionalism, Functionalism, and Universal International Organization." *World Politics* 8 (January 1956): 238-263.

———. "Persistent Themes in Atlantic and European Unity." *World Politics* 10 (July 1958): 614-628.

Halle, Louis J. *Civilization and Foreign Policy: An Inquiry for Americans.* New York: Harper, 1955.

Haviland, H. Field, Jr. *The United States and the Western Community.* Haverford, PA: Haverford College Press, 1957.

Healey, Denis. "'When Shrimps Learn to Whistle'--Thoughts After Geneva." *International Affairs* 32 (January 1956): 1-10.

Hinterhoff, Eugene. *Disengagement.* London: Stevens and Sons, Ltd., 1959.

Hoag, Malcolm W. "NATO: Deterrent or Shield?" *Foreign Affairs* 36 (January 1958): 278-292.

Howard, Michael. "Disengagement and Western Security." *International Affairs* 34 (October 1958): 469-476.

Ingram, Kenneth. *History of the Cold War.* New York: Philosophical Library, 1955.

Kaufmann, William W., ed. *Military Policy and National Security.* Princeton, NJ: Princeton University Press, 1956.

———. "The Crisis in Military Affairs." *World Politics* 10 (July 1958): 579-603.

Kennan, George F. "Disengagement Revisited." *Foreign Affairs* 37 (January 1959): 187-210.

Kennedy, John F. "A Democrat Looks at Foreign Policy." *Foreign Affairs* 36 (October 1957): 44-59.

Kissinger, Henry A. "Force and Diplomacy in the Nuclear Age." *Foreign Affairs* 34 (April 1956): 349-366.

———. "Strategy and Organization." *Foreign Affairs* 35 (April 1957): 279-394.

———. "The Search for Stability." *Foreign Affairs* 37 (July 1959): 537-560.

Knorr, Klaus. *Is the American Defense Effort Enough?* Princeton, N.J.: Center of International Studies, Princeton University, 1957.

———, ed. *NATO and American Security.* Princeton, NJ: Princeton University Press; London: Oxford University Press, 1959.

Kohn, Hans. "The Atlantic Community and the World." *Orbis* 1 (Winter 1958): 418-427.

———. "The Difficult Road to Western Unity." *Orbis* 3 (Fall 1959): 297-312.

Lawson, Ruth C. "Concerting Policies in the North Atlantic Community." *International Organisation* 12 (Spring 1958): 163-179.

Macdonald, H.I. "Disengagement Reconsidered." *International Journal* 14 (Winter 1958/59): 21-32.

Mayo, H.B. "Co-Existence--Is It Possible?" *International Journal* 10 (Summer 1955): 157-170.

McInnis, Edgar. *The Atlantic Triangle and the Cold War.* Toronto: University of Toronto Press for the Canadian Institute of International Affairs, 1959.

McKitterick, T.E.M. and Younger, Kenneth, eds. *Fabian International Essays.* New York: Praeger, 1957. Reprinted 1975 (Essay Index Reprint Service), Arno Press.

McLachlan, Donald and de Freitas, Geoffrey. *NATO Is Not Enough--Two Approaches to an Atlantic Assembly.* London: Friends of Atlantic Union, 1957.

McNamara, Robert S. "Spectrum of Defense." *Survival* 6 (January/February 1964): 2-8.

Moore, Ben T. *NATO and the Future of Europe.* New York: Harper & Row for The Council on Foreign Relations, 1958.

Moulin, Leo. "Anti-Americanism in Europe: A Psychoanalysis." *Orbis* 1 (Winter 1958): 448-458.

Murville, Couve de. "NATO: A French View." *International Journal* 14 (Spring 1959): 85-86.

Niemeyer, Gerhard. "The Probability of War in Our Time." *Orbis* 1 (Summer 1957): 161-183.

———. "NATO's Strength and Weakness." *Orbis* 2 (Spring 1958): 83-95.

Patterson, G. and Furniss, E.S. *NATO: A Critical Reappraisal.* Princeton, NJ: Princeton University Press, 1957.

Pearson, Lester B. "After Geneva: A Greater Task for NATO." *Foreign Affairs* 34 (October 1955): 14-23.

———. "A Measured Defense for the West." *Orbis* 1 (Winter 1958): 428-434.

———. "NATO: Retrospect and Prospects." *International Journal* 14 (Spring 1959): 79-86.

———. *Diplomacy in the Nuclear Age*. Boston, MA: Harvard University Press, 1959.

Pusey, Merlo J. *Eisenhower the President*. New York: Macmillan, 1956.

Reitzel, William; Kaplan, Morton A.; and Coblenz, Constance G. *United States Foreign Policy 1945-1955*. Washington: Brookings Institution, 1956.

Roberts, Henry L. *Russia and America: Dangers and Prospects*. New York: Harper, 1956.

Rogers, Lindsay. "Of Summits." *Foreign Affairs* 34 (October 1955): 141-147.

Salvadori, Massimo. *NATO--A Twentieth-Century Community of Nations*. Princeton, NJ: Van Nostrand Co., 1957.

Schuman, Robert. "The Atlantic Community and Europe." *Orbis* 1 (Winter 1958): 408-410.

Schutz, Wilhelm Wolfgang. "New Initiatives for a New Age: A German View." *Foreign Affairs* 36 (April 1958): 460-471.

Slessor, Sir John. "A New Look at Strategy for the West." *Orbis* 2 (Fall 1958): 320-336.

Spaak, Paul-Henri. "The West in Disarray." *Foreign Affairs* 35 (January 1957): 184-190.

———. "NATO and the Communist Challenge." *International Journal* 13 (Autumn 1958): 243-250.

———. "The Atlantic Community and NATO." *Orbis* 1 (Winter 1958): 411-417.

———. "New Tests for NATO." *Foreign Affairs* 37 (April 1959): 357-365.

———. *Why NATO?* Harmondsworth: Penguin Books, 1959.

Stanley, Timothy W. *American Defense and National Security*. Washington, D.C.: Public Affairs Press, 1956.

Stern, Frederick M. *The Citizen Army: Key to Defense in the Atomic Age*. New York: St. Martin's Press, 1957.

Strausz-Hupe, Robert. *Protracted Conflict.* New York: Praeger, 1958.

"The Military Forces We Need." *Survival* 1 (September/October 1959): 107-116.

Tolmachov, P. "Failure of the Cold War Policy." *International Affairs* (Moscow) 10 (October 1959): 19-27.

Truman, Harry S. *Year of Decisions, 1945.* Garden City, KS: Doubleday, 1955.

─────. *Years of Trial and Hope, 1946-1953.* Garden City, KS: Doubleday, 1956.

Vagts, Alfred. *Defense and Diplomacy: The Soldier and the Conduct of Foreign Relations.* New York: King's Crown Press, 1956.

von Senger und Etterlin, (Gen.) F. "NATO--Disputed Development." *Survival* 1 (May/June 1959): 44-46.

Wolfers, Arnold. "Europe and the NATO Shield." *International Organisation* 12 (Autumn 1958): 425-439.

Woodhouse, C.M. "Attitudes of NATO Countries Toward the United States." *World Politics* 10 (January 1958): 202-218.

1960-1964

Acheson, Dean. "The Practice of Partnership." *Foreign Affairs* 41 (January 1963): 247-260.

─────. *The Evolution of NATO.* (Adelphi Paper No. 5). London: International Institute for Strategic Studies, October, 1963

─────. "The Dilemmas of Our Times." *Atlantic Community Quarterly* 1 (Winter 1963-64): 570-585.

Allais, Maurice. "Preface to a Policy of Atlantic Unity, Part I." *Atlantic Community Quarterly* 2 (Fall 1964): 350-366.

─────. "Preface to a Policy of Atlantic Unity, Part II." *Atlantic Community Quarterly* 2 (Winter 1964-65): 537-556.

Allen, H.C. "The Anglo-American Relationship in the Sixties." *International Affairs* 39 (January 1963): 37-48.

Aptheker, Herbert. *American Foreign Policy and the Cold War: A Marxist-Leninist View.* New York: New Century, 1963.

Aron, Raymond. "The Great Schism: A Reconsideration." *Survey* 50 (January 1964): 3-9.

Ball, George W. "NATO and World Responsibility." *Atlantic Community Quarterly* 2 (Summer 1964): 208-217.

Beaton, Leonard. *The Western Alliance and the McNamara Doctrine*. (Adelphi Paper No. 11). London: International Institute for Strategic Studies, August 1964.

Beaufre, (Gen.) Andre. "NATO in 1962." *Survival* 4 (May/June 1962): 120-124.

───. *Major NATO Problems*. Washington, D.C.: Center for Strategic Studies, Georgetown University, February 1964.

Bell, Carol. *The Debatable Alliance*. London: Oxford University Press, 1964.

Beloff, Max. "The Atlantic Community: The Debate in America." *Survival* 4 (March/April 1962): 69-70.

───. "Britain, Europe and the Atlantic Community." *International Organisation* 17 (Summer 1963): 574-591.

───. *The United States and the Unity of Europe*. Washington: Brookings Institution, 1963. Reprinted by Greenwood Press, 1975.

Bieri, Ernst. *Basic Values of the Atlantic Community*. London: Pall Mall Press, 1962.

Birrenbach, Kurt. "Europe and America: Partners in an Atlantic Community." *Atlantic Community Quarterly* 1 (Summer 1963): 213-218.

───. *The Future of the Atlantic Community: Towards European-American Partnership*. New York: Frederick A. Praeger, 1963.

Blackett, P.M.S. *Students of War*. Edinburgh, Scotland: Oliver and Boyd, 1962.

Bowie, Robert R. "Strategy and the Atlantic Alliance." *International Organisation* 17 (Summer 1963): 709-732.

───. "Tensions Within the Alliance." *Foreign Affairs* 42 (October 1963): 49-69.

───. "Shaping the Future." *Atlantic Community Quarterly* 2 (Fall 1964): 325-349.

───. *Shaping the Future: Foreign Policy in an Age of Transition*. New York: Columbia University Press, 1964.

Brandt, Willy. *The Ordeal of Co-Existence*. Cambridge, MA: Harvard University Press, 1963.

Brentano, Heinrich von. "Goals and Means of the Western Alliance." *Foreign Affairs* 39 (April 1961): 416-429.

Brown, Neville. "A New Policy for NATO?" *The World Today* 20 (October 1964): 423-430.

Brzezinski, Zbigniew. "Threat and Opportunity in the Communist Schism." *Foreign Affairs* 41 (April 1963): 513-525.

———. "Russia and Europe." *Foreign Affairs* 42 (April 1964): 428-44.

Buchan, Alastair. "Strategic Factors and the Summit." *The World Today* 16 (April 1960): 141-149.

———. *NATO in the 1960's: The Implications of Interdependence*. New York: Praeger, 1960.

———. "The Reform of NATO." *Foreign Affairs* 40 (January 1962): 165-182.

——— and Windsor, Philip. *Arms and Stability in Europe*. New York: Frederick A. Praeger, 1963.

Bull, Hedley. *Strategy and the Atlantic Alliance: A Critique of United States Doctrine*. Princeton, NJ: Center of International Studies, Woodrow Wilson School of Public and International Affairs, Princeton University, 1964.

Bundy, McGeorge. "Friends and Allies." *Foreign Affairs* 41 (October 1962): 14-23.

Calvocoressi, Peter. "The Evolution of Europe: The Gaullist Design, Russia and Europe, Europe and the British Question." *Survival* 5 (September/October 1963): 196-205.

Campaigne, Jameson C. *American Might and Soviet Myth*. Chicago, IL: Regnery, 1960.

Cerami, Charles A. *Alliance Born of Danger: America, the Common Market, and the Atlantic Partnership*. New York: Harcourt, Brace and World, 1963.

Chamberlin, William Henry. *Appeasement, Road to War*. New York: Rolton House, 1962.

Church, (Sen.) Frank C. "NATO--Reappraising American Policy." *Survival* 5 (September/October 1963): 232-237.

Coffey, Joseph I. *Old Wine and New Bottles: The U.S. and the Defense of Western Europe*. Ann Arbor, MI: Bendix Systems Division, February 1964.

Coles, Harry L., ed. *Total War and Cold War: Problems in Civilian Control of the Military*. Columbus: Ohio State University Press, 1962.

Cottrell, Alvin J. and Dougherty, James E. *The Politics of the Atlantic Alliance*. New York: Praeger, 1964.

Coulmas, Peter. "The Atlantic Debate: Partnership and Interdependence." *Survival* 5 (July/August 1963): 162-165.

The Defense of Western Europe. (Adelphi Paper No. 4). London: International Institute of Strategic Studies, May 1963.

Donelan, Michael. *The Ideas of American Foreign Policy.* London: Chapman & Hall, 1963.

Dougherty, James E. "European Deterrence and Atlantic Unity." *Orbis* 6 (Fall 1962): 371-421.

Eden, Anthony, Earl of Avon. *Full Circle*; The Memoirs of Anthony Eden. London: Cassell, 1960.

―――. "The Slender Margin of Safety." *Foreign Affairs* 39 (January 1961): 165-173.

Emerson, Rupert. "The Atlantic Community and the Emerging Countries." *International Organisation* 17 (Summer 1963): 628-648.

Erler, Fritz. "The Basis of Partnership." *Foreign Affairs* 42 (October 1963): 84-95; *Survival* 6 (January/February 1964): 16-21.

Etzioni, Amitai. *Winning Without War.* Garden City, KS: Doubleday, 1964.

European Security and the Menace of West German Militarism. Prague: Orbis for the Institute for International Politics and Economics, 1962.

Finletter, Thomas K. *Foreign Policy: The Next Phase.* New York: Harper & Row for the Council on Foreign Relations, 1960.

Fleming, D.F. *The Cold War and Its Origins, 1917-1960, Vol. 1, 1917-1950, Vol. 2, 1950-1960.* Garden City, NY: Doubleday, 1961.

Freymond, Jacques. *Western Europe Since the War.* London: Pall Mall; New York: Praeger, 1964.

Fulbright, (Sen.) J.W. "A Community of Free Nations." *Atlantic Community Quarterly* 1 (Summer 1963): 113-130.

―――. "The Concert of Free Nations." *International Organisation* 17 (Summer 1963): 787-803.

―――. *Prospects for the West.* Cambridge, MA: Harvard University Press, 1963.

―――. "Foreign Policy--Myth and Reality." *Survival* 6 (May/June 1964): 136-141.

———. *Old Myths and New Realities*. New York: Random House, 1964.

Gallois, Pierre M. "New Teeth for NATO." *Foreign Affairs* 39 (October 1960): 67-80.

Gelber, Lionel. "A Marriage of Inconvenience." *Foreign Affairs* 41 (January 1963): 310-322; *Survival* 5 (March/April 1963): 70-77.

———. "Anglo-American Imperatives." *Orbis* 7 (Summer 1963): 250-264.

———. "Peaceful Co-Existence or a Durable Peace?" *Orbis* 8 (Summer 1964): 316-331.

Giffin, S.F. "Untangling an Alliance." *Orbis* 7 (Fall 1963): 465-477.

Gilpatric, Roswell L. "Our Defense Needs: The Long View." *Foreign Affairs* 42 (April 1964): 366-378.

Gladwyn, Lord. "Atlantic Dreams and Realities." *Atlantic Community Quarterly* 2 (March 1964): 81-93.

Goold-Adams, Richard. *John Foster Dulles: A Reappraisal*. New York: Appleton-Century Crofts, 1962.

Graebner, Norman A. "The Cold War: An American View." *International Journal* 15 (Spring 1960): 95-112.

———. *Cold War Diplomacy: American Foreign Policy 1945-1960*. Princeton, NJ: Van Nostrand, 1962.

Haffner, Sebastian. "The Berlin Crisis (1958-1962)." *Survey* 44/45 (October 1962): 37-44.

Halle, Louis J. *American Foreign Policy: Theory and Reality*. London: George Allen and Unwin, 1960.

Hallstein, Walter. "The European Community and Atlantic Partnership." *International Organisation* 17 (Summer 1963): 771-786.

Hartley, Livingston. "On the Political Integration of the Atlantic Community." *Orbis* 6 (Winter 1963): 645-655.

———. "Atlantic Partnership--How?" *Orbis* 8 (Spring 1964): 141-152.

Haviland, H. Field, Jr. "Building a Political Community." *International Organisation* 17 (Summer 1963): 733-752.

Healey, Denis. "The Crisis in Europe." *International Affairs* (London) 38 (April 1962): 144-155.

———. "Strategy and Foreign Policy." *Survey* 50 (January 1964): 17-22.

Herter, Christian A. "Atlantica." *Foreign Affairs* 41 (January 1963): 299-309.

———. *Towards an Atlantic Future*. New York: Harper & Row, 1953.

Hinterhoff, Eugene. "Problems Along NATO's Flanks." *Orbis* 8 (Fall 1964): 607-623.

Hoag, Malcolm W. "What Interdependence for NATO?" *Survival* 2 (May/June 1960): 94-106.

Hodson, H.V., ed. *The Atlantic Future*. London: Longmans, 1964.

Hoffman, Stanley. "Discord in Community: The North Atlantic Area as a Partial International System." *International Organisation* 17 (Summer 1963): 521-549.

Hottelet, Richard C. "Berlin and Beyond." *Orbis* 5 (Fall 1961): 267-291.

Hughes, Emmet John. *The Ordeal of Power: A Political Memoir of the Eisenhower Years*. New York: Atheneum, 1963.

Hunter, Robert. "The Politics of U.S. Defense 1963." *The World Today* 19 (April 1963): 155-166.

Huntington, S.P. *The Common Defense*. New York: Columbia University Press, 1961.

Kaufmann, William W. *The McNamara Strategy*. New York: Harper and Row, 1964.

Kennan, George F. "Peaceful Coexistence: A Western View." *Foreign Affairs* 38 (January 1960): 171-190.

———. "Polycentrism and Western Policy." *Foreign Affairs* 42 (January 1964): 171-183.

———. *On Dealing with the Communist World*. New York: Harper and Row for the Council on Foreign Relations, 1964.

Kennedy, John F. *The Strategy of Peace*. New York: Harper, 1960.

———. "Special Message to Congress on U.S. Defense Policy, 28 March 1961." *Survival* 3 (May/June 1961): 98-105.

———, and Khruschev, Nikita. "K. and K.: Action and Reaction." *Survival* 3 (September/October 1961): 235-242.

———, and Macmillan, Harold. "The Nassau Communique, 21 December 1962." *Survival* 5 (March/April 1963): 46-47.

———. "Europe and the United States." *Atlantic Community Quarterly* 1 (Fall 1963): 305-315.

Kissinger, Henry A. *The Necessity for Choice: Prospects of American Foreign Policy*. London: Chatto and Windus, 1960.

———. "Towards Western Cohesion: An American View." *Survival* 3 (March/April 1961): 69-74.

———. "The Unsolved Problems of European Defense." *Foreign Affairs* 40 (July 1962): 515-541.

———. "European Defense." *Survival* 4 (September/October 1962): 217-225.

———. "Strains on the Alliance." *Foreign Affairs* 41 (January 1963): 261-285.

———. "The United States and Nassau." *Survival* 5 (May/June 1963): 109-125.

———. "Coalition Diplomacy in a Nuclear Age." *Foreign Affairs* 42 (July 1964): 525-545.

Kleiman, R. *Atlantic Crisis: American Diplomacy Confronts a Resurgent Europe*. New York: William Norton, 1964.

———. "A Policy for Atlantic Partnership." *Atlantic Community Quarterly* 2 (Summer 1964): 222-229.

Kohn, Hans. "The U.S. and Western Europe: A New Era of Understanding." *Orbis* 6 (Spring 1962): 13-24.

Kraft, Joseph. *The Grand Design: From Common Market to Atlantic Partnership*. New York: Harper and Row, 1962.

Lange, Halvard. "European Integration and Atlantic Partnership." *Atlantic Community Quarterly* 1 (Winter 1963-64): 512-517.

Lichtheim, G.A. *Europe and America*. London: Thames and Hudson, 1963.

Lippmann, Walter. "The Franco-American Debate: The American Perspective." *Survival* 4 (July/August 1962): 153-158.

———. "How Many Drivers at the Nuclear Wheel?" *Atlantic Community Quarterly* 1 (March 1963): 37-41.

Liska, George. *Europe Ascendant: The International Politics of Unification*. Baltimore, MD: Johns Hopkins Press, 1964.

Lowenstein, Hubertus Prince zu and von Zuhlsdorff, Volkmar. *NATO and the Defense of the West*. New York: Praeger, 1962.

Luard, Evan, ed. *The Cold War*. London: Thames and Hudson, 1964.

Luns, Dr. J.M.A.H. "Independence or Interdependence." *International Affairs* 40 (January 1964): 1-10.

Lukacs, John. *A History of the Cold War.* New York: Doubleday, 1961.

Major, John. "President Kennedy's 'Grand Design': The United States and a United Europe." *The World Today* 18 (September 1962): 383-389.

McNamara, Robert S. "Statement Before the Senate Subcommittee on Department of Defense Appropriations, February 1966." *Survival* 8 (May 1966): 138-146.

Merchant, Livingston T. "Evolving United States Relations with the Atlantic Community." *International Organisation* 17 (Summer 1963): 610-627.

———. "North America and the Atlantic Community." *Atlantic Community Quarterly* 2 (Winter 1964-65): 522-527.

Mosely, Philip E. "The Meanings of Coexistence." *Foreign Affairs* 41 (October 1962): 36-46.

Moulton, J.L. *Defense in a Changing World.* London: Eyre and Spottiswoode, 1964.

Mulley, F.W. *The Politics of Western Defense.* New York: Praeger, 1962.

Munk, Frank. "The Atlantic Community and World Community." *Atlantic Community Quarterly* 2 (March 1964): 53-61.

———. *Atlantic Dilemma: Partnership or Community.* Dobbs Ferry, NY: Oceana Publications, 1964.

Norstad, Lauris. "The Future of the Atlantic Community." *International Organisation* 17 (Summer 1963): 804-812.

———. "European Unification and Atlantic Unity." *Atlantic Community Quarterly* 2 (Summer 1964): 186-191.

Osgood, Robert E. *NATO: The Entangling Alliance.* Chicago, IL: University of Chicago Press, 1962.

Perla, Leo. *Can We End the Cold War? A Study in American Foreign Policy.* New York: Macmillan, 1960.

Rapoport, Anatol. *Strategy and Conscience.* New York: Harper and Row, 1964.

Rock, Vincent P. *A Strategy of Interdependence: A Program for the Control of Conflict Between the United States and the Soviet Union.* New York: Charles Scribner's Sons, 1964.

Rockefeller, Nelson A. "Purpose and Policy." *Foreign Affairs* 38 (April 1960): 370-390.

———. "Voices in Opposition: The Republican Party's Critique of Current U.S. Defense Policy." *Survival* 6 (January/February 1964): 9-15.

Ross, Hugh, ed. *The Cold War: Containment and Its Critics*. Chicago, IL: Rand McNally, 1963.

Rostow, Eugene V. "A New Start for the Alliance." *Atlantic Community Quarterly* 1 (Summer 1963): 207-210.

———. "The Atlantic Debate--Fission or Fusion." *Survival* 5 (July/August 1963): 166-171.

"Russia and the Western Powers: A Chronology Since the Vienna Meeting of 3-4 June 1961." *The World Today* 17 (December 1961): 503-511.

Schaetzel, J. Robert. "The Nuclear Problem and Atlantic Interdependence." *Atlantic Community Quarterly* 1 (Winter 1963-64): 561-569.

Schilling, Warner R. *Strategy, Politics and Defense Budgets*. New York: Columbia University Press, 1962.

Schlesinger, Arthur Jr. "Coexistence vs. Peace." *Survey* 50 (January 1964): 10-16.

Schmidt, Adolph W. "The Atlantic Community." *Atlantic Community Quarterly* 1 (Summer 1963): 219-230.

Schmidt, Helmut. *Defense or Retaliation: A German View*. New York: Praeger, 1962.

Schuman, Frederick L. *The Cold War: Retrospect and Prospect*. Baton Rouge: Louisiana State University Press, 1962.

Schwarz, Urs. "Strengthening Europe's Defensive Power." *Survival* 2 (September/October 1960): 210-213.

Segni, Antonio. "A Goal of Basic Importance." *Atlantic Community Quarterly* 2 (March 1964): 5-9.

Singer, J. David. "From Deterrence to Disarmament." *International Journal* 16 (Autumn 1961): 307-326.

Slambuk, George. *American Military Forces Abroad*. Columbus, OH: Ohio State University Press, 1963.

Slessor, Sir John. *What Price Co-Existence?* New York: Praeger, 1961.

Snyder, Glenn H. *Deterrence and Defense: Towards a Theory of National Security*. Princeton, NJ: Princeton University Press, 1961.

———. "Deterrence, Defense, and Disengagement." *World Politics* 14 (January 1962): 393-403.

Sommer, Theo. "For an Atlantic Future." *Foreign Affairs* 43 (October 1964): 112-125.

Spaak, Paul-Henri. "Hold Fast." *Foreign Affairs* 41 (July 1963): 611-620.

Spinelli, Altiero. "Atlantic Pact or European Unity." *Foreign Affairs* 40 (July 1962): 542-552.

―――――. "Europe and the Nuclear Monopoly." *Atlantic Community Quarterly* 2 (Winter 1964-65): 588-599.

Stambuk, George. *American Military Forces Abroad: Their Impact on the Western State System.* Columbus, OH: Ohio State University Press, 1963.

Steel, Ronald. *The End of Alliance: America and the Future of Europe.* New York: Viking, 1964.

Stern, Frederick M. "Citizen Armies for Multi-Dimensional Defense." *Orbis* 3 (Winter 1960): 469-481.

Strachey, John. *On the Prevention of War.* London: Macmillan, 1962.

Strausz-Hupe, Robert and Dougherty, James. *Building the Atlantic World.* New York: Harper and Row; Toronto: Musson, 1963.

Streit, Clarence K. *Freedom's Frontier: Atlantic Union Now.* New York: Harper, 1961.

Syed, Anwar. "Walter Lippman on Europe and the Atlantic Community." *Orbis* 7 (Summer 1963): 308-335.

Taylor, Maxwell D. *The Uncertain Trumpet.* New York: Harper, 1960.

―――――. "Security Will Not Wait." *Foreign Affairs* 39 (January 1961): 174-184.

Ten Years of Seven-Power Europe. Paris: Western European Union, 1964.

Uri, Pierre. *Partnership for Progress: A Program for Transatlantic Action.* New York: Harper and Row for the Atlantic Institute, 1963.

Verrier, Anthony. "Kennedy and Europe: The End of a Chapter." *The World Today* 20 (January 1964): 39-46.

von Hassel, Kai-Uwe. "Detente Through Firmness." *Foreign Affairs* 42 (January 1964): 184-194.

Warner, Geoffrey. "The Nassau Agreement and NATO." *The World Today* 13 (February 1963): 61-69.

Waskow, Arthur I. "American Military Doctrine." *Survival* 4 (May/June 1962): 106-115.

Watson, Hugh Seton. *Nationalism and Communism: Essays 1946-1963*. New York: Praeger, 1964.

Wilcox, Francis O. "The Atlantic Community and the United Nations." *International Organisation* 17 (Summer 1963): 683-708.

——— and Haviland, H., Jr., eds. *The Atlantic Community*. New York and London: Praeger, 1963.

——— and ———. *The Atlantic Community: Progress and Prospects*. New York: Frederick A. Praeger, 1964.

Wiles, P.J.D. "The Pursuit of Disengagement." *Survival* 2 (January/February 1960): 28-33.

Wilson, Thomas W., Jr. *Cold War and Common Sense*. Greenwich, CT: New York Graphic Society, 1962.

Wolfers, Arnold. *Discord and Collaboration: Essays on International Politics*. Baltimore, MD: Johns Hopkins Press, 1962.

———. "Integration in the West: The Conflict of Perspectives." *International Organisation* 17 (Summer 1963): 753-770; *Atlantic Community Quarterly* 1 (Winter 1963-64): 586-605.

———. *Changing East-West Relations and the Unity of the West*. Baltimore, MD: Johns Hopkins Press, 1964.

1965-1969

Acheson, Dean. "Europe: Decision or Drift." *Foreign Affairs* 44 (January 1966): 198-205.

———. "One of Our 'Firemen' Is Resigning." *Atlantic Community Quarterly* 4 (Summer 1966): 160-165.

———. *Present at the Creation: My Years in the State Department*. New York: W.W. Norton, 1969.

Ailleret, (Gen.) C. "The Character of Strategy." *Survival* 7 (May/June 1965): 109-117.

Amme, Carl H., Jr. *NATO Without France: A Strategic Appraisal*. Stanford, CA: Hoover Institution Press, 1967.

Andreyev, N. "NATO's Role in Europe." *Survival* 8 (May 1966): 150-155.

The Atlantic Community. New York: Foreign Policy Association, 1965.

Bader, William B. Austria Between East and West. Stanford: Stanford University Press, 1966.

Ball, George W. "The Dangers of Nostalgia." Atlantic Community Quarterly 3 (Summer 1965): 167-176.

―――. The Discipline of Power: Essentials of a Modern World Structure. Boston, MA: Atlantic, 1968.

Barnet, Richard J. and Raskin, Marcus G. After 20 Years: Alternatives to the Cold War in Europe. New York: Random House, 1965.

Beaton, Leonard. "NATO After the Soviet Invasion of Czechoslovakia." Atlantic Community Quarterly 7 (Spring 1969): 76-77.

Beaufre, (Gen.) Andre. NATO and Europe. London: Faber and Faber, 1967.

Beer, Francis A. Integration and Disintegration in NATO. Columbus, OH: Ohio State University Press, 1969.

Birnbaum, Karl E. "Ways Towards European Security." Survival 10 (June 1968): 193-199.

Bloomfield, Lincoln P. Western Europe 1965-1975: Five Scenarios. Ann Arbor, MI: Bendix Systems Division, April 1965.

―――. Western Europe to the Mid-Seventies. Cambridge, MA: M.I.T. Press, 1968.

Bohlen, Charles E. The Transformation of American Foreign Policy. New York: W.W. Norton, 1969.

Brandon, Donald. American Foreign Policy: Beyond Utopianism and Realism. New York: Appleton, 1966.

Brandt, Willy. "Detente over the Long Haul." Survival 9 (October 1967): 310-312.

―――. A Peace Policy for Europe. New York; Toronto: Holt, Rinehart and Winston, 1968.

Brinton, Crane. The Americans and the French. Cambridge, MA: Harvard University Press, 1968.

Brodie, Bernard. "The McNamara Phenomenon." World Politics 17 (July 1965): 672-686.

Brosio, Manlio. "The Future of NATO." Atlantic Community Quarterly 3 (Winter 1965-66): 442-450.

―――. "Past and Future Tasks of the Alliance: An Analysis of the Harmel Report." Atlantic Community Quarterly 6 (Summer 1968): 231-237.

———. "Twenty NATO Years." *Atlantic Community Quarterly* 7 (Summer 1969): 209-211.

———. "Justified Gesture." *Atlantic Community Quarterly* 7 (Winter 1969-70): 480-493.

Brown, Harold. "Planning Our Military Forces." *Foreign Affairs* 45 (January 1967): 277-290.

Brown, Seyom. "An Alternative to the Grand Design." *World Politics* 17 (January 1965): 232-42.

———. *The Faces of Power: Constancy and Change in United States Foreign Policy from Truman to Johnson.* New York: Columbia University Press, 1968.

Brzezinski, Zbigniew. *Alternative to Partition: For a Broader Conception of America's Role in Europe.* New York: McGraw-Hill for the Council on Foreign Relations, 1965.

———. "America and a Larger Europe." *The World Today* 21 (October 1965): 419-427.

———. "The Framework of East-West Reconciliation." *Foreign Affairs* 46 (January 1968): 256-275.

Buchan, Alastair. "The Changed Setting of the Atlantic Debate." *Foreign Affairs* 43 (July 1965): 574-586.

———. *Europe's Futures, Europe's Choices: Models of Western Europe in the 1970's.* New York: Columbia University Press, 1969.

Bull, Hedley. "Strategic Studies and Its Critics." *World Politics* 20 (July 1968): 593-605.

Bundy, McGeorge. "Atlantic Alliance Is Not America's Alone." *Atlantic Community Quarterly* 4 (Fall 1966): 330-339.

"Call for a European Conference, March 1969." *Survival* 11 (May 1969): 159-161.

Calleo, David. *Europe's Future: The Grand Alternatives.* New York: Horizon Press, 1965.

Campbell, John C. *American Policy Towards Communist Eastern Europe: The Choices Ahead.* Minneapolis, MN: University of Minnesota Press, 1965.

Catlin, George. *Creating the Atlantic Community.* London: Fabian Society, 1965.

———. *The Atlantic Commonwealth.* Harmondsworth: Penguin, 1969.

Cerny, K.H. and Briefs, H.W. *NATO in Quest of Cohesion.* New York: Praeger, 1965.

Church, Frank G. "Towards a More Perfect Union." *Atlantic Community Quarterly* 3 (Fall 1965): 285-292.

―――. "U.S. Policy and the 'New Europe.'" *Foreign Affairs* 45 (October 1966): 49-57.

Cleveland, Harlan. "NATO After the Invasion." *Foreign Affairs* 47 (January 1969): 251-265.

―――. "The United States and the Future of NATO." *Atlantic Community Quarterly* 7 (Summer 1969): 216-220.

Cleveland, Harold van B. *The Atlantic Idea and Its European Rivals.* New York: McGraw-Hill, 1966.

―――, and Cleveland, Joan B. *The Atlantic Alliance: Problems and Prospects.* New York: Foreign Policy Association, 1966.

―――. "The Atlantic Idea." *Atlantic Community Quarterly* 4 (Winter 1966-67): 494-508.

―――. "The Real Deterrent." *Survival* 9 (December 1967): 378-383.

―――. "The Rejuvenation of NATO." *Atlantic Community Quarterly* 5 (Winter 1967-68): 512-519.

―――. "The Irrelevance of Anti-Commitment." *Atlantic Community Quarterly* 6 (Winter 1968-69): 520-530.

Coffey, Joseph I. *Strategy, Alliance Policy and Nuclear Proliferation.* Ann Arbor, MI: Bendix Systems Division, 1965.

Collier, David S., and Glaser, Kurt, eds. *The Conditions for Peace in Europe: Problems of Detente and Security.* Washington, D.C.: Public Affairs Press, 1969.

Combeaux, (Gen.) Edmond. "Debate on the Atlantic Alliance." *Orbis* 10 (Summer 1966): 360-389.

"Communique and Annexe." *Survival* 10 (February 1968): 62-64.

Connery, Robert H., ed. *The 'Atlantic Community' Reappraised.* New York: Academy of Political Science, 1968.

Conquest, Robert. "The Limits of Detente." *Foreign Affairs* 46 (July 1968): 733-742.

Crane, Robert Dickson. "A New Cold War?" *Survival* 7 (March/April 1965): 79-82.

Critchley, Julian. *The Future of NATO.* London: Conservative Political Centre, 1968.

Cromwell, William C., ed. *Political Problems of Atlantic Partnership: National Perspectives.* Bruges: College of Europe, 1969.

Dawson, Raymond and Rosecrance, Richard. "Theory and Reality in the Anglo-American Alliance." *World Politics* 19 (October 1966): 21-51.

de Borchgrave, Arnaud. "Europe Looks Again to U.S. Leadership." *Atlantic Community Quarterly* 5 (Winter 1967-68): 564-568.

"Declaration of Ministers of Foreign Affairs of Warsaw Pact." *Survival* 11 (December 1969): 394-395.

"Declaration of Strengthening Peace and Security in Europe." *Survival* 8 (September 1966): 289-293.

De Staercke, Andre. "As Tacitus Said..." *Atlantic Community Quarterly* 7 (Summer 1969): 212-215.

Deutsch, Karl W. *France, Germany and the Western Alliance: A Study of Elite Attitudes on European Integration and World Politics.* New York: Charles Scribner's Sons, 1967.

Deutscher, Isaac. *Ironies of History: Essays on Contemporary Communism.* New York: Oxford University Press, 1966.

Druks, Herbert. *Harry S. Truman and the Russians, 1945-1953.* New York: Robert Speller, 1967.

Duchene, Francois. *Beyond Alliance.* (The Atlantic Papers, NATO Series I). Paris: The Atlantic Institute, 1965.

Dulles, Eleanor Lansing and Crane, Robert Dickson, eds. *Detente: Cold War Strategies in Transition.* New York: Praeger, 1965.

Duroselle, J.B. "The Future of the Atlantic Community." *International Journal* 21 (Autumn 1966): 421-446.

Eisenhower, Dwight D. *The White House Years.* New York: Doubleday, 1965.

―――. *Waging Peace 1956-1961: The White House Years.* Garden City, NY: Doubleday, 1965.

―――. "Promise Is Now a Fact." *Atlantic Community Quarterly* 7 (Summer 1969): 221-223.

Ellsworth, Robert. "The Future of the Atlantic Alliance." *Atlantic Community Quarterly* 7 (Fall 1969): 315-320.

Fedder, E.H. and Robinson, J.A. *Beyond Hegemony: The U.S. and the Future of NATO.* Columbus, OH: Ohio State University, 1967.

Fontaine, Andre. *History of the Cold War: From the Korean War to the Present.* New York: Pantheon Books, 1969.

Fox, William T.R. and Fox, Annette Baker. *NATO and the Range of American Choice.* New York: Columbia University Press, 1967.

Fraser, Blair. "Can We Succeed in NATO Without Really Trying?" *Atlantic Community Quarterly* 3 (Spring 1965): 50-55.

Freymond, Jacques. "Alternative to Partition." *Survey* 58 (January 1966): 128-133.

Furniss, Edgar S., Jr., ed. *The Western Alliance: Its Status and Prospects.* Columbus, OH: Ohio State University Press, 1965.

Garnett, John. "The United States and Europe: Defense, Technology and the Western Alliance." *International Affairs* 44 (April 1968): 282-288.

Gasteyger, Curt. *The American Dilemma: Bipolarity or Alliance Cohesion.* (Adelphi Paper No. 24). London: International Institute for Strategic Studies, January 1966.

──────. *Europe in the Seventies.* (Adelphi Paper No. 37). London: International Institute for Strategic Studies, 1967.

──────. "Europe in the Seventies." *Atlantic Community Quarterly* 5 (Fall 1967): 317-335.

Geiger, Theodore. "The Ending of an Era in Atlantic Policy." *Atlantic Community Quarterly* 5 (Spring 1967): 87-98.

Gelber, Lionel. *The Alliance of Necessity: Britain's Crisis, the New Europe and American Interests.* New York: Stein and Day, 1966.

Gladwyn, Lord. "NATO Today." *Atlantic Community Quarterly* 4 (Summer 1966): 215-223.

Goldwin, Robert A., ed. *Beyond the Cold War.* Chicago, IL: Rand McNally, 1966.

Gordenker, Leon. "International Organization and the Cold War." *International Journal* 23 (Summer 1968): 357-368.

Graebner, Norman A. "Whither Containment?" *International Journal* 24 (Spring 1969): 246-263.

Griffith, William E. and Rostow, Walt W. *East-West Relations: Is Detente Possible?* Washington, D.C.: American Enterprise Institute for Public Policy Research, 1969.

Gutteridge, William. "Defense or Disarmament." *International Affairs* (London) 41 (October 1965): 676-681.

Hackett, (Gen.) Sir John. "Letter to 'the Times' 6 February 1968." *Atlantic Community Quarterly* 6 (Summer 1968): 291-293.

Halle, Louis J. "The Turning Point." *Survey* 58 (January 1966): 168-176.

————. "A Multitude of Cold Wars." *International Journal* 23 (Summer 1968): 335-343.

Hammond, Paul Y. *The Cold War Years*. New York: Harcourt Brace and World, Inc., 1969.

Haroche, C. "American Bases in Europe." *International Affairs* 7 (1966): 32-38.

Harrison, Dr. S.L.R. "America's 1969 Option." *Atlantic Community Quarterly* 7 (Fall 1969): 334-341.

Hartley, Livingston. *Atlantic Challenge*. New York: Oceana Publications, Inc., 1965.

————. "Towards an Atlantic Assembly." *Atlantic Community Quarterly* 4 (Spring 1966): 104-113.

Hassner, Pierre and Newhouse, John. *Diplomacy in the West*. New York: 20th Century Fund, 1966.

————. *Change and Security in Europe, Part I: The Background*. (Adelphi Paper No. 45). London: International Institute for Strategic Studies, February 1968.

————. *Change and Security in Europe, Part II: In Search of a System*. (Adelphi Paper No. 49). London: International Institute for Strategic Studies, July 1968.

Hastings, Paul. *The Cold War 1945-1969*. London: Ernest Benn, 1969.

Heldring, J.L. "Atlantic Partnership: European Unity." *Survival* 7 (January/February 1965): 30-37.

Herz, Martin. *Beginnings of the Cold War*. Bloomington, IN: Indiana University Press, 1966.

Heusinger, Adolf Ernst. "Vietnam and the U.S. Role in Europe." *Atlantic Community Quarterly* 3 (Winter 1965-66): 486-495.

Hoffman, Stanley. *Gulliver's Troubles, or the Setting of American Foreign Policy*. New York: McGraw-Hill for Council for Foreign Relations, 1968.

Holifield, Chet. "Nuclear Controls in NATO." *Atlantic Community Quarterly* 4 (Winter 1965-1966): 496-498.

Hooson, Emlyn. "NATO's Future." *Survival* 8 (June 1966): 182-185.

Horowitz, David. *The Free World Colossus: A Critique of American Foreign Policy in the Cold War.* London: MacGibbon and Kee, 1965.

―――. *From Yalta to Vietnam: American Foreign Policy in the Cold War.* Harmondsworth: Penguin Books, 1969.

Hudson, G.F. *The Hard and Bitter Peace: World Politics Since 1945.* New York: Frederick A. Praeger, 1967.

Huizinga, J.H. "Which Way Europe?" *Foreign Affairs* 43 (April 1965): 487-500.

Humphrey, Hubert H. "The Need for Common Effort." *Atlantic Community Quarterly* 3 (Winter 1965-66): 451-455.

Hunter, Robert. "The Future of Soviet-American Detente." *The World Today* 24 (July 1968): 281-290.

―――. *Security in Europe.* London: Elek, 1969.

Huntley, James R. *The NATO Story.* New York: Manhattan Publishing Co., 1969.

Jackson, Henry M. "The Decisive Area." *Atlantic Community Quarterly* 4 (Spring 1966): 25-36.

―――. *The Atlantic Alliance: Senate Sub-Committee Hearings and Findings.* New York: Frederick A. Praeger, 1967.

Jacquet, L.G.M., ed. *European and Atlantic Cooperation.* The Hague: Martinus Nijhoff, 1965.

Javits, Jacob K. "The United States and Europe--After Vietnam." *Atlantic Community Quarterly* 6 (Fall 1968): 361-368.

Johnson, Lyndon B. "Our View of NATO." *Atlantic Community Quarterly* 2 (Summer 1966): 156-160.

―――. "LBJ and Europe." *Survival* 8 (December 1966): 378-379.

―――. "Making Europe Whole: An Unfinished Task." *Atlantic Community Quarterly* 4 (Winter 1966-67): 487-493.

Joyce, J.A. *End of an Illusion.* London: Allen and Unwin, 1969.

Kahn, Herman and Pfaff, William. "Our Alternatives in Europe." *Foreign Affairs* 44 (July 1966): 587-600.

Kaplan, Morton A. "Old Realities and New Myths." *World Politics* 17 (January 1965): 334-367.

―――――. *NATO and the Policy of Containment.* Boston, MA: D.C. Heath and Co., 1968.

―――――. *Recent American Foreign Policy: Conflicting Interpretations.* Homewood, IL: Dorsey Press, 1969.

Kennan, George F. *Memoirs: 1925-1950.* Boston, MA: Little, Brown & Co., 1967.

Kennedy, Robert F. *Thirteen Days: A Memoir of the Cuban Missile Crisis.* London: Macmillan; New York: Norton, 1969.

Kim, Young Hum, ed. *Twenty Years of Crises: The Cold War Era.* Englewood Cliffs, NJ: Prentice-Hall, 1968.

Kindleberger, Charles P. "The Marshall Plan and the Cold War." *International Journal* 23 (Summer 1968): 369-382.

Kirk, Peter. "Rethinking NATO." *The World Today* 22 (January 1966): 28-31.

Kissinger, Henry A. *The Troubled Partnership: A Reappraisal of the Atlantic Alliance.* New York: McGraw-Hill, 1965.

―――――. "What About the Future?" *Atlantic Community Quarterly* 4 (Fall 1966): 317-329.

―――――, ed. *Problems of National Strategy.* New York and London: Praeger and Pall Mall, 1966.

―――――. "What Kind of Atlantic Partnership?" *Atlantic Community Quarterly* 7 (Spring 1969): 18-38.

―――――. *American Foreign Policy: Three Essays.* New York: W.W. Norton and Co., 1969.

Knapp, Wilfred. "Cold War Origins." *Survey* 58 (January 1966): 153-158.

―――――. *A History of War and Peace 1939-1965.* London: Oxford University Press for the Royal Institute of International Affairs, 1967.

―――――. "The Cold War Revised." *International Journal* 23 (Summer 1968): 344-356.

Knorr, Klaus. *NATO: Past, Present and Future.* New York: Foreign Policy Association, 1969.

Kohn, Hans. "Nationalism in the Atlantic Community." *Atlantic Community Quarterly* 3 (Fall 1965): 293-313.

―――――. *Nationalism in the Atlantic Community.* Philadelphia, PA: University of Pennsylvania, 1965.

Kolodziej, Edward A. *The Uncommon Defense and Congress 1945-1963.* Columbus, OH: Ohio State University Press, 1966.

Kovrig, Bennett. "Spheres of Influence: A Reassessment." *Survey* 70/71 (Winter/Spring 1969): 102-120.

LaFeber, Walter. *America, Russia and the Cold War 1945-1966*. New York: Wiley, 1968.

―――. *America in the Cold War 1947-1967*. London: John Wiley, 1969.

Laloy, Jean. *Western and Eastern Europe: The Changing Relationship*. (Adelphi Paper No. 33). London: International Institute for Strategic Studies, March 1967.

Lemnitzer, Lyman L. "The Most Formidable Conventional Armed Forces in the World Today." *Atlantic Community Quarterly* 6 (Winter 1968-69): 501-507.

Lerche, Charles O., Jr. *The Cold War and After*. Englewood Cliffs, NJ: Prentice-Hall, 1965.

―――. *Last Chance in Europe*. Chicago: Quadrangle Books, 1967.

Lerner, Daniel and Gorden, Morton. *Euratlantica: Changing Perspectives of the European Elites*. Cambridge, MA: M.I.T. Press, 1969.

Lodge, John Davis. "Can NATO Be Restored?" *Orbis* 10 (Fall 1966): 724-736.

Luard, Evan. "Conciliation and Deterrence: A Comparison of Political Strategies in the Interwar amd Postwar Periods." *World Politics* 19 (January 1967): 167-189.

Macmillan, Harold. *Tides of Fortune 1945-1955*. (The Macmillan Memoirs, Vol. 2). New York: Harper & Row, 1969.

Mally, Gerhard. "Proposals for Integrating the Atlantic Community." *Orbis* 9 (Summer 1965): 378-392.

―――. "A 'Forward Strategy' for Atlantica." *Atlantic Community Quarterly* 3 (Fall 1965): 318-325.

Mansfield, Mike; Dodd, Thomas J.; and Javits, Jacob K. "The Great Debate on Europe." *Atlantic Community Quarterly* 5 (Spring 1967): 12-33.

Maudling, Reginald. "Europe and the Atlantic Community." *Atlantic Community Quarterly* 4 (Spring 1966): 48-56.

―――. "The Real Threat to the West." *Atlantic Community Quarterly* 5 (Fall 1967): 344-346.

McCloy, John J. *The Atlantic Alliance: Its Origin and Its Future*. New York: Columbia University Press for Carnegie-Mellon University, 1969.

McNamara, Robert S. "American Strategy Now: Statement to the House Armed Services Committee." *Survival* 7 (May/June 1965): 98-107.

——. *The Essence of Security: Reflections in Office.* New York: McGraw-Hill, 1968.

——. "Report to the Senate Armed Services Committee, February 1968." *Survival* 10 (April 1968): 106-114.

Middleton, Drew. *The Atlantic Community: A Study in Unity and Disunity.* New York: McKay, 1965.

Morgan, Carlyle. "NATO: A New Desire to Exist." *Atlantic Community Quarterly* 7 (Spring 1969): 53-58.

Morgonthau, Hanson. *A New Foreign Policy for the United States.* New York: Praeger for the Council on Foreign Relations, 1969.

Moynihan, Daniel P. "The NATO Committee on Challenges of Modern Society." *Atlantic Community Quarterly* 7 (Winter 1969-70): 530-537.

"NATO and the Defense of Europe." *Survival* 7 (October 1965): 266-267.

Nixon, Richard M. "The Time to Save NATO." *Atlantic Community Quarterly* 6 (Winter 1968-69): 479-484.

——. "NATO: Facing the Truth of Our Times." *Atlantic Community Quarterly* 7 (Summer 1969): 203-208.

"Non-Military Functions of NATO." *Atlantic Community Quarterly* 3 (Winter 1965-66): 425-441.

Northedge, F.S., ed. *The Foreign Policies of the Powers.* London: Faber, 1968.

"Nuclear Weapons and the Atlantic Alliance." Washington, D.C.: H.Q. Department of the Army, 1965.

Orvik, Nils. "The Role of the Small Member." *International Journal* 21 (Spring 1966): 173-185.

——. "NATO, NAFTA and the Smaller Allies." *Orbis* 12 (Summer 1968): 455-464.

Pasternak, E. *U.S. Concepts of Crisis Diplomacy.* New York: McGraw-Hill, 1968.

Patijn, C.L. "The Future of the Atlantic Alliance." *Atlantic Community Quarterly* 6 (Winter 1968-69): 512-519.

Pfaltzgraff, Robert L., Jr. "Alternative Designs for the Atlantic Alliance." *Orbis* 9 (Summer 1965): 358-377.

———. *The Atlantic Community: A Complex Imbalance.* New York: Van Nostrand Reinhold, 1969.

Philip, Andre. *Counsel from an Ally: Reflections on Changes Within the Atlantic Community.* Columbia, MO: University of Missouri Press, 1966.

"Picking Up Nato's Pieces." *Atlantic Community Quarterly* 4 (Fall 1966): 361-365.

Pierre, Andrew J. "Implications of the Western Response to the Soviet Intervention in Czechoslovakia." *Atlantic Community Quarterly* 7 (Spring 1969): 59-75.

"Policy Statement." *Atlantic Community Quarterly* 3 (Winter 1965-66): 419-424.

Posvar, Wesley W. *American Defense Policy.* Baltimore, MD: Johns Hopkins Press, 1965.

Quaroni, Pietro. "'Open Door to the East' Swings Shut." *Atlantic Community Quarterly* 6 (Winter 1968-69): 508-511.

Ranger, Robert. "NATO's Reaction to Czechoslovakia: The Strategy of Ambiguous Response." *The World Today* 25 (January 1969): 19-26.

Rees, David. *The Age of Containment.* London: Macmillan, 1967.

"The Reform of NATO--The Conference Debate." *Atlantic Community Quarterly* 3 (Winter 1965-66): 464-478.

Reid, Escott. "The Birth of the North Atlantic Alliance." *International Journal* 22 (Summer 1967): 426-440.

Roach, J.R., ed. *The United States and the Atlantic Community: Issues and Prospects.* Austin, TX: University of Texas Press, 1969.

Rostow, Eugene V. "Prospects for the Alliance." *Atlantic Community Quarterly* 3 (Spring 1965): 34-42.

———. "The Road Before Us." *Atlantic Community Quarterly* 5 (Summer 1967): 161-172.

———. "The Next Stage of the Alliance." *Atlantic Community Quarterly* 5 (Winter 1967-68): 475-485.

———. "Europe and the United States--The Partnership of Necessity." *Atlantic Community Quarterly* 6 (Summer 1968): 216-227.

———. "The Future of the Atlantic Community." *Atlantic Community Quarterly* 7 (Winter 1969-70): 467-479.

Rusk, Dean. "Don't Dismantle the Dam." *Atlantic Community Quarterly* 4 (Summer 1966): 166-172.

Sapin, Burton M. *The Making of United States Foreign Policy*. Washington, D.C.: Brookings Institution, 1966.

Sathyamurthy, T.V. "From Containment to Interdependence." *World Politics* 20 (October 1967): 142-177.

Schaetzel, J. Robert. "The Necessary Partnership." *Foreign Affairs* 44 (April 1966): 417-433.

Schlesinger, Arthur, Jr. "Origins of the Cold War." *Foreign Affairs* 46 (October 1967): 22-52.

Schmidt, Helmut. "The Brezhnev Doctrine." *Survival* 11 (October 1969): 307-313.

Schwarz, Urs. "The Citizen Army in the Atomic Age." *Survival* 7 (July 1965): 232-235.

Seabury, Paul. *The Rise and Decline of the Cold War*. New York: Harvard University Press, 1967.

────── and Wildavsky, Aaron, eds. *U.S. Foreign Policy: Perspectives and Proposals for the 1970's*. New York: McGraw-Hill, 1969.

Seton-Watson, Hugh. "The Khruschev Era." *Survey* 58 (January 1966): 187-195.

Sherman, Michael. "Guarantees and Nuclear Spread." *International Journal* 21 (Autumn 1966): 484-490.

Shulman, Marshall D. "'Europe' Versus 'Detente'?" *Foreign Affairs* 45 (April 1967): 389-402.

──────. "A European Security Conference." *Survival* 11 (December 1969): 373-381.

Smith, Mark E., and Johns, Claude J., eds. *American Defense Policy*. Baltimore, MD: Johns Hopkins Press, 1968.

Spaak, Paul-Henri. "The Search for Consensus, A New Effort to Build Europe." *Foreign Affairs* 43 (January 1965); 199-208.

──────. "Chaos in Europe." *Atlantic Community Quarterly* 4 (Summer 1966): 211-214.

──────. "The Alliance Must Go On." *Atlantic Community Quarterly* 5 (Summer 1967): 199-208.

──────. *The Crisis of the Atlantic Alliance*. Columbus, OH: Ohio State University Press, 1697.

──────. "The Indispensable Alliance." *Atlantic Community Quarterly* 5 (Winter 1967-68): 497-503.

―――. "The Fundamental Reality." *Atlantic Community Quarterly* 6 (Winter 1968-69): 485-492.

Speidel, (Gen.) Hans. "The Essential Basis of Detente." *Atlantic Community Quarterly* 7 (Winter 1969-70): 506-509.

Spinelli, Altiero. "Some Aspects of Nuclear Interdependence." *Atlantic Community Quarterly* 3 (Fall 1965): 335-339.

Stanley, Timothy W. *NATO in Transition: The Future of the Atlantic Alliance.* New York: Praeger, 1965.

―――. "Patterns for the Future." *Atlantic Community Quarterly* 3 (Summer 1965): 188-196.

Starobin, Joseph R. "Communism in Western Europe." *Foreign Affairs* 44 (October 1965): 62-77.

―――. "Origins of the Cold War: The Communist Dimension." *Foreign Affairs* 47 (July 1969): 681-696.

Stehlin, Paul. "Necessity and Possibility Within the Alliance." *Atlantic Community Quarterly* 5 (Winter 1967-68): 485-496.

Steibel, Gerald L. *Detente: Dilemma of Disaster?* New York: National Strategy Information Center, Inc., July 1969.

―――. *Detente: Promises and Pitfalls.* New York: Crane, Russak, and Co., 1974.

Stikker, Dirk U. "NATO--The Shifting Western Alliance." *Atlantic Community Quarterly* 3 (Spring 1965): 7-17.

―――. *Men of Responsibility.* New York: Harper and Row, 1966.

―――. "Nationalism Threatens Atlantic Cooperation." *Atlantic Community Quarterly* 6 (Summer 1968): 228-230.

Strauss, Dr. Franz Josef. "An Alliance of Continents." *International Affairs* 41 (April 1965): 191-203.

Strausz-Hupe, Robert. "The Real Communist Threat." *International Affairs* 41 (October 1965): 611-623.

―――. "The World Without NATO." *Orbis* 10 (Spring 1966): 79-90.

Szent, Miklosy, Istvan. *The Atlantic Union Movement: Its Significance in World Politics.* New York: Fountainhead Publishers, 1965.

Tompkins, John S. *The Weapons of World War III: The Long Road Back from the Bomb.* Garden City, KS: Doubleday, 1966.

Tornudd, Klaus. "'The Finnish Model', Neutral States and European Security." *International Journal* 24 (Spring 1969): 349-355.

Twining, (Gen.) Nathan F. *Neither Liberty Nor Safety: A Hard Look at U.S. Military Policy and Strategy.* New York: Holt, Rinehart and Winston, 1966.

van der Beugel, Ernst H. "The Clash in Europe." *Atlantic Community Quarterly* 3 (Spring 1965): 27-33.

―――. "From Marshall Aid to Atlantic Partnership." *Atlantic Community Quarterly* 4 (Spring 1966): 5-16.

―――. "Relations Between Europe and the United States." *Atlantic Community Quarterly* 5 (Summer 1967): 173-176.

―――. "The Need for Atlantic Solidarity." *Atlantic Community Quarterly* 5 (Winter 1967-68): 507-511.

von Hassel, Kai-Uwe. "Organizing Western Defense." *Foreign Affairs* 43 (January 1965): 209-216.

von Riekhoff, Harald. "The Changing Function of NATO." *International Journal* 21 (Spring 1966): 157-172.

―――. *NATO: Issues and Prospects.* Toronto: Canadian Institute of International Affairs, 1967.

Warburg, James. *The United States in the Postwar World: A Critical Appraisal.* London: Gollancz, 1966.

"Western Europe's Defense." *Survival* 10 (April 1968): 115-117.

Windsor, Philip. "Recent Developments in NATO." *The World Today* 22 (June 1966): 227-234.

―――. "NATO and European Detente." *The World Today* 23 (September 1967): 361-369.

―――. "NATO Confronts Its Future." *The World Today* 24 (March 1968): 121-126.

―――. "The Boundaries of Detente." *The World Today* 25 (June 1969): 255-264.

Winton, John. *The War at Sea*, Volume I. New York: William Morrow, 1968.

Wolfers, Arnold, ed. *Alliance Policy in the Cold War.* Baltimore, MD: Johns Hopkins Press, 1959.

Yarmolinsky, Adam. "The Atlantic Alliance." *Survival* 11 (February 1969): 57-62.

Zoppo, Ciro Elliott. "Nuclear Technology, Multipolarity, and International Stability." *World Politics* 18 (July 1966): 579-606.

1970-1974

"Abolish NATO!--But Then What?" *NATO's Fifteen Nations* 15 (February-March 1970): 80-86.

Acheson, Dean. *This Vast External Realm*. New York: Norton, 1973.

Allison, Graham; May, Ernest; and Yarmolinsky, Adam. "Limits to Intervention." *Foreign Affairs* 48 (January 1970): 245-261.

―――. "Cool It: The Foreign Policy of Young America." *Foreign Policy* 1 (Winter 1970-71): 144-160.

―――. *Essence of Decision: Explaining the Cuban Missile Crisis*. Boston: Little, Brown, 1971.

Alperovitz, Gar. *Cold War Essays*. New York: Doubleday, Anchor Books, 1970.

Aron, Raymond. *The Imperial Republic: The United States and the World 1945-1973*. Englewood Cliffs, NJ: Prentice-Hall, 1974.

Aronson, James. *The Press and the Cold War*. New York: Bobbs-Merrill, 1970.

Aspects of the NATO Alliance. McLean, VA: Research Analysis Corp., (November 1970): 102.

The Atlantic Allies and the Future of Europe. Paris: North Atlantic Treaty Association, 1973.

The Atlantic Papers: Political and Strategic Studies. New York: Dunellen, 1970.

Bailey, (Maj.) Jerry T. *NATO: Then and Now*. Maxwell AFB, AL: Air Command and Staff College, 1974.

Ball, George W. "The USSR and the West, 1972." *Atlantic Community Quarterly* 10 (Summer 1972): 188-193.

―――. "Parochialism in Europe; 'Creeping Gaulism' in America." *Atlantic Community Quarterly* 11 (Summer 1973): 161-170.

Ball, Robert. "Rethinking the Defense of Europe." *Fortune* 87 (February 1973): 60-65.

―――. "NATO Needs a Fresh Breeze." *Fortune*, February 1974, pp. 112, 104-109, 112, 116-117.

Balniel, Lord. "European Defense and European Security." *Survival* 13 (May 1971): 168-172.

Barber, (Comdr.) James A., Jr. "The Nixon Doctrine and the Navy." *Naval War College Review* 23 (June 1971): 5-15.

Barclay, (Brig.) C.N. "What Happens to Europe if the Americans Leave? A British View." *Army* 23 (November 1973): 7-11.

Barnet, Richard J. "The Illusion of Security." *Foreign Policy* 2 (Spring 1971): 71-89.

―――. *Roots of War*. New York: Atheneum, 1972.

Bell, Carol. "Strategic Problems of the Atlantic." *Survival* 12 (March 1970): 98-101.

Bertram, Christoph. "Internal Pressures on Defense Policy." *Survival* 13 (January 1971): 13-16.

Birgi, Nuri. "The Atlantic Alliance: Its Present Problems and Its Aims; Lecture Delivered at the NATO Defense College on 4 March 1970." *NATO's Fifteen Nations* 15 (December 1970-January 1971): 31-38.

Birnbaum, Karl E. *Peace in Europe: East-West Relations 1966-1968*. London: Oxford University Press, 1967.

―――. "Pan-European Perspectives After the Berlin Agreement." *International Journal* 27 (Winter 1972): 32-44.

Birrenbach, Kurt. "The United States and Western Europe: Partners or Rivals?" *Orbis* 17 (Summer 1973): 405-414.

―――. "Europe's Security in the Changed World." *Aussen Politik* (Fall 1973): 285-297.

Blaney, Harry C. "NATO's New Challenges to the Problems of Modern Society." *Atlantic Community Quarterly* 11 (Summer 1973): 236-247.

Bletz, Donald F. *The Role of the Military Professional in U.S. Foreign Policy*. London: Pall Mall; New York: Praeger, 1972.

Bloomfield, Lincoln P. *In Search of American Foreign Policy: The Humane Use of Power*. New York: Oxford University Press, 1974.

Bohlen, Charles E. *Witness to History, 1929-1969*. New York: W.W. Norton, 1973.

Braeman, J., ed. *Twentieth Century American Foreign Policy.*
Columbus, OH: State University Press, 1971.

Brandon, Henry. *The Retreat of American Power: Nixon's and Kissinger's Foreign Policy--and Its Effects.* Garden City, NY: Doubleday, 1973.

Brandt, Willy. "Europe's New Self-Awareness." *Survival* 15 (July/August 1973): 193-194.

Brosio, Manlio. "Will NATO Survive Detente?" *The World Today* 27 (June 1971): 231-241. *Atlantic Community Quarterly* 9 (Summer 1971): 143-155.

———. "An Account of Stewardship." *Atlantic Community Quarterly* 9 (Winter 1971-72): 451-459.

———. "Europe and the Atlantic Alliance Today." *Atlantic Community Quarterly* 10 (Fall 1972): 285-294.

———. "Consultation and the Atlantic Alliance." *Survival* 16 (May/June 1974): 115-120. *Atlantic Community Quarterly* 12 (Fall 1974): 308-318.

Brown, Neville. "An Unstable Balance of Terror?" *The World Today* 26 (January 1970): 38-46.

———. *European Security 1972-1980.* London: R.U.S.I., 1972.

Brzezinski, Zbigniew. "America and Europe." *Foreign Affairs* 49 (October 1970): 11-30.

———. "The Balance of Power Delusion." *Foreign Policy* 7 (Summer 1972): 54-59.

———. "How the Cold War Was Played." *Foreign Affairs* 51 (October 1972): 181-209.

———. "U.S. Foreign Policy: The Search for Focus." *Foreign Affairs* 51 (July 1973): 708-727.

———. "Recognizing the Crisis." *Foreign Policy* 17 (Winter 1974-1975): 63-74.

———. "Shifting Mood and System--Subjective and Objective Changes Affect US-EC Relations." *Atlantic Community Quarterly* 12 (Fall 1974): 319-326.

Buchan, Alastair. "The Purpose of NATO and Its Future Development." *Atlantic Community Quarterly* 8 (Spring 1970): 49-56.

———. *Power and Equilibrium in the 1970's.* New York: Praeger, 1972.

———. *Europe and America: From Alliance to Coalition.* Paris: Atlantic Institute for International Affairs, 1973.

————. *The End of the Post-War Era: A New Balance of World Power*. London: Weidenfeld and Nicolson, 1974.

Bundy, McGeorge. "America's Enduring Links with Europe." *Atlantic Community Quarterly* 8 (Spring 1970): 17-30.

Bundy, William P. "International Security Today." *Foreign Affairs* 53 (October 1974): 24-44.

Burgess, W. Randolph and Huntley, James Robert. *Europe and America: The Next Ten Years*. New York: Walker & Co., 1970.

Burrows, Sir Bernard and Irwin, Christopher. *The Security of Western Europe: Towards a Common Defense Policy*. London: Charles Knight, 1972.

Burt, Richard, and Kemp, Geoffrey. *Congressional Hearings on American Defense Policy: 1947-1971: An Annotated Bibliography*. Lawrence, KS: University Press of Kansas, 1974.

Bussmann, Bernard. "A European Security Conference." *Survival* 12 (March 1970): 81-85.

Calleo, David. *The Atlantic Fantasy: The U.S., NATO, and Europe*. Baltimore, MD: Johns Hopkins Press, 1970.

Camps, Miriam. "Sources of Strain in Transatlantic Relations." *International Affairs* 48 (October 1972): 559-578.

Canby, Steven L. "The Wasteful Ways of NATO." *Survival* 15 (January/February 1973): 21-26.

————. "NATO Muscle: More Shadow Than Substance." *Military Review* 53 (February 1973): 65-74.

Chace, James. "The Concert of Europe." *Foreign Affairs* 52 (October 1973): 96-108.

"The Challenge of Success." *NATO's Fifteen Nations* 19 (April-May 1974): 50-56.

Clemens, Diane Shaver. *Yalta: A Study in Soviet-American Relations*. New York: Oxford University Press, 1970.

Clemens, Walter C., Jr. "The Impact of Detente on Chinese and Soviet Communism." *Journal of International Affairs* 28 (October 1974): 133-157.

Cleveland, Harlan. "The Golden Rule of Consultation." *Atlantic Community Quarterly* 8 (Fall 1970): 334-350.

————. *NATO--The Transatlantic Bargain*. New York: Harper and Row, 1970.

Cobb, (Maj.) Tyrus W. "The Durability of Detente." *Military Review* 54 (April 1974): 3-15.

Collins, John M. "Maneuver Instead of Mass: The Key to Assured Stability." *Orbis* 18 (Fall 1974): 750-762.

Combeaux, (Gen.) Edmond. *The Atlantic Alliance and Defense Problems*. Paris: Atlantic Treaty Association, September, 1970.

Cottrell, Alvin J., and Theberge, James D., eds. *The Western Mediterranean: Its Political, Economic and Strategic Importance*. New York: Praeger, 1973.

Cox, (Capt.) G.W. "An Alliance Initiative." *United States Naval Institute Proceedings* 100 (November 1974): 45-53.

Crankshaw, Edward. "Where Khrushchev Left Off." *Survival* 12 (November 1970): 374-375.

Davidow, Mike. "USA: Detente, Crises and Problems." *International Affairs* (NSSR) 4 (April 1974): 64-71.

Davis, Lynn Etheridge. *The Cold War Begins: Soviet-American Conflict over Western Europe*. Princeton, NJ: Princeton University Press, 1974.

Davison (Gen.) Michael S. "The Role and Capability of United States Ground Forces in Europe." *RUSI Journal* 118 (December 1973): 3-9.

Davydov, Y. "U.S.A.-Western Europe: A 'New Relationship.'" *International Affairs* (USSR) 1 (January 1974): 35-41.

Debre, Michel. "The Defense of Europe and Security in Europe." *Atlantic Community Quarterly* 11 (Spring 1973): 93-118.

"Declaration of Atlantic Relations, 26 June 1974." *Survival* 16 (September/October 1974): 246-248.

"Declaration on Atlantic Relations Approved and Published by the North Atlantic Council in Ottawa." *NATO Review* 11 (1974): 6-8.

de Gara, John P. *Nuclear Proliferation and Security*. New York: Carnegie Foundation for International Peace, May 1970.

de Staercke, Andre. "Where Does the Atlantic Alliance Stand Today?" *Atlantic Community Quarterly* 11 (Winter 1973-1974): 448-455.

Dobney, Frederick J., ed. *Selected Papers of Will Clayton*. Baltimore, MD: Johns Hopkins Press, 1971.

Dodd, (Col.) Norman. "25 Years in NATO." *Defense* 5 (July 1974): 308-310.

Duchene, Francois. "Salt, the *Ostpolitik* and the Post-Cold War Context." *The World Today* 26 (December 1970): 500-511.

―――――. "The Future of Europe: Ways Forward." *The World Today* 27 (November 1971): 457-462.

―――――. "A New European Defense Community." *Foreign Affairs* 50 (October 1971): 69-82.

―――――. "The Strategic Consequence of the Enlarged European Community." *Survival* 15 (January/February 1973): 2-7.

Ecobescu, Nicolae and Celac, Sergia. "Security and Co-operation in Europe." *Survival* 13 (June 1971): 203-207.

Ellsworth, Robert. "Europe, America and the Era of Negotiation." *Survival* 13 (April 1971): 114-122.

Elwood, (Lt. Col.) Niles T. *U.S. vs. Allied Contribution to the Support of NATO*. (Professional Study). Maxwell AFB, AL: Air War College, 1974.

Erhardt, Carl A. "Disenchantment Between Europe and America." *Aussen Politik* (Winter 1973): 377-392.

European Security, Disarmament and Other Problems. Anlanko, Finland: Pugwash Conference, 1973.

"European Security." *Survival* 15 (September/October 1973): 236-242.

"Extracts from President Nixon's Foreign Policy Report to Congress of 25 February 1971." *NATO Review* 19 (May/June 1971): 23-29.

Feis, Herbert. *From Trust to Terror: The Onset of the Cold War, 1945-1950*. New York: Norton, 1971.

Fontaine, Andre. "The Real Divisions of Europe." *Foreign Affairs* 49 (January 1971): 302-314.

Foster, Richard B., ed. *Strategy for the West: American-Allied Relations in Transition*. New York: Russak, 1974.

Fox, William T. and Schilling, Warner R., eds. *European Security and the Atlantic System*. New York: Columbia University Press, 1973.

Freeland, Richard M. *The Truman Doctrine and the Origins of McCarthyism*. New York: Knopf, 1972.

Fried, Anne. "Finlandization Is Not a Curse Word." *Worldview* 16 (January 1973): 17-21.

Full Committee Consideration of the Report of the Ad Hoc Committee on U.S. Military Commitments to Europe. Washington, D.C.: Government Printing Office, 1974.

Gaddis, John Lewis. *The United States and the Origins of the Cold War, 1941-1947.* New York: Columbia University Press, 1972.

―――. "Was the Truman Doctrine a Real Turning Point?" *Foreign Affairs* 52 (January 1974): 386-402.

Galtung, Johan, ed. *Co-Operation in Europe.* New York: Humanities Press, 1971.

Gamson, William A. and Modigliani, Andre. *Untangling the Cold War: A Strategy for Testing Rival Theories.* Boston: Little, Brown, 1971.

Gardner, Lloyd C. *Architects of Illusion: Men and Ideas in American Foreign Policy, 1941-1949.* Chicago: Quadrangle Books, 1970.

―――; Schlesinger, Arthur, Jr.; and Morgenthau, Hans J. *The Origins of the Cold War.* Waltham, MA: Ginn-Blaisdell, 1970.

Gasteyger, Curt. "Europe and America: Between Co-operation and Competition." *NATO Review* 20 (May/June 1972): 12-15.

―――. "Europe and America at the Crossroads." *Atlantic Community Quarterly* 10 (Summer 1972): 154-166.

―――. "Europe Cool to US Suggestions on Revitalized Charter." *Atlantic Community Quarterly* 11 (Fall 1973): 319-321.

Gati, Charles. "What Containment Meant." *Foreign Policy* 7 (Summer 1972): 22-40.

Geiger, Theodore. *The Fortunes of the West: The Future of the Atlantic Nations.* Bloomington, IN: Indiana University Press, 1973.

Gelb, Leslie H. and Halperin, Morton H. "Why West Europe Needs 300,000 G.I.'s?" *Atlantic Community Quarterly* 9 (Spring 1971): 56-60.

Gilmour, I.H.J. "The Prospects for NATO." *NATO's Fifteen Nations* 19 (February-March 1974): 22-25.

Gladwyn, Lord. "The Defense of Western Europe." *Foreign Affairs* 51 (April 1973): 588-597.

Godson, Joseph, ed. *Transatlantic Crisis: Europe and America in the 1970's.* London: Alcove Press Ltd., 1974.

Goldmann, Kjell. "East-West Tension in Europe, 1946-1970: A Conceptual Analysis and a Quantitative Description." *World Politics* 26 (October 1973): 106-125.

———. *Tension and Detente in Bipolar Europe.* Stockholm: Esselte Studium, Scandinavian University Books, 1974.

Goldwater, Barry. "The Perilous Conjuncture: Soviet Ascendancy and American Isolationism." *Orbis* 15 (Spring 1971): 53-64.

———. "NATO's Future." *NATO's Fifteen Nations* 19 (February-March 1974): 26-27.

Goodpaster, Andrew J. "New Challenges, New Problems, New Dangers." *Atlantic Community Quarterly* 10 (Winter 1972-1973): 457-469.

———. "Remarks at the NATO Defense College, Rome, Italy, 13 July 1973." *NATO's Fifteen Nations* 18 (December 1973-January 1974): 24-29.

———. "NATO: A Successful Product of Political-Military Engineering." *Vital Speeches of the Day* 40 (15 April 1974): 389-393.

———. "NATO and U.S. Forces: Challenges and Prospects." *Strategic Review* 2 (Winter 1974): 6-17.

Graubard, Stephen R. *Kissinger: Portrait of a Mind.* New York: W.W. Norton, 1973.

Greenhill, Denis. "The Future Security of Western Europe." *International Affairs* 50 (January 1974): 1-14.

Gregg, Robert W. and Kegley, Charles W., Jr., eds. *After Vietnam: The Future of American Foreign Policy.* Garden City, KS: Doubleday & Co., 1971.

Grey, Collin S. "Mini-nukes and Strategy." *International Journal* 29 (Spring 1974): 216-241.

Griffith, William E. *Cold War and Co-existence: Russia, China and the United States.* Englewood Cliffs, NJ: Prentice-Hall, 1971.

———. "NATO: Alliance to Disarray." *Reader's Digest* 105 (August 1974): 56-60.

Griffiths, Franklyn. "Cooperation as a Form of Conflict." *Atlantic Community Quarterly* 12 (Winter 1974-1975): 481-499.

Hadik, Laszlo. "The Process of Detente in Europe." *Atlantic Community Quarterly* 8 (Fall 1970: 325-333.

Hadley, Guy. *Transatlantic Partnership and Problems: An Enquiry into Relations Between Western Europe and the United States.* Kent, England: Free Trade Association Trust, 1974.

Halperin, Morton H. "The Good, the Bad and the Wasteful."
Foreign Policy 6 (Spring 1972): 69-83.

Hammond, Paul Y. *Changing Bargaining Relations in the Atlantic Alliance.* Santa Monica, CA: Rand Corp., June 1973.

Hanreider, Wolfram, ed. *The United States and Western Europe: Political, Economic and Strategic Perspectives.* Cambridge, MA: Winthrop, 1974.

Harrison, Stanley R. "Congress and Presidential Conflict: Foreign Policy and NATO." *NATO's Fifteen Nations* 17 (June-July 1972): 83-87.

──────. "Strategy for Tomorrow: America's Need for Future Security in Europe." *Military Review* 52 (August 1972): 57-70.

Hartley, Anthony. "Europe Between the Superpowers." *Foreign Affairs* 49 (January 1971): 271-282.

──────. "JFK's Foreign Policy." *Foreign Policy* 4 (Fall 1971): 77-100.

Hartman, Arthur A. "Department Gives Views on U.S. Commitments to NATO." *The Department of State Bulletin* 70 (11 March 1974): 243-247.

Hassner, Pierre. *Change and Security in Europe.* (Adelphi Paper No. 45). London: Institute for Strategic Studies, 1968.

──────. "Europe in the '70's: Stability and Conflicts." *Revue de defense nationale* (May 1970): 723-736.

──────. "The New Europe: From Cold War to Hot Peace." *International Journal* 27 (Winter 1972): 1-17.

──────, and Steel, Ronald. "'Spheres of What?' An Exchange." *Foreign Policy* 6 (Spring 1972): 142-152.

──────. *Europe in the Age of Negotiation.* Beverly Hills, CA: Sage Publications; published for the Georgetown Center for Strategic and International Studies, 1973.

──────. "How Troubled a Partnership?" *International Journal* 29 (Spring 1974): 166-185.

Head, Richard G. and Rokke, Erwin J., eds. *American Defense Policy.* Baltimore, MD: Johns Hopkins Press, 1973.

Hill, R.J. "MBFR." *International Journal* 29 (Spring 1974): 242-255.

Hoffmann, Stanley. "Weighing the Balance of Power." *Foreign Affairs* 50 (July 1972): 618-643.

———. "After the Creation, or the Watch and the Arrow." *International Journal* 18 (Spring 1973): 175-184.

———. *Force in Modern Societies: Its Place in International Politics.* (Adelphi Paper No. 102). London: International Institute for Strategic Studies, 1973.

Hogglund, (Maj.) Gustav. "United States NATO Strategy." *Military Review* 54 (January 1974): 39-49.

Hollander, Paul. *Soviet and American Society: A Comparison.* New York: Oxford University Press, 1973.

Horton, Frank B., ed. *Comparative Defense Policy.* Baltimore, MD: Johns Hopkins Press, 1974.

Howard, Michael. "NATO and the Year of Europe." *Survival* 16 (January/February 1974): 21-27.

Howe, Quincy. *Ashes of Victory: World War II and Its Aftermath.* New York: Simon and Schuster, 1972.

Hunter, Robert. "Troops, Trade and Diplomacy." *Atlantic Community Quarterly* 9 (Fall 1971): 283-292.

Huntington, S.P., and Manshell, Warren D. "'X' Plus 25: Interview with George Kennan." *Foreign Policy* 7 (Summer 1972): 3-21.

Huntley, James Robert. *Man's Environment and the Atlantic Alliance.* Brussels: NATO Information Service, 1971.

———. "The United States and the European Community." *Atlantic Community Quarterly* 10 (Winter 1972-1973): 527-540.

———. "The United States and the European Community." *NATO's Fifteen Nations* 17 (June-July 1972): 73-80.

"In the Same Boat." *Atlantic Community Quarterly* 11 (Fall 1973): 314-318.

I.I.S.S. *The Military Balance 1974-75.* London: International Institute for Strategic Studies, yearly since 1972.

Irwin, Christopher. "Nuclear Aspects of West European Defence Integration." *International Affairs* 47 (October 1971): 679-691.

Janowitz, Morris. "The Future of NATO." *Survival* 13 (December 1971): 412-415.

———. "Toward a Redefinition of Military Strategy in International Relations." *World Politics* 26 (July 1974): 473-508.

Jaquet, L.G.M., ed. "The Role of NATO Military Forces as Part of the Alliance's Overall Objectives." *NATO Review* 22 (December 1974): 6-13.

Jenner, Peter. "NATO Solidarity and Undiminished Defence Basis for Progress Towards Detente." *NATO Review* 6 (1973): 3-5.

Jennings, (Col.) Richard M. "The Thrust of the Nixon Doctrine." *Military Review* 52 (February 1972): 3-9.

Jones, David C. "Reappraising the Prospects for NATO." *Strategic Review* 2 (Fall 1974): 9-12.

Jordan, Robert S., ed. *Europe and the Superpowers: Perceptions of European International Politics.* Boston, MA: Allyn and Bacon, 1971.

Joshua, Wynfred and Hahn, Walter F. *Nuclear Politics: America, France, and Britain.* (The Washington Papers, V-1. 1). Beverly Hills, CA: Sage Publications, 1973.

Kaiser, Karl. "Europe and America: A Critical Phase." *Foreign Affairs* 52 (July 1974): 725-741.

──────. *Europe and the United States: The Future of the Relationship.* Washington, D.C.: Columbia Books, 1973.

Kaiser, Robert G. *Cold Winter, Cold War.* New York: Stein and Day, 1974.

Kaltefleiter, Werner. "Europe and the Nixon Doctrine: A German Point of View." *Orbis* 17 (Spring 1973): 75-94.

Kaplan, Morton A. *The Rationale for NATO: European Collective Security--Past and Future.* Stanford, CA: Hoover Institution; Washington, D.C.: American Enterprise Institute for Public Policy Research, 1973.

──────. *Great Issues of International Politics.* Chicago, IL: Aldine, 1974.

Kennan, George F. "After the Cold War: American Foreign Policy in the 1970s." *Foreign Affairs* 51 (October 1972): 210-227.

──────. *Memoirs 1950-1963.* Boston, MA: Atlantic (Little, Brown), 1972.

──────. "Europe's Problems, Europe's Choices." *Foreign Policy* 14 (Spring 1974): 3-16.

Kiep, Walther L. *A New Challenge for Western Europe: A View from Bonn.* New York: Mason and Lipscomb, 1974.

Kintner, William R. and Klaiber, Wolfgang. *Eastern Europe and European Security*. New York: Dunellen, 1971.

──── and Foster, Richard B., eds. *National Strategy in a Decade of Change*. Lexington, MA: Lexington Books, D.C. Heath, 1973.

Kissinger, Henry A. "A New Atlantic Charter." *Survival* 15 (July/August 1973): 188-192.

────. "Creativity Together or Irrelevance Apart." *Atlantic Community Quarterly* 11 (Winter 1973-74): 413-421.

────. "Detente with the Soviet Union: The Reality of Competition and the Imperative of Cooperation." *The Department of State Bulletin* 71 (14 October 1974): 505-519.

Klaiber, Wolfgang. *Era of Negotiations: European Security and Force Reductions*. Lexington, MA: Lexington Books, D.C. Heath, 1973.

Knorr, Klaus E. *The Atlantic Alliance: A Reappraisal*. New York: Foreign Policy Association, 1974.

Kohl, Wilfrid L. and Taubman, William. "American Policy Toward Europe: The Next Phase." *Orbis* 17 (Spring 1973): 51-74.

Kolko, Joyce and Gabriel. *The Limits of Power: The World and U.S. Foreign Policy 1945-1954*. New York: Harper and Row, 1972.

Komer, Robert. *Treating NATO's Self-Inflicted Wound*. Santa Monica, CA: Rand Corp., October 1973.

Korbel, Josef. *Detente in Europe: Real or Imaginary?* Princeton, NJ: Princeton University Press, 1972.

Kruls, (Gen.) H.J. "Twenty-Five Years of NATO!" *NATO's Fifteen Nations* 19 (February-March 1974): 19-21.

Kuklick, Bruce. *American Policy and the Division of Germany: The Clash with Russia over Reparations*. Ithaca, NY: Cornell University Press, 1972.

Lacqueur, Walter, ed. *A Dictionary of Politics*. New York: The Free Press, 1973.

La Feber, Walter, ed. *The Origins of the Cold War, 1941-1947*. New York: Wiley, 1971.

Laloy, Jean. "Does Europe Have a Future?" *Foreign Affairs* 51 (October 1972): 154-166.

Landau, David. *Kissinger: The Uses of Power*. Boston: Houghton Mifflin, 1972.

Legvold, Robert. "European Security Conference." *Survey* 76 (Summer 1970): 41-52.

―――. "The Problem of European Security." *Problems of Communism* 23 (January/February 1974): 13-33.

Leifer, Michael, ed. *Constraints and Adjustments in Foreign Policy*. London: Allen and Unwin, 1972.

Luns, Joseph M.A.H. "The Future of the Atlantic Alliance in the Light of Present European Developments." *Atlantic Community Quarterly* 10 (Summer 1972): 194-202.

―――. "NATO in the 1970s." *RUSI Journal* 4 (December 1972): 3-9.

―――. "NATO View of Security Conferences." *Atlantic Community Quarterly* 11 (Spring 1973): 55-64.

―――. "NATO's 25th Birthday." *Atlantic Community Quarterly* 12 (Spring 1974): 7-11.

―――. "The North Atlantic Alliance Commemorates Its Twenty-Fifth Anniversary; Address by Secretary General Joseph Luns." *NATO Review* 22 (June 1974): 5-7.

―――. "NATO: Reflections on the 25th Anniversary." *Millennium* 3 (Autumn 1974): 166-168.

―――. "Prospect for the Alliance." *NATO Review* 22 (1974): 3-7.

Lyon, Peyton V. *NATO as a Diplomatic Instrument*. Toronto: The Atlantic Council of Canada, December 1970.

―――. "Beyond NATO." *International Journal* 29 (Spring 1974): 268-278.

MacLaren, (Col.) William G., Jr. *"Europeanization"; Some Considerations Concerning the Application of the Nixon Doctrine to NATO*. (Professional Study No. 4400). Maxwell AFB, AL: Air War College, 1971.

McGee, (Sen.) Gale. "The Atlantic Union Resolution." *Atlantic Community Quarterly* 10 (Winter 1972/1973): 541-544.

McGeehan, Robert. *The German Rearmament Question: American Diplomacy and European Defense After World War II*. Urbana, IL: University of Illinois Press, 1971.

――― and Warnecke, Steven J. "Europe's Foreign Policies: Economics, Politics, or Both?" *Orbis* 17 (Winter 1974): 1251-1279.

Maddox, Robert James. *The New Left and the Origins of the Cold War*. Princeton, NJ: Princeton University Press, 1973.

Mally, Gerhard. *The European Community in Perspective.* Lexington, MA: Lexington Books for the Atlantic Council for the United States, 1973.

———. *Interdependence: The European-American Connection in the Global Context.* Lexington, MA: Published for Atlantic Council of the United States, 1976.

———. *The New Europe and the United States.* Franborough: Saxon House, 1974.

Mathias, (Sen.) Charles McC., Jr. *Europe and America in the 1970's: Part I: Between Detente and Confrontation.* (Adelphi Paper No. 70). London: International Institute for Strategic Studies, November 1970.

Menaul, Stewart W.B. "Strategy for Europe." *NATO's Fifteen Nations* 18 (October-November 1973): 24-35.

Mendershausen, Horst. *Union or Concert in Europe?* Santa Monica, CA: Rand Corp., August 1972.

———. *The Atlantic Defense Relationships: Core, Troubles, Prospects.* Santa Monica, CA: Rand Corp., July 1974.

Mensonides, Louis J. and Kuhlman, James A. *The Future of Inter-Bloc Relations in Europe.* New York: Praeger, 1974.

Miller, Lynn H. and Pruessen, Ronald W., eds. *Reflections on the Cold War: A Quarter Century of American Foreign Policy.* Philadelphia, PA: Temple University Press, 1974.

Milton, (Gen.) T.R. "Behind NATO's Shiny Facade--A Troubled Future?" *Air Force Magazine* 55 (August 1972): 49-52.

———. "NATO and the Aging Process." *Strategic Review* 2 (Winter 1974): 39-43.

Mogensen, (Capt.) Ebbe. "American Strategy for Western Europe in the 70's." *Military Review* 53 (August 1973): 3-15.

Mondale, Walter F. "Beyond Detente: Toward International Economic Security." *Foreign Affairs* 53 (October 1974): 1-23.

Morgan, Roger. "West-East Relations in Europe: Political Perspectives." *International Affairs* 49 (April 1973): 177-189.

Morgenthau, Hans J. "Changes and Chances in American-Soviet Relations." *Foreign Affairs* 49 (April 1971): 429-441.

Morse, Edward L. "Why the Malaise?" *Foreign Affairs* 51 (January 1973): 367-379.

Moulton, Harland B. *From Superiority to Parity.* Westport, CT: Greenwood Press, 1973.

Nash, Henry T. *American Foreign Policy: Response to a Sense of Threat.* Homewood, IL: The Dorsey Press, 1973.

NATO Facts and Figures. Brussels: NATO Information Service, 1971.

"NATO Glossary of Terms and Definitions for Military Use (English and French)." Brussels: NATO, Military Agency for Standardization, 1974.

Newhouse, John. *U.S. Troops in Europe: Issues, Costs, and Choices.* Washington, D.C.: The Brookings Institution, 1971.

──────. "Stuck Fast." *Foreign Affairs* 51 (January 1973): 353-366.

"Nineteenth Annual Session of the North Atlantic Assembly." *NATO Review* 21 (1973): 19-25.

Nixon, (President) Richard M. "Europe and the Atlantic Alliance." *Atlantic Community Quarterly* 11 (Fall 1973): 293-313.

Noble, G. Bernard. *Christian A. Herter.* New York: Cooper Square Publishers, 1970.

"North Atlantic Council Ministerial Meeting Adopts Declaration on Atlantic Relations." *The Department of State Bulletin* 71 (8 July 1974): 37-44.

Northedge, F.S., ed. *The Use of Force in International Relations.* New York: Free Press, 1974.

Nuechterlein, Donald E. *United States National Interests in a Changing World.* Lexington, KY: University Press of Kentucky, 1973.

Nunn, (Sen.) Sam. *Policy, Troops and the NATO Alliance.* Washington, D.C.: U.S. Government Printing Office, 1974.

────── and Bartlett, (Sen.) Dewey F. *NATO and the New Soviet Threat, Report of Senator Sam Nunn and Senator Dewey F. Bartlett to the Committee on Armed Services, United States Senate.* Washington, D.C.: U.S. Government Printing Office, 1977.

Orvik, Nils. "Semi-neutrality and Canada's Security." *International Journal* 29 (Spring 1974): 186-215.

Osgood, Robert E. *America and the World: From the Truman Doctrine to Vietnam.* Baltimore, MD: Johns Hopkins Press, 1970.

Ottoman, (Col.) Raymond H. *NATO in the 1970's: A Prognosis.* (Professional Study No. 3975). Maxwell AFB, AL: Air War College, 1970.

Owen, David. *The Politics of Defense.* London: Jonathan Cape, 1972.

Palmer, Michael. "The Prospects for a European Security Conference." *Atlantic Community Quarterly* 9 (Fall 1971): 293-300.

———. "A European Security Conference: Preparation and Procedure." *The World Today* 28 (January 1972): 36-46.

———. "The European Community and a Security Conference." *The World Today* 28 (July 1972): 296-303.

Parker, W.H. *The Superpowers: The United States and the Soviet Union Compared.* New York: Halstead Press, 1972.

Paterson, Thomas G., ed. *Cold War Critics: Alternatives to American Foreign Policy in the Truman Years.* Chicago, IL: Quadrangle Books, 1971.

———. *Soviet-American Confrontation: Postwar Reconstruction and the Origins of the Cold War.* Baltimore, MD: Johns Hopkins Press, 1973.

Paul, Roland A. *American Military Commitments Abroad.* New Brunswick: Rutgers University Press, 1973.

Pfaltzgraff, Robert L., Jr. "NATO and European Security: Prospects for the 1970's." *Orbis* 15 (Spring 1971): 154-177.

———. "The United States and Europe: Partners in a Multipolar World?" *Orbis* 17 (Spring 1973): 31-50.

Pick, Otto. "Atlantic Defense and the Integration of Europe." *Atlantic Community Quarterly* 10 (Summer 1972): 174-184.

——— and Critchley, Julian. *Collective Security.* London: Macmillan, 1974.

Pierre, Andrew J. "Nuclear Diplomacy: Britain, France and America." *Foreign Affairs* 49 (January 1971): 283-301.

———. "America Down, Russia Up: The Changing Political Role of Military Power." *Foreign Policy* 4 (Fall 1971): 163-187.

———. "Europe and America in a Pentagonal World." *Survey* 18 (Winter 1972): 183-201.

———. "Can Europe's Security Be 'Decoupled' from America?" *Foreign Affairs* 51 (July 1973): 761-777.

———. "What Happened to the Year of Europe?" *The World Today* 30 (March 1974): 110-118.

"President Nixon Visits NATO Headquarters and the Soviet Union." *The Department of State Bulletin* 71 (29 July 1974): 165-173.

Proxmire, (Sen.) William. *Report from Wasteland: America's Military Industrial Complex.* New York: Praeger, 1970.

Quester, George H. *Nuclear Diplomacy: The First Twenty-Five Years.* New York: Dunnellen, 1971.

Radovanovic, Ljubomir. "The Atlantic Declaration." *Review of International Affairs* 25 (August 1974): 13-14.

Rapoport, Anatol. *The Big Two: Soviet-American Perceptions of Foreign Policy.* New York: Pegasus, 1971.

Richards, Ivor. "A European Defence Policy." *Survival* 12 (March 1970): 75-80.

Richardson, Elliot. "The United States and Western Europe." *Survival* 12 (March 1970): 86-90.

Richardson, J.L. "Cold-War Revisionism: A Critique." *World Politics* 24 (July 1972): 579-612.

Ritchie, Ronald S. "The Atlantic Condition." *International Journal* 29 (Spring 1974): 155-165.

Roberts, Chalmers M. *The Nuclear Years: The Arms Race and Arms Control 1945-1970.* New York: Praeger, 1970.

―――. "How Containment Worked." *Foreign Policy* 7 (Summer 1972): 41-53.

Rogers, William P. "Our Permanent Interests in Europe." *Atlantic Community Quarterly* 10 (Spring 1972): 21-26.

Rose, Eugene J., ed. *American Defense and Detente: Readings in National Security Policy.* New York: Dodd, Mead & Co., 1973.

Rosecrance, Richard and Stein, Arthur. "Interdependence: Myth or Reality?" *World Politics* 26 (October 1973): 1-27.

Rosen, Steven, ed. *Testing the Theory of the Military Industrial Complex.* Lexington, MA: Lexington Books, D.C. Heath, 1973.

Rosenfeld, Stephen S. "Pluralism and Policy." *Foreign Affairs* 52 (January 1974): 263-272.

Rosenthal, Benjamin S. "America's Move." *Foreign Affairs* 51 (January 1973): 380-391.

Rostow, Eugene V. *Peace in the Balance: The Future of American Foreign Policy.* New York: Simon and Schuster, 1972.

———. "Atlantic Relations: Perspectives Towards the Future." *NATO Review* 21 (1973): 7-10.

Rothstein, Robert L. "New Perspectives on NATO." *International Organization* 24 (Summer 1970): 566-577.

Ruhl, Lothar. *The Nine and NATO*. Paris: Atlantic Institute for International Affairs, 1974.

———. "NATO's Political Limitations." *Atlantic Community Quarterly* 12 (Winter 1974-75): 463-469.

Rush, Kenneth. "The NATO Alliance: The Basis for an Era of Negotiation." *The Department of State Bulletin* 68 (June 18, 1973): 867-871.

———. "The NATO Alliance: The Basis for an Era of Negotiation." *Atlantic Community Quarterly* 11 (Fall 1973): 327-334.

Sarkesian, Sam C., ed. *The Military-Industrial Complex: A Reassessment*. Beverly Hills and London: Sage Publications, 1972.

Schaetzel, J. Robert. "Some European Questions for Dr. Kissinger." *Foreign Policy* 12 (Fall 1973): 66-78.

Schilling, Warner R. *American Arms and a Changing Europe: Dilemmas of Deterrence and Disarmament*. New York: Columbia University Press, 1974.

Schmidt, Helmut. "European Security: Perspectives of the Alliance." *Survival* 12 (February 1970): 43-46.

———. *The Balance of Power*. London: William Kimber, 1971.

Schoenthal, Klaus. "Bonn-Washington: The Maturing Alliance." *Aussenpolitic* 1 (1970): 42-52.

Schuckburgh, (Sir) Evelyn. *The Atlantic Alliance and Political Problems*. Paris: Atlantic Treaty Association, 1970.

Schwarz, Hans Peter. "A Doubtful Device--The European Security Conference." *Survival* 13 (February 1971): 49-55.

Schwelien, Joachim. "Era of Negotiation? Harsh Words--Friendly Dialogues." *Survival* 13 (January 1971): 29-31.

Serfaty, Simon. "America and Europe in the 1970's: Integration or Disintegration?" *Orbis* 17 (Spring 1973): 95-109.

———. *America and Europe in the 1970's: Integration or Disintegration?* Bologna: Johns Hopkins University, February 1974.

Shulman, Marshall D. *Soviet-American Relations and World Order: The Two and the Many.* (Adelphi Paper No. 66). London: International Institute for Strategic Studies, 1970.

———. "What Does Security Mean Today?" *Foreign Affairs* 49 (July 1971): 607-618.

———. "Toward a Western Philosophy of Coexistence." *Foreign Affairs* 52 (October 1973): 35-58.

Smart, Ian. "The New Atlantic Charter." *The World Today* 29 (June 1973): 238-242.

Smith, Gaddis. *Dean Acheson.* New York: Cooper Square Publishers, 1972.

———. "The Shadow of John Foster Dulles." *Foreign Affairs* 52 (January 1974): 403-408.

Smith, Jean Edward, ed. *The Papers of General Lucius D. Clay: Germany 1945-1949.* Bloomington, IN: Indiana University Press, 1974.

Smith, (Lt. Col) Paul G. *Toward a Reduced U.S. Profile in NATO.* (Professional Study). Maxwell AFB, AL: Air War College, 1972.

Solberg, Carl. *Riding High: America in the Cold War.* New York: Mason and Lipscomb, 1973.

Sommer, Theo. "Detente and Security: The Options." *Atlantic Community Quarterly* 9 (Spring 1971): 34-49.

Sorenson, Theodore C. "Most-Favored-Nation and Less Favorite Nations." *Foreign Affairs* 52 (January 1974): 273-386.

Spanier, John W. *American Foreign Policy Since World War II.* New York: Praeger, 1960.

Stanley, Timothy W. *A Conference on European Security? Problems, Prospects and Pitfalls.* Washington, D.C.: The Atlantic Council of the United States, 1970.

——— and Whitt, Darnell M. "Detente in the 1970s." *Atlantic Community Quarterly* 8 (Fall 1970): 313-324.

——— and ———. *Detente Diplomacy: United States and European Security in the 1970's.* New York: Dunellen, 1970.

Status of the World's Nations. (Geographic Bulletin, Publication 8735). Washington, D.C.: Department of State, Bureau of Intelligence and Research, September 1973.

Steel, Ronald. "A Sphere of Influence Policy." *Foreign Policy* 5 (Winter 1971-72): 107-118.

Stewart, (Maj.) Leslie W., Jr. *NATO in a World of Detente.* (Research Study). Maxwell AFB, AL: Air Command and Staff College, 1974.

Steinhoff, (Gen.) Johannes. "The Road to Detente." *Atlantic Community Quarterly* 10 (Winter 1972-73): 446-456.

Strauss, Franz Josef. *Challenge and Response: A Programme for Europe.* New York: Athenaeum, 1970.

Tatu, Michel. "The Great Power Triangle: Washington-Moscow-Peking." *The Atlantic Papers* 3. Paris: The Atlantic Institute, 1970.

―――. "Something More Than an Interlude." *Atlantic Community Quarterly* 9 (Spring 1971): 50-56.

Taylor, Maxwell D. "The Legitimate Claims of National Security." *Foreign Affairs* 52 (April 1974): 577-594.

Tillema, Herbert K. *Appeal to Force: American Military Intervention in the Era of Containment.* New York: Crowell, 1973.

Trager, Frank and Kronenberg, eds. *National Security and American Society.* Lawrence, KS: The University Press of Kansas, 1973.

Trotman, J.H. "NATO in Theory and Practice." *Survival* 13 (December 1971): 406-411.

―――. "NATO Uncertainties and Palliatives." *Canadian Defense Quarterly* 3 (Autumn 1973): 15-20.

Tuthill, John W. "Strategy Drift in the Atlantic." *Atlantic Community Quarterly* 9 (Summer 1971): 156-173.

Tuttle, Donald J. *Troubled Alliance.* (Professional Study). Maxwell AFB, AL: Air War College, 1974.

Twitchett, K.J., ed. *International Security.* London: Oxford University Press, 1971.

Ulam, Adam B. *The Rivals: America and Russia Since World War II.* New York: The Viking Press, 1971.

―――― and Windsor, Philip. "Moscow Plays the Balance ... But Europe Shouldn't." *Foreign Policy* 8 (Fall 1972): 86-101.

"United States Foreign Policy." *International Journal* 28 (Spring 1973): (theme issue).

van der Beugel, Ernst H. and Kohnstamm, Max. "Western Europe and America in the Seventies." *Atlantic Community Quarterly* 10 (Fall 1972): 295-311.

Vayrynen, Raimo. *Two Approaches to European Security: Arms Control and Cooperation.* Tampere: Tampere Peace Research Institute, 1974.

Vernon, Raymond. "Apparatchiks and Entrepreneurs: U.S.-Soviet Economic Relations." *Foreign Affairs* 52 (January 1974): 249-262.

―――. "Rogue Elephant in the Forest: An Appraisal of Transatlantic Relations." *Foreign Affairs* 51 (April 1973): 573-587.

von Groll, Gotz. "The Foreign Ministers in Helsinki." *Aussenpolitik* 24 (1973): 255-274.

―――. "The Helsinki Consultations." *Aussenpolitik* 24 (1973): 123-129.

Wagner, Wolfgang. "Through Different Eyes (The Four-Power Negotiation over Berlin)." *Survival* 13 (July 1971): 244-247.

Wall, Patrick. "NATO Looks Ahead." *Defense* 5 (March 1974): 98-99.

Walton, Richard J. *Cold War and Counter-Revolution: The Foreign Policy of John F. Kennedy.* New York: The Viking Press, 1972.

Warner, Geoffrey. "The United States and the Origins of the Cold War." *International Affairs* 46 (July 1970): 529-544.

Warnke, Paul C. and Gelb, Leslie H. "Security or Confrontation. The Case for a Defense Policy." *Foreign Policy* 1 (Winter 1970-71): 6-30.

Watson, Alan. *Europe at Risk.* London: George C. Harrap and Co., Ltd., 1972.

Weidenbaum, Murray L. *The Economics of Peacetime Defense.* London: Pall Mall, 1974.

"West Europe, 1973." *Current History* (April 1973): 145-185, (theme issue).

Western European Security Trends: Implications for the U.S. Military Role. McLean, VA: Research Analysis Corp., June 1970.

Wheeler-Bennett, Sir John and Nicholls, Anthony. *The Semblance of Peace: The Political Settlement After the Second World War.* New York: St. Martin's Press, 1972.

Whetten, Lawrence L. "The Mediterranean Threat: Has Strategic Parity Been Achieved?" *Survey* 74/75 (Winter/Spring 1970): 270-281.

———. A European View of NATO Strategy." *Military Review* 51 (September 1971): 25-37.

———. *Contemporary American Foreign Policy: Minimal Diplomacy, Defensive Strategy and Detente Management.* Lexington, MA: Lexington Books, D.C. Heath, 1974.

Williams, Geoffrey Lee and Williams, Alan Lee. *Crisis in European Defense: The Next Ten Years.* New York: St. Martin's Press, 1974.

Windsor, Philip. "Current Tensions in NATO." *The World Today* 26 (July 1970): 289-295.

Wohlstetter, Albert. "Is There a Strategic Arms Race?" *Foreign Policy* 15 (Summer 1974): 3-20.

———. "Rivals, But No Race." *Foreign Policy* 16 (Fall 1974): 48-81.

———. "Threats and Promises of Peace: Europe and America in the New Era." *Orbis* 17 (Winter 1974): 1107-1144.

Wolf, Charles, Jr. "Is United States Foreign Policy Being Militarized?" *Orbis* 14 (Winter 1971): 819-828.

Wyle, Frederick S. "Is European Security Negotiable?" *Survival* 12 (June 1970): 189-193.

———. "The United States and West European Security." *Survival* 14 (January/February 1972): 8-15.

Yarmolinsky, Adam. "The Military Establishment (Or How Political Problems Become Military Problems)." *Foreign Policy* 1 (Winter 1970-71): 78-79.

Yochelson, John. "The American Military Presence in Europe: Current Debate in the United States." *Orbis* 15 (Fall 1971): 784-807.

Yost, Charles. *The Conduct and Misconduct of Foreign Affairs: Reflections on U.S. Foreign Policy Since World War II.* New York: Random House, 1972.

"Z." (Pseud.) "The Year of Europe?" *Foreign Affairs* 52 (January 1974): 237-248.

Zellentin, Gerda. "Institutions for Detente and Co-operation." *The World Today* 29 (January 1973): 8-15.

1975-1979

Aliano, Richard A. *American Defense Policy from Eisenhower to Kennedy.* Columbus, OH: Ohio State Unierrsity Press, 1975.

Andren, Nils and Birnbaum, Karl. *Beyond Detente: Prospects for East-West Cooperation and Security in Europe.* Leyden: Sijthoff, 1976.

Aron, Raymond. *In Defense of Decadent Europe.* South Bend, IN: Regnery/Gateway, translated from French, 1979.

Bailey, Thomas A. *The Marshall Plan Summer: An Eyewitness Report on Europe and the Russians in 1947.* Stanford, CA: Hoover Institution Press, 1977.

Beaufre, Andre. *Strategy for Tomorrow.* New York: Crane-Russak Co., 1975.

Bergsten, C. Fred. "Interdependence and the Reform of International Institutions." *International Organisation* 30 (Spring 1976): 361-372.

Bertram, Christoph and Holst, Johan. *New Strategic Factors in the North Atlantic.* Oslo: Universitetesforlaget, 1977.

Bonnart, Frederick. "Hanging Together--Reflections on Relations Between Europe and the United States." *NATO's Fifteen Nations* 24 (August-September 1979): 39-40.

Booth, Ken. "Security Makes Strange Bedfellows: NATO's Problems from a Minimalist Perspective." *Journal for Defense Studies* 120 (December 1975): 3-14.

Bowman (Brig. Gen.) Richard C. "NATO in a Time of Crisis." *Air Force Magazine* 58 (April 1975): 49-54.

Brown, (Gen.) George. "Why U.S. Forces Are in Europe." *Commanders Digest* 17 (6 March 1975): 8.

Campbell, John C. "The Mediterranean Crisis." *Foreign Affairs* 53 (July 1975): 605-624.

─────. "Soviet-American Relations: Detente and Dispute." *Current History* 69 (October 1975): 113-166ff.

Canby, Steven L. "NATO Defense: The Problem Is Not More Money." *Policy Studies Journal* 8 (Autumn 1979): 46-53.

─────. "NATO: Reassessing the Conventional Wisdoms." *Survival* 19 (July/August 1977): 164-168.

Carter, Jimmy. "30th Anniversary of NATO: A Proclamation." *Federal Register* 44 (March 16, 1979): 17993-17994.

Chace, James and Ravenal, Earl C., eds. *Atlantis Lost: U.S.-European Relations After the Cold War.* New York: New York University Press for the Council on Foreign Relations, 1976.

"Change of Parties--Support for NATO Continues." *NATO's Fifteen Nations* 6 (December '79-January '80): 94.

Chaplin, Dennis. "NATO's Defense in Depth--Conundrum or Challenge?" *Military Review* 55 (December 1975): 3-6.

Clark, John J. "Is the NATO Alliance Structure Appropriate for the 1980's?" *Military Review* 59 (April 1979): 25-34.

Cleveland, Harlan. "The Third Phase of NATO." *NATO Review* (December 1979): 14.

"Coalition Government Falls." *NATO's Fifteen Nations* 5 (Oct.-Nov. 1979): 91.

Coffey, J.I. "Detente, Arms Control and European Security." *International Affairs* (London) 52 (January 1976): 39-52.

―――. *Arms Control, Tactical Nuclear Forces and European Security.* (Occasional Paper No. 2). Pittsburgh, PA: Center for Arms Control and International Security Studies; University Center for International Studies, 1976.

DePort, Anton W. *Europe Between the Superpowers: The Enduring Balance.* Cambridge, MA: Harvard University Press, 1979.

"Detente in Check." *Atlantic Community Quarterly* 14 (Spring 1976): 45-48.

Dougherty, James E. and Pfaltzgraff, Diane. *Eurocommunism and the Atlantic Alliance.* Cambridge, MA: Institute for Foreign Policy Analysis, January 1977.

Drummond (Maj.) Dennis M. "Getting Traffic Moving on NATO's Two-Way Street." *Air University Review* 30 (September/October 1979): 26-34.

Enthoven, Alain C. "U.S. Forces in Europe: How Many? Doing What?" *Foreign Affairs* 53 (April 1975): 513-532.

Erickson, John. "NATO's Balancing Act." *Current History* 77 (November 1979): 145-147, 180, 196.

"Europe: NATO Ministerial Meeting Held in Brussels." *Department of State Bulletin* 79 (January 1979): 34-36.

"Final Communique of the Defence Planning Committee." *NATO's Fifteen Nations* 24 (June/July 1979): 109-110.

Finger, Seymour Maxwell. "United States Policy Toward International Institutions." *International Organisation* 30 (Spring 1976): 347-360.

Fouquet, David. "The Atlantic Arms 'Race.'" *European Community* (August-September 1976): 26-29.

Franks, H. George. "How the U.S.-Soviet Relationship Has Developed: Can the Detente Policy Succeed?" *NATO's Fifteen Nations* 20 (February-March 1975): 36-38.

Freymond, Jacques. "An Atlanticist or European Europe." *The World Today* 31 (May 1975): 214-221.

Friedland, Edward. *The Great Detente Disaster: Oil and the Decline of American Foreign Policy.* New York: Basic Books, Inc., 1975.

Frisbee, John L. "New Parameters for Old Perils." *Air Force Magazine* 58 (January 1975): 2.

Galtung, Johan. "European Security and Co-operation: A Skeptical Contribution." *Journal of Peace Research* 12 (1975): 165-173.

Gasteyger, Curt. "The Super-Powers in the Mediterranean." *Survival* 17 (November/December 1975): 270-275; *Atlantic Community Quarterly* 14 (Spring 1976): 49-58.

Gelber, Lionel. *Crisis in the West: American Leadership and the Global Balance.* London: Macmillan, 1975.

Gessert, Robert A. "NATO and the Warsaw Pact: Should NATO Deploy New Nuclear Weapons?" *Worldview* 22 (November 1979): 25-26.

Gladwyn, Lord. "Western Europe's Collective Defence." *International Affairs* 51 (April 1975): 166-174.

Glass, George A. "The United States and West Germany: Cracks in the Security Foundation?" *Orbis* 23 (Fall 1979): 535-47.

Godson, Joseph. "Is NATO Still Necessary?" *Military Review* 57 (March 1977): 22-27.

Goodman, Eliot R. *The Fate of the Atlantic Community.* New York: Praeger for the Atlantic Council of the United States, 1975.

Gordon, Colin, ed. *The Atlantic Alliance: A Selected Bibliography.* New York: Nichols Pub., 1978.

Graham, Daniel O. *A New Strategy for the West: NATO After Detente.* Washington, D.C.: Heritage Foundation, 1977.

Gray, Robert C. "Deterrence, Defence and Detente: The Military and Political Challenges Facing NATO." *NATO Review* 27 (October 1979): 28-31.

Griffiths, Franklyn. *A Northern Foreign Policy.* Toronto: Canadian Institute of International Affairs, 1979.

Hahn, Walter F. and Pflatzgraff, Robert L., Jr., eds. *Atlantic Community in Crisis: A Redefinition of the Transatlantic Relationship.* Elmsford, NY: Pergamon Press, Inc., 1979.

──────. "NATO's Quiet Crisis." *Strategic Review* 5 (Summer 1977): 26-39.

Haig, Alexander M., Jr. "NATO--An Agenda for the Future." *NATO Review* 27 (June 1979): 3-5.

Handwork, Bertrand. *The Nordic Arc: A Vital Region.* Carlisle Barracks: U.S. Army War College, 1977.

Hartley, Anthony. *American Foreign Policy in the Nixon Era.* (Adelphi Paper No. 110). London: International Institute for Strategic Studies, 1975.

Hassner, Pierre. "Detente and Political Change in Europe." *Survival* 18 (March/April 1976): 68-72.

──────. "Eurocommunism and Detente." *Survival* 19 (November/December 1977): 251-255.

Hewish, Mark. "How NATO Can Survive." *New Scientist* 82 (17 May 1979): 554-557.

Heyhoe, D.C.R. *The Alliance and Europe: Part VI: The European Programme Group.* (Adelphi Paper No. 129). London: International Institute for Strategic Studies, 1976/77.

Hill-Norton, Peter. "Crisis Management." *Atlantic Community Quarterly* 17 (Spring 1979): 78-88.

Hirsch, Mario. "Influence Without Power: Small States in European Politics." *The World Today* 32 (March 1976): 112-118.

Hoffman, Stanley. "New Variations on Old Themes." *International Security* 4 (Summer 1979): 88-107.

Holst, Johan Jorgen. "A Strategic Arms Race? What Is Really Going On?" *Foreign Policy* 19 (Summer 1975): 155-169.

────── and Nerlich, Uwe, eds. *Beyond Nuclear Deference: New Aims, New Arms.* New York: Crane, Russak and Co., Inc., 1977.

Holtzel, Michael, ed. *Helsinki, Belgrade and Detente.* Berlin: Aspen Institute, October 1976.

Howard, Michael. "Social Change and the Defense of the West." *Washington Quarterly* 2 (Autumn 1979): 18-31.

Huntington, Samuel P. "American Foreign Policy: The Changing Political Universe." *Washington Quarterly* 2 (Autumn 1979): 45-53.

Hussain, Farooq. "Rationalizing NATO." *New Scientist* 82 (10 May 1979): 447-449.

Janczewski, George H. *Detente and Eastern Europe.* Washington, D.C.: Strategic Research Group, National War College, 1975.

Jordan, Robert S. *Political Leadership in NATO: A Study in Multilateral Diplomacy.* Boulder, CO: Westview Press, 1979.

Kissinger, Henry A. "Detente: The American View." *Survival* 17 (January/February 1975): 35-42.

———. "The Future of NATO." *Washington Quarterly* 2 (Autumn 1979): 3-17.

———. "NATO: The Next Thirty Years." *Survival* 21 (November/December 1979): 264-268.

Knorr, Klaus, ed. *Historical Dimensions of National Security Problems.* Lawrence, KS: The University Press of Kansas, 1976.

Kochenour, Robert W. "The United States, NATO and the Decade Ahead." *Military Review* 56 (July 1976): 14-24.

Kohl, Wilfrid L. "The Nixon-Kissinger Foreign Policy System and U.S.-European Relations: Patterns of Policy Making." *World Politics* 28 (October 1975): 1-43.

Komer, Robert. "Ten Suggestions for Rationalizing NATO." *Atlantic Community Quarterly* 15 (Summer 1977): 192-200.

———. "Looking Ahead." *International Security* 4 (Summer 1979): 108-116.

Korkegi, Robert H. "AGARD's Role in NATO." *NATO Review* 27 (June 1979): 25-26.

Kozicharow, Eugene. "NATO Leaders Optimistic Despite Major Problems." *Aviation Week* 110 (March 12, 1979): 55-58.

Kristol, Irving. "Does NATO Exist?" *Washington Quarterly* 2 (Autumn 1979): 45-53.

Laird, Melvin R. "Is This Detente?" *Reader's Digest* (July 1975).

Landes, David, ed. *Western Europe: The Trials of Partnership.* Lexington, MA: Lexington Books, D.C. Heath, 1977.

Lane, (Maj.-Gen.) Thomas A. "Prospects for the Atlantic Alliance." *Strategic Review* 3 (Winter 1975): 39-45.

Le Bailly, Louis. "Need for NATO Maritime Forces." *R.U.S.I. and Brassey's Defense Yearbook, 1976/1977* (1976): 122-141.

Lemnitzer, Lyman L. "NATO's 30th Anniversary." *Nato's Fifteen Nations* 24 (1979): 32-33.

Link, Werner and Feld, Werner J., eds. *The New Nationalism: Implications for Transatlantic Relations.* Elmsford, NY: Pergamon Press, Inc., 1979.

Luciolli, Mario. "The Atlantic Alliance in a Changed World." *NATO Review* 27 (October 1979): 12-15.

Ludz, Peter Christian. *Dilemmas of the Atlantic Alliance.* New York: Praeger, 1975.

Luns, Joseph. "Thirty Years Later: Aims of the Alliance Still Valid." *NATO Review* 27 (April 1979): 3-8.

MacNeil, Robert. "NATO and the Price of Peace." *Atlantic Community Quarterly* 13 (Fall 1975): 308-311.

Mally, Gerhard. *Interdependence.* Lexington, MA: Lexington Books, 1976.

Manor, F.S. "NATO in Disarray." *Alternative* 10 (March 1977): 10-12.

Meany, George. "Detente and the Workingman." *Atlantic Community Quarterly* 14 (Spring 1976): 37-41.

Menaul, Stewart W.B. "The Military Balance and Its Implications: A European View." *Strategic Review* 5 (Summer 1977): 47-59.

Mendershausen, Horst. *Who Is Leading Whom in the Atlantic Alliance?* Santa Monica, CA: Rand Corp., July 1975.

──────. *Outlook on Western Solidarity: Political Relations in the Atlantic Alliance System.* Santa Monica, CA. Rand Corporation, June 1976.

Milton (Gen.) T.R. "NATO Turns Thirty." *Air Force* 62 (February 1979): 23.

──────. "NATO's 30th Anniversary." *Retired Officer* 35 (April 1979): 14-18.

Mondale, Walter F. and Brzezinski, Zbigniew. "Europe: NATO's Fourth Decade--Defense and Detente." *Department of State Bulletin* 79 (November 1979): 32-36.

Morse, John H. "Questionable NATO Assumptions." *Strategic Review* 5 (Winter 1977): 21-29.

Moskowitz, Harry and Roberts, Jack. *Nuclear Weapons and NATO: Analytical Survey of Literature.* Washington, D.C.: Superintendent of Documents, January 1975.

Myers, Kenneth. *North Atlantic Security: The Forgotten Flank?* (The Washington Papers, No. 62): Beverly Hills, CA: Sage Publications, Inc., 1979.

Nathan, James A. "The Missile Crisis: His Finest Hour Now." *World Politics* (January 1975): 256-281.

"NATO--An Analysis of Its Priorities." *Defense and Foreign Affairs Digest* 3 (February 1975): 7-12.

"NATO and the Defence of Europe After Thirty Years." *Canadian Defense Quarterly* 9 (Summer 1979): 4-5.

"NATO Exacerbates the Mediterranean Situation." *International Affairs, Moscow* 1 (1975): 89-92.

"NATO--30 Years After." *U.S. Department of State Bulletin* 79 (April 1979): 1-3.

"NATO Ministerial Meeting." *Department of State Bulletin* 79 (August 1979): 46-47.

Nerlich, Uwe. "Western Europe's Relations with the United States." *Daedalus* (Winter 1979): 87-111.

Nitze, Paul H., Sullivan, Leonard, Jr., and the Atlantic Council Working Group on Securing the Seas. *Securing the Seas: The Soviet Naval Challenge and Western Alliance Options.* Boulder, CO: Westview Press, 1979.

Northedge, F.S. *East-West Relations: Detente and After.* Ife, Nigeria: University of Ife Press, 1975.

Polmar, Norman. "Outflanking NATO?" *Atlantic Community Quarterly* 14 (Fall 1976): 349-357.

Pranger, Robert J., ed. *Detente and Defense.* Washington, D.C.: American Enterprise Institute for Policy Research, 1976.

Prina, L. Edgar. "A New Look at NATO." *Military Review* 57 (July 1977): 25-33.

Rattinger, Hans. "Armaments, Detente and Bureaucracy: The Case of the Arms Race in Europe." *Journal of Conflict Resolution* 19 (December 1975): 571-595.

Rendel, Alexander. "The Alliance's Anxious Birth." *NATO Review* 27 (June 1979): 15-20.

Roberts, Adam. *Nations in Arms.* London: Chatto and Windus, 1976.

Rosecrance, Richard. "Détente or Entente." *Foreign Affairs* 53 (April 1975): 464-481.

Rummel, Rudolph. *Understanding Conflict and War: Volume I, The Dynamic Psychological Field.* New York: Sage Publications, Inc., 1975.

Salpeter, Eliahu. "Recession Takes Its Toll: The (Sorry) State of NATO." *New Leader* 60 (April 25, 1977): 4-6.

Saulle, Maria R. *NATO and Its Activities: A Political and Juridicial Approach to Consultation.* Dobbs Ferry: Oceana, 1979.

Schaetzel, J. Robert. *The Unhinged Alliance: America and the European Community.* New York: Harper and Row for the Council on Foreign Relations, 1975.

Schlesinger, James R. "American Defence Policy 1975." *Survival* 17 (May/June 1975): 133-140.

---------. "NATO and Mutual Security." *Atlantic Community Quarterly* 13 (Fall 1975): 302-307.

---------. "A Testing Time for America." *Atlantic Community Quarterly* 14 (Spring 1976): 7-19.

Scott, P.H. "Beyond the Eurogroup: New Developments in European Defense." *The World Today* 32 (January 1976): 31-38.

Shulman, Marshall D. "Priorities for Detente." *Survival* 18 (January/February 1976): 27-28. *Atlantic Community Quarterly* 14 (Spring 1976): 42-44.

Skikker, Dirk V. "Past and Present." *NATO's Fifteen Nations* 24 (1979): 30-31.

Sloss, Leon. *NATO Reform: Prospects and Priorities.* (Washington Papers, No. 30). Beverly Hills and London. Sage Publications for the Center for Strategic and International Studies, Georgetown University, Washington, D.C., 1975.

Steinbrunner, John D. *The Cybernetic Theory of Decision: New Dimensions of Political Analysis.* Princeton, N.J.: Princeton University Press, 1974.

Steinhoff, (Gen.) Johannes. "Editorial: Strength in Unity." *NATO's Fifteen Nations* 24 (April-May 1979): 17-18.

Tatu, Michel. "The Devolution of Power: A Dream?" *Foreign Affairs* 53 (July 1975): 668-682.

Taylor, (Gen.) Maxwell D. "Changing Military Priorities." *Policy and Defense Review* 1 (1979): 2-13.

Trezise, Philip H. *The Atlantic Connection: Prospects, Problems and Policies.* Washington, D.C.: The Brookings Institution, 1975.

Tucker, Gardiner L. "Standardization and the Joint Defense." *NATO Review* 23 (January 1975): 10-14.

Urban, G.R., ed. *Detente.* London: Maurice Temple Smith, 1976.

United States, International Communication Agency. Office of Research. *West European Public Perceptions of NATO and Mutual Defense Issues.* Helen M. Crossley. December 10, 1979. (Research Report R27-79). Washington, D.C. 20547.

van Campen, S.I.P. "NATO: A Balance Sheet After Thirty Years." *Orbis* 23 (Summer 1979): 261-271.

Vest, George S. "NATO: On Turning Thirty." *Signal* 33 (April 1979): 21-22.

―――. "Review of U.S. Policy in Europe." *Atlantic Community Quarterly* 17 (Fall 1979): 319-336.

Wall, Patrick. "The Work of the North Atlantic Assembly in 1978." *Navy International* 84 (April 1979): 47-49.

―――. "The Planned Destruction of the West." *Sea Power* 22 (Novemver 1979): 17-22.

Wallace, William. "Atlantic Relations: Policy Co-Ordination and Conflict." *International Affairs* (London) 52 (April 1976): 163-179.

Warnke, Paul C. "Apes on a Treadmill." *Foreign Policy* 18 (Spring 1975): 12-29.

"We Are Moving into a New World." *U.S. News & World Report* 98 (23 June 1975): 20-24.

Williams, Keith. "20th Annual Session of the North Atlantic Assembly." *NATO Review* 23 (January 1975): 20-24.

Windsor, Philip. "The State of NATO." *The World Today* 31 (August 1975): 318-325.

―――. "A Watershed for NATO: Despite Its Many Remaining Problems, the Atlantic Alliance Is Showing More Purpose and More Confidence Than Have Been Evident for Many Years." *World Today* (London) 33 (November 1977): 409-416.

1980-1981

Adler, Kenneth and Wertman, Douglas. "Is NATO in Trouble?" *Public Opinion* 4 (August/September 1981): 8-12.

Allen, Richard V. The Atlantic Alliance at a Crossroad (effect of new United States policy directions: based on conference presentation]. *Strategic Review* 9 (Fall 1981): 9-14.

Brown, (Dr.) James. "Challenges and Uncertainty: NATO's Southern Flank." *Air University Review* 31 (May/June 1980): 3-16.

Collins, John M. *U.S.-Soviet Military Balance: Concepts and Capabilities 1960-1980*. Englewood Cliffs: McGraw-Hill Publications Co., 1980.

Cordier, Sherwood. *The Air and Sea Lanes of the North Atlantic: Their Security in the 1980's*. Washington, D.C.: University Press of America, Inc., 1981.

Czempiel, Ernst-Otto, et al., eds. *United States Interests and Western Europe: Arms Control, Energy and Trade*. Frankfort: Campus Verlag GMBH, 1981 for Peace Research Institute, Frankfort, FDR.

Eaker, (Lt. Gen., Ret.) Ira C. "The Trouble with NATO." *Air Force Times* 40 (June 23, 1980): 19-20.

Ellsworth, Robert F. "Reagan and NATO." *Armed Forces Journal International* 118 (January 1981): 29-30.

"European/American Relations: Divergent Attitudes?" Theme of the 27th Annual Assembly of the Atlantic Treaty Association, London, September 29-October 2, 1981." *Atlantic Community Quarterly* 19 (Winter, 1981/1982): 395-434.

Flynn, Gregory and others. *The International Fabric of Western Society*. Totowa, NJ: Allanheld, Osmun (for the Atlantic Institute for International Affairs), 1981.

Forum: "Reagan's Foreign and Defense Policies [five essays]." *Orbis* 25 (Fall 1981): 487-410.

Foster, Charles R. "Political-Military Factors in the Atlantic Relationship: Outlook Under Reagan." *Atlantic Community Quarterly* 19 (Fall 1981): 304-311.

Genscher, Hans-Dietrich. "Toward an Overall Western Strategy for Peace, Freedom and Progress." *Foreign Affairs* 61 (Fall 1982): 42-66.

Goldsborough, James Oliver. *Rebel Europe: How America Can Live with a Changing Continent.* New York: Macmillan, Inc., 1982.

Goldstein, Walter. "The Opportunity Costs of Acting as a Superpower: U.S. Military Strategy in the 1980's." *Journal of Peace Research* 18 (No. 3, 1981): 241-260.

Hahn, Walter F. "Does NATO Have a Future?" *International Security Review* 5 (Summer 1980): 151-172.

Haig, Alexander M., Jr. "A New Direction in U.S. Foreign Policy." *Atlantic Community Quarterly* 19 (Summer 1981): 131-137.

Hoffmann, Stanley and Vance, Cyrus. *Building the Peace: U.S. Foreign Policy for the Next Decade.* Washington, D.C.: Center for National Policy, 1982.

Ireland, Timothy P. *Creating the Entangling Alliance: The Origins of the North Atlantic Treaty Organization.* Westport, CT: Greenwood Press, 1981.

Jablonsky, David. "NATO's Long-Term Defense Planning: Will It Work?" *Parameters* 11 (June 1981): 75-82.

Jaroch, (Maj.) Roger M. "NATO: Past, Present and Future." *Marine Corps Gazette* 64 (June 1980): 29-40.

Jefferies, (Maj.) Chris L. "NATO and Oil: Conflict and Capabilities." *Air University Review* 31 (January/February 1980): 35-46.

Kaplan, Lawrence S. "NATO and the Nixon Doctrine Ten Years Later." *Orbis* 24 (Spring 1980): 149-164.

────── and Clawson, Robert W. *NATO After Thirty Years.* Wilmington, DE: Scholarly Resources, Inc., 1981.

Killick, Sir John. "Is NATO Relevant to the 1980s?" *World Today* (London) 36 (January 1980): 4-10.

Kirby, Stephen. "Reagan, Congress and National Security." *World Today* (London) 37 (July/August 1981): 270-276.

Kissinger, Henry A. "The Realities of Security." *Foreign Policy and Defense Review* 3 (No. 6, 1982): 11-16.

Makins, Christopher J. and Wasserman, Sheri L. "In Search of a Security Blanket." *Europe* (January/February 1982): 2-5.

McGeehan, Robert. "The Atlantic Alliance and the Reagan Administration." *World Today* (London) 37 (July/August 1981): 254-262.

McGowan, Pat and Kegley, Charles W., Jr., eds. *Threats, Weapons and Foreign Policy.* Beverly Hills: Sage Publications, Inc., 1980.

Mets, David R. *NATO: Alliance for Peace.* New York: Simon and Schuster, 1981.

Myers, Kenneth A., ed. *NATO--The Next Thirty Years: The Changing Political, Economic & Military Setting.* Boulder, CO: Westview Press, 1980.

"NATO Ministers Meet." December 12-14, 1979. *Department of State Bulletin* 80 (February 1980): 15-23.

North Atlantic Treaty Organization Information Service. *NATO Handbook, 1981.* Brussels: North Atlantic Treaty Organization, 1981.

O'Leary, James P. "Can NATO Survive Eurocommunism?" *International Security Review* 5 (Spring 1980): 73-90.

Orvik, Nils. "NATO and the Northern Rim." *Nato Review* 1 (February 1980): 10-13.

Osgood, Robert E. "The Revitalization of Containment." *Foreign Affairs* 60 (No. 3, 1982): 465-502.

Pfaltzgraff, Robert L., Jr. "The Reagan Administration and the Common Defense: Moving Toward Assured Survival." *American Spectator* 14 (December 1981): 7-12.

Rona, Thomas P. *Our Changing Geopolitical Premises.* New Brunswick, NJ: Transaction Books, Inc., published by National Strategy Information Center, Inc., 1982.

Sanders, John S. "Health Is Not Valued Till Sickness Comes: A Report on NATO." *Defense and Foreign Affairs* 9 (February 1981): 6-9ff.

Sestanovich, Stephan. "Renewing a Beautiful Relationship: Our Allies in NATO Are Different Now." *American Spectator* 13 (November 1980): 13-18.

Snyder, Jed. "Strengthening the NATO Alliance: Toward a Strategy for the 1980s." *Naval War College Review* 34 (March-April 1981): 18-37.

Stoessel, Walter T., Jr. "Conflict or Cooperation in the 1980's?" *Atlantic Community Quarterly* 19 (Winter 1981/1982): 441-448.

Taylor, William and Fairlamb, John. *Toward Understanding the Northern Theatre: Scandinavian Defense Policy Decision Making.* Washington, D.C.: National Defense University Press, 1981.

Train (ADM) Harry D. II. "Preserving the Atlantic Alliance."
U.S. Naval Inst Proc. 107 (January 1981): 24-28.

Turner, Derek. "Extending the Tentacles ... Can the U.S. and Europe Work Closer?" *Defense and Foreign Affairs* 9 (February 1981): 27-28.

United States. Senate Committee on Foreign Relations. *Turkey, Greece and NATO: The Strained Alliance; a Staff Report, March 1980.* Binnendijk, Hans and Alfred Friendly, Jr. Washington, D.C.: U.S. Government Printing Office, 1980.

United States. Congress. Senate. Committee on Foreign Relations. *NATO--A Status Report.* 96th Congress, 2nd Session, 1980, Washington, D.C., 1980.

United States National Defense University. *Planning U.S. Security.* Krinenberg, Philip S., ed. Washington, D.C.: Superintendent of Documents, 1981.

United States House Committee on Foreign Affairs. *Issues in Relations Between the United States and Western Europe, Fall 1981: Report of a Study Mission to Western Europe, November 4-13, 1981.* 97th Congress, 2nd Session. Washington, D.C.: Government Printing Office, 1981.

United States. House Committee on Foreign Affairs. Subcommittee on Europe and the Middle East. *Hearings on United States-Western European Relations in 1980: June 15-September 22, 1980.* 96th Congress, 2nd Session, 1980. Washington, Government Printing Office, 1980.

United States. House. Committee on Foreign Affairs. *Transatlantic Cooperation and Perspectives on East-West Relations: Copenhagen, 1980; Report, June 30, 1981, of the Seventeenth Meeting of Members of Congress and of the European Parliament, November 13-14, 1980.* Washington, D.C.: Government Printing Office, 1981.

United States. Senate. Committee on Foreign Relations. *Crisis in the Atlantic Alliance: Origins and Implications.* Prepared by Foreign Affairs and National Defense Division, Congressional Research Service, Library of Congress, 97th Congress, 2nd Session. Washington, D.C.: Government Printing Office, 1982.

United States. Senate. Committee on Foreign Relations. *International Security Policy: Hearing, July 27, 1981.* 97th Congress, 1st Session. Washington, D.C.: Government Printing Office, 1981.

United States. Senate. Committee on Foreign Relations. *International Security Policy: Hearing, July 27, 1981.* 97th

Congress, 1st Session. Washington, D.C.: Government Printing Office, 1981.

United States. Senate. Committee on Foreign Relations. *NATO Today: The Alliance in Evolution; a Report, April 1982.* 97th Congress, 2nd Session. Washington, D.C.: Government Printing Office, 1982.

Vest, George S. "Security of the Western Alliance." *Department of State Bulletin* 80 (February 1980): 1-4.

Wall, Patrick. "Peace or War? A View from Europe." *Sea Power* 24 (January 1981): 41-43.

Weiss, Seymour and Adelman, Kenneth. "A Critical Phase in Trans-Atlantic Relations." *Strategic Review* 9 (Spring 1981): 24-34.

West, F.J., Jr. "NATO II: Common Boundaries for Common Interests." *Naval War College Review* 34 (January-February 1981): 59-67.

"The Year of Europe." *Foreign Affairs* 52 (January 1974): 237-248.

Yochelson, John N. "The American Military Presence in Europe: Current Debate in the United States." *Orbis* (Fall 1971): 796-802.

Yost, Charles. *The Conduct and Misconduct of Foreign Affairs: Reflections on U.S. Foreign Policy Since World War II.* New York: Random House, 1972.

Zellentin, Gerda. "Institutions for Detente and Cooperation." *The World Today* 29 (January 1972): 8-15.

MEMBER STATES

BELGIUM

Boel, Baron Rene. "European Community-Atlantic Community." *Atlantic Community Quarterly* 1 (March 1963): 72-78.

Bonnart, Frederick. "The Defense Policy of Belgium (An Interview with Frank Swaelen, Minister of Defense, Belgium)." *Nato's Fifteen Nations* 26 (June-July 1981): 99.

de Smedt (Lt. Gen.) M. "The Belgian Air Force." *Nato's Fifteen Nations* Special Issue Number 2: (1979): 38-40.

Howard, (Col.) G.B. "The Role of Belgium in NATO." *Military Review* 51 (July 1971): 17-22.

CANADA

Alexander, Fred. *Canadians and Foreign Policy*. Toronto: University of Toronto Press, 1960.

Barkway, Michael. "Canada's Changing Role in NATO Defense." *International Journal* 14 (Spring 1959): 99-110.

Barrett, Jane R. and Beaumont, Jane. *A Bibliography of Works on Canadian Foreign Relations, 1976-1980*. Toronto: Canadian Institute of International Affairs, 1982.

Beaton, Leonard, "The (1964) Canadian White Paper on Defense." *International Journal* 19 (Summer 1964): 364-370.

Bothwell, Robert. "Canada and the World in the Seventies." *Current History* 62 (April 1972): 194-197, 213, 214.

Brewin, Andrew. *Debate on Defence. Canada Within the North Atlantic Community*. Toronto: Ontario Woodsworth Memorial Foundation, 1960.

---. *Stand on Guard: The Search for a Canadian Defence Policy.* Toronto and Montreal, Canada: McClelland and Stewart, 1965.

Byers, R.B. "Canadian Defense: The ASW Dilemma." *Survival* 18 (July/August 1976): 154-161.

"Canadian Defense White Paper, March 1964." *Survival* 6 (May/June 1964): 105-111.

Clarkson, Stephen, ed. *An Independent Foreign Policy for Canada?* Toronto, Canada: McClelland and Stewart for the University League for Social Reform, 1968.

Clokie, H.M. "Canada and the North Atlantic Treaty." *International Journal* 4 (Summer 1949): 244-249.

Conant, Melvin. "Canada and Continental Defense: An American View." *International Journal* 15 (Summer 1960): 219-228.

---. *The Long Polar Watch: Canada and the Defence of North America.* London: Oxford University Press; Hamish Hamilton. New York: Harper for the Council on Foreign Relations; Toronto: Musson Book., 1962.

---. "Canada's Role in Western Defense." *Foreign Affairs* 40 (April 1962): 431-442.

---. "Canada and Nuclear Weapons: An American View." *International Journal* 18 (Spring 1963): 207-210.

---. *A Perspective of Defence: The Canadian-United States Compact.* Toronto: Canadian Institute of International Affairs, 1974.

Dobell, Peter C. *Canada's Search for New Roles: Foreign Policy in the Trudeau Era.* London: Oxford University Press for the Royal Institute of International Affairs, 1972.

---. "Europe: Canada's Last Chance?" *International Journal* 27 (Winter 1971): 113-133.

Eayrs, James. *In Defence of Canada: Peacemaking and Deterrence.* Toronto: University of Toronto Press, 1965-1977, 3V.

Ferguson, George. "Canada and the 'Atlantic Alliance.'" *International Journal* 12 (Spring 1957): 83-89.

Gellner, John. "Canada's Contribution to the Defense of Europe." *NATO's Fifteen Nations* 24 (April-May 1979): 45-57.

Gibson, James A. "Canadian Foreign Policy: A Forward View." *International Journal* 4 (Spring 1949): 109-118.

Gray, Colin S. *Canada and Norad: A Study in Strategy*. Toronto: Canadian Institute of International Affairs, 1972.

———. *Canadian Defense Priorities: A Question of Relevance*. Toronto: Clark, Irwin, 1972.

Harrison, Eric. "Strategy and Policy in the Defense of Canada." *International Journal* 4 (Summer 1949): 212-243.

Harrison, W.E.C. "Canadian-American Defense." *International Journal* 5 (Summer 1950): 189-200.

———. *Canada in World Affairs, 1949-1950*. Toronto: Oxford University Press for the Canadian Institute of International Affairs, 1957.

Holmes, John W. "Canada and the United States in World Politics." *Foreign Affairs* 40 (October 1961): 105-117.

———. "Canada in Search of Its Role." *Foreign Affairs* 41 (July 1963): 659-672.

———. "The New Perspectives of Canadian Foreign Policy." *The World Today* 25 (October 1969): 450-460.

———. "Canada and the United States: Political and Security Issues." *Atlantic Community Quarterly* 8 (Fall 1970): 398-416.

———. "Canada: The Reluctant Power." *Orbis* 15 (Spring 1971): 292-304.

Jockel, Joseph T., and Sokolsky, Joel J. "Emphasizing the Assets: A Proposal for the Restructuring of Canada's Military Contribution to NATO." *Canadian Defence Quarterly* 9 (Autumn 1979): 17-20.

Kennedy, Floyd D., Jr. "Canadian Defenses: Canada Plays a Vital Role in the Defense of North America and as a NATO Partner." *National Defense* 66 (September 1981): 42-48.

Kent, Tom. "The Changing Place of Canada." *Foreign Affairs* 35 (July 1957): 581-592.

Knorr, Klaus. "Canada and Western Defense." *International Journal* 18 (Winter 1962): 1-16.

Kronenberg, Vernon J. *All Together Now: The Organization of the Department of National Defence in Canada*. Toronto: Canadian Institute of International Affairs, 1973.

Lentner, Howard H. "Foreign Policy Decision Making: The Case of Canada and Nuclear Weapons." *World Politics* 29 (October 1976): 29-66.

Macdonald, R. St. J. *The Arctic Frontier*. University of Toronto Press with the Canadian Institute of International Affairs and the Arctic Institute of North America; London: Oxford University Press, 1966.

Mackenzie, (Lt Gen) G.A. "The Canadian Armed Forces: Air Command." *NATO's Fifteen Nations*, Special Issue Number 2 (1979): 42+.

Martin, Paul. "Canada and the Atlantic Alliance." *Atlantic Community Quarterly* 3 (Summer 1965): 251-253.

─────. *Canada and the Quest for Peace*. New York: Columbia University Press, 1967.

─────. "NATO's Value to Canada." *Atlantic Community Quarterly* 5 (Summer 1967): 177-185.

Matthews, Roy A. "A New Atlantic Role for Canada." *Foreign Affairs* 47 (January 1969): 334-347.

McLin, John B. *Canada's Changing Defence Policy 1957-1963*. Baltimore, MD: Johns Hopkins, 1967.

Modar, Daniel. "Foreign Policy Objectives, Country Studies and Planning Theory." *Canadian Public Administration* (Toronto): 23 (Fall 1980): 380-399.

Orvik, Nils. "Semi-Neutrality and Canada's Security." *International Journal* 29 (Spring 1974): 186-215.

Pearson, Lester B. "Canada and the North Atlantic Alliance." *Foreign Affairs* 27 (April 1949): 369-378.

─────. "The Development of Canadian Foreign Policy." *Foreign Affairs* 30 (October 1951): 17-30.

─────. "Canada's Northern Horizon." *Foreign Affairs* 31 (July 1953): 581-591.

─────. "Western European Union: Implications for Canada and NATO." *International Journal* 10 (Winter 1954-55): 1-11.

Ranger, Robin. "Canadian Foreign Policy in an Age of Super-Power Detente." *The World Today* 28 (December 1972): 546-554.

Ritchie, Ronald S. "Problems of a Defense Policy for Canada." *International Journal* 14 (Summer 1959): 202-212.

Schneider, Fred D. "Exploring the Third Option: Canadian Foreign Policy and Defense." *Current History* 79 (November 1980): 121-124.

Sokolsky, Joel J. "Canada's Future in NATO." *U.S. Naval Institute Proceedings* 106 (January 1980): 66-73.

Spencer, Robert A. *Canada in World Affairs: From U.N. to NATO 1946-1949.* Toronto: Oxford University Press for the Canadian Institute of International Affairs, 1959.

―――. "Triangle into Treaty: Canada and the Origins of NATO." *International Journal* 14 (Spring 1959): 87-98.

Stacey, C.P. *Canada and the Age of Conflict: Vol. 2, 1921-1948; A History of External Policies; the Mackenzie King Era.* Toronto: University of Toronto Press, 1981.

Starnes, John. "Quebec, Canada and the Alliance." *Survival* 19 (September/October 1977): 212-216.

Sutherland, R.J. "Canada's Long-Term Strategic Situation." *International Journal* 17 (Summer 1962): 199-223.

Thompson, R.W. "Canada, A United Europe and NATO." *International Journal* 12 (Summer 1957): 220-226.

Thorardson, Bruce. *Trudeau and Foreign Policy: A Study in Decision Making.* London and Toronto: Oxford Universtiy Press, 1972.

Warnock, John W. *Partner to Behemoth: The Military Policy of a Satellite Canada.* Toronto: New Press, 1970.

DENMARK

Andersen, K.B. "Denmark and NATO." *The Atlantic Community Quarterly* 11 (Fall 1973): 322-326.

―――. "Denmark and NATO." *NATO Review* 21 (No. 3, 1973): 3-8.

Bjol, Erling. "Foreign Policy Making in Denmark." *Cooperation and Conflict* 1 (1966): 1-17.

―――. "NATO and Denmark." *Cooperation and Conflict* 3 (1968): 93-107.

Denmark Between the Super-Powers. Copenhagen: Danish Foreign Policy Society, 1977.

Haagerup, Niels J. "Denmark's Security Policy." *Survival* 13 (May 1971): 172-177.

―――. "Denmark's Defense Reform." *Survival* 15 (July/August 1973): 171-177.

Haekkerup, Per. "Europe: Basic Problems and Perspectives-- A Danish View." *International Affairs* 41 (January 1965): 1-10.

———. "Why Denmark Should Stay in NATO." *Atlantic Community Quarterly* 6 (Fall 1968): 347-352.

Hansen, Peter. "Denmark and European Integration." *Cooperation and Conflict* 4 (1969): 13-46.

Holstsorensen (Maj Gen) Neils. "The Royal Danish Air Force." *NATO's Fifteen Nations* Special Issue Number 2 (1979): 46-47+.

Nesbitt, (Maj.) Robert L. *Denmark: The Cork in the Baltic Bottle.* (Research Study). Maxwell Air Force Base, AL: Air Command and Staff College, 1973.

Petersen, Nikolaj. "Danish Security Policy in the Seventies: Continuity or Change?" *Cooperation and Conflict* 3/4 (1972): 139-170.

Wilkinson, Joe R. "Denmark and NATO: The Problem of a Small State in a Collective Security System." *International Organization* 10 (Summer 1956): 390-401.

FRANCE

Ailleret, (Gen.) C. "French Strategy--Directed Defense." *Survival* 10 (February 1968): 38-43.

Alphand, Herve. "The 'European Policy' of France." *International Affairs* 29 (April 1953): 141-148.

———. "France and Her Allies." *Orbis* 7 (Spring 1963): 17-31.

Aron, Raymond. "Alone at Last." *Atlantic Community Quarterly* 4 (Summer 1966): 208-211.

———. "The Franco-American Debate: The French Perspective." *Survival* 4 (July/August 1962): 159-162.

———. "French Public Opinion and the Atlantic Treaty." *International Affairs* 28 (January 1952): 1-8.

———. "Gaullist Word and Reality." *Atlantic Community Quarterly* 4 (Winter 1966/67): 529-531.

———. "From Independence to Neutrality." *Atlantic Community Quarterly* 6 (Summer 1968): 267-269.

———. "National Defense and European Unification." *Revue de defense nationale*, April 1970, pp. 556-570.

Bellini, James. *French Defense Policy.* London: R.U.S.I., 1974.

Bernos, Roger. "Gaullist Foreign Policy in Retrospect." *The World Today* 30 (August 1974): 345-354.

Chambost, G. "France and NATO: An Ambiguous Relationship." *International Defense Review* 21 (No. 4, 1979): 526-530.

Cobban, Alfred. "Security and Sovereignty in French Foreign Policy." *International Journal* 8 (Summer 1953): 172-180.

Courtade, Pierre. "France and the United States." *International Affairs* (Moscow), No. 2 (1958), pp. 31-37.

Couve de Murville, Maurice. "NATO: A French View." *International Journal* 14 (Spring 1959): 85-86.

———. "The Role of France." *Atlantic Community Quarterly* 2 (Summer 1964): 255-261.

———. "French Policy Today." *Atlantic Community Quarterly* 2 (Winter 1964/65): 614-626.

———. "France and Her Destiny." *Atlantic Community Quarterly* 4 (Summer 1966): 197-204.

Crabb, Cecil V., Jr. "The Gaullist Revolt Against the Anglo-Saxons." *Atlantic Community Quarterly* 2 (March 1964): 35-44.

Crozier, Brian. *De Gaulle*. New York: Charles Scribner's Sons, 1973.

Dabezies, Pierre. "French Political Parties and Defense Policy: Divergences and Consensus." *Armed Forces and Society* 8 (Winter 1982): 239-256.

Debre, Michel. "The Principles of Our Defense Policy." *Survival* 12 (November 1970): 376-383.

———. "France's Global Strategy." *Foreign Affairs* 49 (April 1971): 395-406.

———. "The Defense of Europe and Security in Europe." *Atlantic Community Quarterly* 11 (Spring 1973): 93-118.

de Carmoy, Guy. *The Foreign Policies of France 1944-1968*. Chicago: University of Chicago Press, 1970.

———. "The Last Year of De Gaulle's Foreign Policy." *International Affairs* 45 (July 1969): 424-435.

Defourneaux, Marc. "France and a European Armaments Policy." *NATO Review* 27 (October 1979): 19-24.

de Gaulle, Charles. "President de Gaulle's First Press Conference." *Survival* 1 (May/June 1959): 47-48.

―――. "The Atlantic Alliance." *Survival* 5 (September/ October 1963): 238-239.

―――. "Long Live France." *Atlantic Community Quarterly* 3 (Summer 1965): 155-158.

―――. *Memoirs of Hope: Renewal and Endeavour.* New York: Simon and Schuster, 1971.

Delarue, Maurice. "France--for a European Europe." *Aussenpolitik* 25 (1974): 134-145.

Eisenhammer, J.S. "The French Communist Party, the General Confederation of Labour, and the Nuclear Debate." *West European Politics* 4 (October 1981): 252-266.

Fontaine, Andre. "What Is French Policy?" *Foreign Affairs* 45 (October 1966): 58-76.

Fontaine, Francois. "The Impossible Schism." *Atlantic Community Quarterly* 2 (Fall 1964): 367-376.

Francois-Poncet, Andre. "L'Enfant Terrible." *Atlantic Community Quarterly* 4 (Summer 1966): 205-207.

"The French Army." *Survival* 6 (March/April 1964): 67-68.

"The French Army: Yesterday and Tomorrow." *Survival* 5 (March/ April 1963): 64-70.

Friedrich, P.J. "Defense and the French Political Left." *Survival* 16 (July/August 1974): 165-171.

Fromm, Ernst Ulrich. "President de Gaulle's Vision of Europe." *Atlantic Community Quarterly* 4 (Summer 1966): 224-225.

Furniss, Edgar S. "France, NATO and European Security." *International Organization* 10 (Autumn 1956): 544-558.

―――. "de Gaulle's France and NATO: An Interpretation." *International Organization* 15 (Summer 1961): 349-365.

Gallois, Pierre M. "The Raison d'Etre of French Defense Policy." *International Affairs* 39 (October 1963): 497-510.

Geneste, Marc. "Deterrence Through Terror or Deterrence Through Defense: The Emerging Nuclear Debate [France]." *Armed Forces and Society* 8 (Winter 1982): 223-238.

Giscard d'Estaing, President Valery. "French Defense Policy." *Survival* 18 (September/October 1976): 225-230.

Goldhammer, Herbert. "The U.S.-Soviet Strategic Balance as Seen from London and Paris." *Survival* 19 (September/October 1977): 202-207.

Goldsborough, James O. "France, The European Crisis and the Alliance." *Foreign Affairs* 52 (April 1974): 538-555.

Gooch, G.P. "Franco-German Coexistence at Last?" *Foreign Affairs* 37 (April 1959): 432-442.

Goodman, Elliot R. "de Gaulle's NATO Policy in Perspective." *Orbis* 10 (Fall 1966): 690-723.

Goormaghtigh, John. "France and the European Defense Community." *International Journal* 9 (Spring 1954): 96-106.

Griswold, Lawrence. "France, the Third Force?" *Sea Power*, August 1973, pp. 6-12.

―――. "France and Europe: A New Look." *Sea Power*, April 1974, pp. 21-26.

Grosser, Alfred. "General de Gaulle and the Foreign Policy of the Fifth Republic." *International Affairs* 39 (April 1963): 198-213.

―――. "French Strategy--Doubts About Defense." *Survival* 10 (February 1965): 33-43.

―――. *French Foreign Policy Under de Gaulle*. Boston, MA: Little, Brown & Co., 1967.

Harrison, Michael M. *The Reluctant Ally: France and Atlantic Security*. Baltimore, MD: Johns Hopkins University Press, 1981.

Hazan, Joseph. "Why France Belongs to NATO." *Alternative* 10 (Fall 1977): 17-18.

Hill, R.J. "French Strategy After de Gaulle." *International Journal* 23 (Spring 1968): 244-253.

Hoffman, Stanley. "de Gaulle, Europe and the Alliance." *International Organization* 18 (Winter 1964): 1-28.

Hunt, Kenneth. *NATO Without France: The Military Implications*. Adelphi Paper no. 32. (December 1966): London: I.S.S.

Kieval, Hillel J. "Legality and Resistance in Vichy, France: The Rescue of Jewish Children." *Proceedings of the American Philosophical Society* 124, October 10, 1980: 339-66.

Kolodziej, Edward A. "France Ensnared: French Strategic Policy and Bloc Politics After 1968." *Orbis* 15, Winter 1972, pp. 1085-1108.

―――. *French International Policy Under de Gaulle and Pompidou: The Politics of Grandeur*. Ithaca: Cornell University Press, 1974.

―――. "French Security Policy: Decisions and Dilemmas." *Armed Forces and Security* 8 (Winter 1982): 185-222.

Kulski, W.W. *de Gaulle and the World; The Foreign Policy of the Fifth French Republic.* Syracuse: Syracuse University Press, 1966.

Leites, Nathan, and del la Malene, Christian. "Paris from EDC to WEU." *World Politics* 9 (January 1957): 193-219.

Lerner, Daniel and Aron, Raymond, eds. *France Defeats EDC.* New York: Praeger, 1957.

Luthy, Herbert. "De Gaulle: Pose and Policy." *Foreign Affairs* 43 (July 1965): 561-573.

Macridis, Roy C. "The New French Maginot Line: A Note on French Strategy." *Journal of Political and Military Sociology*, Spring 1974, pp. 105-112.

Marshall, D. Bruce. "De Gaulle and the Shaping of French Foreign Policy." *Orbis* 19 (Spring 1975): 255-264.

―――. "Mitterand's Defense Policies: The Early Signals." *Strategic Review* 9 (Fall 1981): 39-50

Martin, Michael L., ed. "Defense and Military Institutions in Contemporary France." [Special Issue of] *Armed Forces and Society* 8 (Winter 1982): 179-345.

Mendl, Wolf. "French Policy in Europe." *The World Today* 23 (January 1967): 23-29.

―――. "Perspectives of Contemporary French Defense Policy." *The World Today* 24 (February 1968): 50-57.

―――. "French Defense Policy." *Survival* 10 (April 1968): 115-116.

Mery, (Gen.) Guy. "French Defense Policy." *Survival* 18 (September/October 1976): 226-228.

Messmer, Pierre. "The French Military Establishment of Tomorrow." *Orbis* 6 (Summer 1962): 205-216.

―――. "The Atom, Cause and Means of an Autonomous Military Policy." *Atlantic Community Quarterly* 6 (Summer 1968): 270-277.

Moisi, Dominique. "Mitterand's Foreign Policy: The Limits of Continuity." *Foreign Affairs* 60 (Winter 1981/1982): 347-357.

Mollet, Guy. "France and the Defense of Europe." *Foreign Affairs* 32 (April 1954): 365-373.

Morgan, Roger. "Anglo-French Relations Today." *The World Today* 27 (July 1971): 285-290.

Morse, Edward L. *Foreign Policy and Interdependence in Gaullist France.* Princeton, NJ: Princeton University Press, 1973.

Nerlich, Uwe. "West European Defense Identity: The French Paradox." *The World Today* 30 (May 1974): 187-198.

Newhouse, John. *de Gaulle and the Anglo-Saxons.* London: Andre Deutsch; New York: Viking Press, 1970.

Norstad, (Gen.) Lauris. "Defending Europe Without France." *Atlantic Community Quarterly* 4 (Summer 1966): 178-188.

Pick, Otto. "Theme and Variations: The Foreign Policy of France." *The World Today* (London) 36 (October 1980): 398-405.

Pickles, Dorothy. *The Uneasy Entente: French Foreign Policy and Franco-British Misunderstandings.* London: Oxford University Press, 1966.

Piele, Otto. "Theme and Variations: The Foreign Policy of France." *World Today* 36 (October 1980): 398-405.

Pleven, Rene. "France in the Atlantic Community." *Foreign Affairs* 38 (October 1959): 19-30.

Pompidou, Georges. "France: The Real Europe." *Atlantic Community Quarterly* 3 (Fall 1965): 326-331.

Rasmussen, (Maj.) Kenneth H. "France, NATO, and United States Interests." Maxwell AFB, AL: Air Command and Staff College, 1974. (Research Study).

Rocheron, Pierre. "The Paris View of Brussels." *Defense and Foreign Affairs Digest* 3 (February 1975): 13-15.

Rose, Francois de. "The Relationship of France with NATO." *Foreign Policy and Defense Review* (No. 1, 1982): 23-27.

Rotvand, Georges. "NATO--A French View." *International Journal* 7 (Spring 1952): 107-115.

Saint Brides, John Morrice Cairn James, Baron. "Foreign Policy of Socialist France." *Orbis* 26 (Spring 1982): 35-47.

Scheinman, Lawrence. "The Politics of Nationalism in Contemporary France." *International Organization* 23 (Autumn 1969): 834-858.

Schuman, Robert. "France and Europe." *Foreign Affairs* 31 (April 1953): 349-360.

Serfaty, Simon. *France, de Gaulle and Europe.* Baltimore: Johns Hopkins Press, 1968.

Shub, Joyce Lasky, ed. "French Security Issues: A Symposium." *Foreign Policy and Defense Review* 4 (No. 1, 1982): 3-48.

Soustelle, Jacques. "France and Europe: A Gaullist View." *Foreign Affairs* 30 (July 1952): 545-553.

———. "France, Europe and Peace." *Foreign Affairs* 26 (April 1948): 497-504.

———. "France Looks at Her Alliances." *Foreign Affairs* 35 (October 1956): 116-130.

Stares, Paul. "The Future of the French Strategic Nuclear Force." *International Security Review* 5 (Summer 1980): 231-257.

Stikker, Dirk U. "France and Its Diminishing Will to Cooperate." *Atlantic Community Quarterly* 3 (Summer 1965): 197-205.

Strausz-Hupe, Robert. "de Gaulle: Prophet for Europe or Disturber of the Peace." *Atlantic Community Quarterly* 2 (March 1964): 45-52.

Tatu, Michel. "European Security Conference: It Might Actually Take Place." *Atlantic Community Quarterly* 8 (Fall 1970): 309-312.

Ullman, Marc. "Security Aspects in French Foreign Policy." *Survival* 15 (November/December 1973): 262-267.

Unwin, Peter. "Britain's Foreign Policy Opportunities: The Global Context." *International Affairs* (London) 57 (Spring 1981): 225-235.

Van Hunn, (Lt. Col.). "NATO and France After de Gaulle." Maxwell AFB, AL: Air War College, 1974. (Professional Study).

Vernant, Jacques. "France and Nassau." *Survival* 5 (May/June 1963): 106-109.

von Riekhoff, Harald. "NATO Without France." *International Journal* 23 (Spring 1968): 281-286.

Warner, Geoffrey. "President de Gaulle's Foreign Policy." *The World Today* 18 (August 1962): 320-327.

———. "Gaullist Foreign Policy." *The World Today* 21 (March 1965): 112-119.

Weinstein, Adelbert. "France Strategic Concepts: Only Towards the East." *Survival* 11 (July 1969): 211-212.

Willis, F. Ray. *France, Germany and the New Europe 1945-1967.* Stanford, CA: Stanford University Press, 1968.

Yost, David. [Review Essay] "The Socialists in the French Defense Debate." *Armed Forces and Society* 8 (Winter 1982): 334-335.

GREAT BRITAIN

Allison, (Wing Comdr.) Duncan. "Royal Air Force, Britain's Defense Objectives in the 1980's." *Military Review* (November 1973): 20-29.

Amery, Julian. *The British Commonwealth and Western Europe*. London: Longmans, Green, 1952.

Amme, Carl H., Jr. "National Strategies Within the Alliance: Great Britain." *NATO's Fifteen Nations* 17 (October-November 1972): 18+.

Anatolyev, G. "Britain and European Security." *International Affairs* (Moscow) 2 (1966): 42-45.

Argument About NATO. London: The British Peace Committee, 1968.

Attlee, Clement R. "Britain and America: Common Aims, Different Opinions." *Foreign Affairs* 32 (January 1954): 190-202.

Baylis, John. *British Defence Policy in a Changing World*. London: Croom Helm, 1977.

Beetham (ACM) Michael. "The Royal Air Force." *NATO's Fifteen Nations* Special Issue Number 1 (1979): 80-82.

Bellini, James and Geoffrey, Pattie. "British Defense Options: A Gaullist Perspective." *Survival* 19 (September/October 1977): 217-224.

Beloff, Max. *The Future of British Foreign Policy*. London: Secker and Warburg; New York: Taplinger, 1969.

Bevan, Aneurin. "Britain and America at Loggerheads." *Foreign Affairs* 36 (October 1957): 60-67.

Blackaby, F.T., and Paige, D.C. "Defense Expenditure--Burden or Stimulus?" *Survival* 2 (November/December 1960): 242-247.

Bolton, (Comdr.) David. "European Defence--Britain's Choice." *RUSI Journal* 118 (September 1973): 43-48.

Bridge, T.D. "Britain Decides upon Trident." *Army Quarterly* 110 (July 1980): 280-284.

———. "UK Defense: The Next Ten Years." *Army Quarterly* 111 (July 1981): 267-281.

Britain and the Cold War: The Future of British Foreign Policy. London: Westminister Press Provincial Newspapers, 1952.

"Britain Rallies to the Aid of NATO." *NATO's Fifteen Nations* 18 (February-March 1973): 16-20.

Britain in Western Europe: WEU and the Atlantic Alliance. London: Royal Institute of International Affairs, 1956.

"Britain's Defense Axe Looks Somewhat Blunted: 'NATO Has First Call on Our Resources.'" *NATO's Fifteen Nations* 19 (June-July 1974): 13-15.

"British Defense Policy: The Labour Party's Manifesto 1964." *Survival* 6 (November/December 1964): 256-257.

Brodie, Bernard. "How Strong Is Britain?" *Foreign Affairs* 26 (April 1948): 432-449.

Brown, George. "Voices in Opposition." *Survival* 6 (January/February 1964): 23-24.

Brown, (Lord) George. *In My Way.* London: Victor Gollancz, 1971; Harmondsworth: Pelican, 1972.

Brown, Neville. "Some Features of the British Defense Review." *The World Today* 22 (April 1966): 171-176.

———. *Arms Without Empire.* Harmondsworth: Penguin, 1967.

———. "British Arms and the Switch Towards Europe." *International Affairs* 43 (July 1967): 468-482.

Buchan, Alastair. "Europe, America and NATO: A British View." *Survival* 4 (January/February 1962): 9-12.

———. "The Choices for British Defense Policy." *International Journal* 18 (Summer 1963): 281-290.

Callahan, James. "Britain and NATO." *NATO Review* 22 (August 1974): 13-15.

Calleo, David P. *Britain's Future.* New York: Horizon Press, 1969.

Chalfont, Alun. "The British Army in Germany." *Survival* 6 (January/February 1964): 37-38.

Coates, W.P., and Zelda, K. *A History of Anglo-Soviet Relations.* London: Lawrence and Wishert, 1943.

Cordier, Sherwood S. *Britain and the Defence of Western Europe in the 1970's.* New York: Exposition Press, 1973.

Crane, Peggy. *Argument About NATO: The Case for and Against the Renewal of the Treaty in 1969.* London: British Peace Committee, 1968.

de Kadt, Emanuel J. *British Defence Policy and Nuclear War.* London: Frank Cass, 1964; New York: Humanities Press, 1966.

DeWeerd, H.A. "Britain's Changing Military Policy." *Foreign Affairs* 34 (October 1955): 102-116.

―――. *Britain Defense Policy and NATO.* Santa Monica, CA: Rand Corporation, June 1963.

Eden, Anthony. "Britain in World Strategy." *Foreign Affairs* 29 (April 1951): 341-350.

Epstein, Leon D. "British Labour's Foreign Policy." *World Politics* 6 (October 1953): 106-121.

―――. *Britain--Uneasy Ally.* Chicago: University of Chicago Press, 1954.

―――. "Partisan Foreign Policy: Britain in the Suez Crisis." *World Politics* 12 (January 1960): 201-224.

Evans, (ACM) David. "United Kingdom Air Force (UKAIR)." *NATO's Fifteen Nations* Special Issue Number 2 (1979): 18+.

Fowles, John S. "Britain's Defense Forces: The 1977 Defense White Paper, with Comments." *Military Review* 57 (September 1977): 16-20.

Frankel, Joseph. *British Foreign Policy 1954-1973.* London: Oxford University Press for the Royal Institute on International Affairs, 1975.

Frankland, Noble. "Britain's Changing Strategic Position." *International Affairs* 33 (October 1957): 416-426.

Freedman, Lawrence. "Britain's Contribution to NATO." *International Affairs* (London) 5 (January 1978): 30-47.

―――. *Britain and Nuclear Weapons.* London: Royal Institute of International Affairs, 1980.

―――. "Britain: The First Ex-nuclear Power?" *International Security* 6 (Fall 1981): 80-104.

The Future of NATO. London: Conservative Political Centre, October 1968.

Gelber, Lionel. *America in Britain's Place: The Leadership of the West and Anglo-American Unity.* New York: Praeger, 1961.

Goldberg, Alfred. "The Atomic Origins of the British Nuclear Deterrent." *International Affairs* 40 (July 1964): 409-429.

Goldstein, Walter. *The Dilemma of British Defence: The Imbalance Between Commitments and Resources.* Columbus: Ohio State University Press, 1966.

Goodfellow, Robin, and Goodwin, Roger. "The Royal Air Force in Germany." *NATO's Fifteen Nations* 18 (December 1973-January 1974): 85-92.

Goold-Adams, Richard. "The British Army in the Nuclear Age." *Survival* 1 (November/December 1959): 155-163.

Great Britain. Secretary of State for Defense. *Statement on the Defense Estimates, 1981,* 2 vols. London: Her Majesty's Stationery Office, 1981.

Greenwood, David. "The 1974 Defense Review in Perspective." *Survival* 17 (September/October 1975): 223-229.

Gwyn, William B. and Rose, Richard. *Britain: Progress and Decline.* London: Macmillan, 1980.

Harlech, Lord. "Suez Snafu, Skybolt Sabu." *Foreign Policy* 2 (Spring 1971): 38-50.

Hawtrey, R.G. *Western European Union: Implications for the United Kingdom.* London: Royal Institute of International Affairs, 1949.

Heath, Edward. "Realism in British Foreign Policy." *Foreign Affairs* 48 (October 1969): 39-50.

----------. *Old World, New Horizons: Britain, the Common Market and the Atlantic Alliance.* (The Godkin Lectures at Harvard). London: Oxford University Press, 1970.

Hogg, Quintin. "Britain Looks Forward." *Foreign Affairs* 43 (April 1965): 409-425.

Howard, Michael. "Britain's Defenses: Commitments and Capabilities." *Foreign Affairs* 39 (October 1960): 81-91. *Survival* 3 (January/February 1961): 35-40.

Hugo, Grant. *Britain in Tomorrow's World: Principles of Foreign Policy.* New York: Columbia University Press, 1969.

Kaiser, Karl, and Morgan, Roger, eds. *Britain and West Germany: Changing Societies and the Future of Foreign Policy.* London: Oxford University Press for the Royal Institute of International Affairs, 1971.

Layton, (Lord) C.H. "Little Europe and Britain." *International Affairs* 29 (July 1953): 292-301.

Maclean, Donald. *British Foreign Policy: The Years Since Seuz, 1956-1968.* New York: Stein and Day, 1970.

———. *At the End of the Day, 1961-1963.* (The Macmillan Memoirs, Vol. 5). London: Macmillan, 1973.

Macmillan, Harold. "The Justification of Nassau." *Survival* 5 (March/April 1963): 48-49.

Madzojewski, S. "The Security of Britain and Anglo-American Relations." *International Affairs* (Moscow) No. 10: 45-52.

Marriott, John. "45 Commando Royal Marines; Britain's Arctic Warfare Unit Assigned to NATO." *NATO's Fifteen Nations* 19 (June-July 1974): 31-35.

Martin, Kingsley. "NATO—A British View." *International Journal* 6 (Autumn 1951): 292-299.

Mason, Roy. "Britain's Security Interests." *Survival* 17 (September/October 1975): 217-222.

Mayhew, Christopher. "British Foreign Policy Since 1945." *International Affairs* 26 (October 1956): 477-486.

———. *Britain's Role Tomorrow.* London: Hutchinson, 1967.

Menaul, (AVM) Stewart W.B. "Great Britain and NATO Theater Nuclear Forces." *Strategic Review* 9 (Spring 1981): 61-66.

Middleton, Drew. *The Supreme Choice: Britain and Europe.* New York: Knopf, 1963.

Nagel, (Lt. Col.) Richard A., Jr. *Conventional Reinforcements for NATO in the UK.* (Professional Study). Maxwell AFB, AL: Air War College, 1974.

Neild, Robert. *How to Make Up Your Mind About the Bomb.* London: Andre Deutsch Limited, 1981.

Newman, (Wing Comdr.) Anthony T. *Britain's Contribution to NATO: A New Perspective.* (Professional Study). Maxwell AFB, AL: Air War College, 1972.

"The Next Five Years: Suggestions for the British Defense Review 1962." *Survival* 4 (January/February 1962): 43-44.

Nicholas, Herbert. *The United States and Britain.* Chicago: University of Chicago Press, 1975.

Northedge, F.S. *British Foreign Policy: The Process of Readjustment 1945-1961.* New York: Praeger, 1962.

———. "Britain as a Second-Rank Power." *International Affairs* 46 (January 1970): 37-47.

Nott, John. "Decisions to Modernize UK's Nuclear Contribution to NATO Strengthen Deterrence." *Atlantic Community Quarterly* 19 (Fall 1981): 339-345.

Nunnerly, David. *President Kennedy and Britain*. New York: St. Martin's Press, 1972.

Paice, Anthony. *A Defence for Britain*. (Unservile State Paper No. 15). London: Liberal Party Research and Information Department, 1969.

Powell, Enoch. "The Tories and Defense." *Survival* 7 (December 1965): 319-320.

Reynolds, P.A. "Recent Trends in British Foreign Policy." *International Journal* 15 (Summer 1960): 200-209.

Roberts, Henry L., and Wilson, Paul A. *Britain and the United States: Problems in Co-operation*. New York: Published for the Council of Foreign Relations, Harper, 1953.

Short, John. "Defense Spending in the U.K. Regions." *Regional Studies* (London) 15 (No. 2, 1980): 101-110.

Slessor, Sir John. "The Place of the Bomber in British Policy." *International Affairs* 29 (July 1953): 302-307.

―――. "British Defense Policy." *Foreign Affairs* 35 (July 1957): 551-563.

Snyder, William P. *The Politics of British Defense Policy 1945-1962*. Columbus: Ohio State University Press, 1964.

Steel, Sir Christopher. "Anglo-German Relations: A British View." *International Affairs* 39 (October 1963): 521-532.

Stewart, Michael. "Britain, Europe and the Alliance." *Foreign Affairs* 48 (July 1970): 648-659.

Strachan, Hew. "Britain's Deterrent." *Political Quarterly* 51 (Oct/Dec 1980): 424-440.

"The Tory Warpath." *Labour Research* 69 (July 1980): 150-151.

Unwin, Peter. "Britain's Foreign Policy Opportunities: The Global Context." *International Affairs* (London) 57 (Spring 1981): 225-235.

"U.S. Bases in Britain." *The World Today* 16 (August 1960): 319-325.

Van Wingen, John and Tillema, Herbert K. "British Military Intervention After WW II: Militance in a Second-Rank Power." *Journal of Peace Research* 17 (No. 4, 1980): 291-303.

Verrier, Anthony. "British Defense Policy Under Labor." *Foreign Affairs* 42 (January 1964): 282-292.

―――. *An Army for the Sixties: A Study in National Policy, Contract and Obligation*. London: Secker and Warburg, 1966.

Volkov, Fyodor. "Duplicity" (Diplomatic Negotiations and Events of the Spring and Summer of 1939 Involving Britain, France, Russia and Germany). *New Times* (Moscow) No. 36 (September 1980): 27-30.

Walker, P.C. Gordon. "The Labor Party's Defense and Foreign Policy." *Foreign Affairs* 42 (April 1964): 391-398.

Warren, Jenny. "British Arms: Peace on Earth?" *Labour Monthly* 60 (January-February 1978): 28-34.

Watt, D.C. *Britain Looks to Germany*. London: O. Wolff, 1965.

Watt, Donald Cameron. "British Opinion and the Oder-Neisse Line." *Survey* 61 (October 1966): 118-128.

Webster, (Prof.) Sir Charles, et al. *United Kingdom Policy: Foreign, Strategic, Economic*. London: Royal Institute of International Affairs, 1950.

Williams, Francis. *A Prime Minister Remembers*. London: Wm. Heinemann, 1961.

Williams, Roger. "British Scientists and the Bomb: The Decisions of 1980." *Government and Opposition* 16 (Summer 1981): 267-292.

Wilmot, Chester. "Britain's Strategic Relationship to Europe." *International Affairs* 29 (October 1963): 409-417.

Wilson, Duncan. "Anglo-Soviet Relations: The Effect of Ideas on Reality." *International Affairs* 50 (July 1974): 380-393.

Woodhouse, C.M. *British Foreign Policy Since the 2nd World War*. New York: Praeger, 1962.

Worsthorne, Peregrine. "Trust America More." *Survival* 5 (March/April 1963): 52-53.

Younger, Kenneth. *Changing Perspectives in British Foreign Policy*. London: Oxford University Press, 1964.

GREECE

Anghelatos, A.G. "New-Found Political Stability in Greece." *The World Today* 18 (March 1962): 102-111.

Boll, Michael M. "Greek Foreign Policy in the 1980's: Decade for Decision." *Parameters* 10 (December 1980): 72-81.

Clarke, Nick. "Greece: The Odd Man In? Greece Will Be Next to Join the EEC; But Is She Ready for the Shock Treatment of Opening Her Economy to the Nine?" *Vision* (Paris) (September 1980): 17-20.

Couloumbis, Theodore. *Greek Political Reaction to American and NATO Influences*. New Haven, CT: Yale University Press, 1966.

Demetracopoulos, Elias P. "Greece--12 Years After the Coup." *Vital Speeches of the Day* 45 (6 April 1979): 615-618.

Dobell, W.M. "Stability in the Northeast Mediterranean." *International Journal* 27 (Autumn 1972): 546-559.

Eliou, Chris G. "View from Athens--New Efforts to Bring Greece Back into NATO's Military Structure." *NATO's Fifteen Nations* 25 (February-March 1980): 44.

Murphy, Patrick. "The Rise of the New Greece." *Defense and Foreign Affairs* 8 (October 1980): 6-9+.

Pavid, Radovan. "Greece and U.S. and NATO Military Bases." *Review of International Affairs* 25 (20 September 1974): 11-12.

Pipinelis, Panayotis. "The Greco-Turkish Feud Revived." *Foreign Affairs* 37 (January 1959): 306-316.

Sulzberger, C.L. "Greece Under the Colonels." *Foreign Affairs* 48 (January 1970): 300-311.

Tsakalogannis, Panos. "The European Community and the Greek-Turkish Dispute (over Cypress)." *Journal of Common Market Studies* 19 (September 1980): 35-54.

Vatikiotis, P.J. "Greece and the Mediterranean Crisis." *Survival* 18 (January/February 1976): 23-28.

ICELAND

Amason, Robert. "Iceland, Greenland, and North Atlantic Security." *The Washington Quarterly* 2 (Spring 1981): 68-81.

―――. *Political Parties and Defense: The Case of Iceland 1945-1980*. Kingston: Center for International Relations, Queens University, 1980.

Benediktsson, Bjarni. "Iceland: Atlantic Link." *Atlantic Community Quarterly* 4 (Fall 1966): 416-420.

Bittner, Donald. "The British Occupation of Iceland, 1940-1946." *The Army Quarterly and Defence Journal* 103 (October 1972): 81-90.

Iceland

Bjarnason, Bjorn. "The Security of Iceland." *Conciliation and Conflict* 7 (1972): 193-208.

―――. "Iceland's Security Policy." *New Strategic Factors in the North Atlantic*. Oslo: Universitetsforlaget, 1977.

―――. "Iceland's Position in NATO." *Atlantic Community Quarterly* 4 (Winter 1977-78): 393-403.

Campbell, (Lt. Cmdr.) Craig S. "The Influence of Domestic Politics on the Defense Policy of Iceland." *Naval War College Review* 23 (December 1970): 76-99.

"Constitution and Government." *Iceland 1874-1974*. Reykjavik: The Central Bank of Iceland, 1975.

Croker, F.P.U. "Iceland and the Maritime Threat to NATO." *Royal United Service Institution Journal* 117 (June 1972): 51-54.

Eggertsson, T. "Determinants of Icelandic Foreign Relations." *Conciliation and Conflict* Nos. 1-2 (1975): 94-99.

Fairlamb, John. "Icelandic Threat Perceptions." *The Naval War College Review* 34 (September-October 1981): 66-77.

Fliegel, (LCDR) Robert A. "Iceland: Unique in NATO." *U.S. Naval Institute Proceedings* 106 (August 1980): 32-37.

"Foreign Relations." *Iceland 874-1974*. Reykjavik: The Central Bank of Iceland, 1975.

Grondal, Benedikt. *Iceland: From Neutrality to NATO Membership*. Oslo: Universitetsforlaget, 1971.

―――. "Iceland's Role in NATO." *NATO's Fifteen Nations* 5 (Oct.-Nov. 1979): 70.

Hainl, (Col.) Robert D., Jr. "Iceland's Closure of U.S. Base Will Cripple U.S./NATO Defense." *Armed Forces Journal* 108 (August 1971): 20.

Hallgrimsson, Geir. "Iceland and the Atlantic Alliance." *The Atlantic Community Quarterly* 4 (Winter 1977-78): 389-392.

"Iceland's New Permanent Representative at NATO." *NATO's Fifteen Nations* 4 (Aug.-Sept. 1979): 90.

―――. "View from Reykjavik." *NATO's Fifteen Nations* (Apr.-May 1980): 55.

McCartney, (Lt. Comdr.) R. Scott, and Triemer (Lt. Comdr.) William L. "Iceland and NATO: Problems and Prospects." (Unpublished Group Research Project Report.) Newport, RI: U.S. Naval War College, 1972.

Neuchterlein, Donald E. *Iceland, Reluctant Ally*. Ithaca: Cornell University Press, 1961.

O'Connor, Neil. *Iceland--Troubled Ally*. Norfolk, VA: The Naval War College, 1975.

Ruhl, Lothat. "Iceland's Vital Value to NATO Strategy." *Atlantic Community Quarterly* 14 (Spring 1976): 66-68.

Schneider, Andrew. "Living in Iceland: It's as Cold as You Make It." *Air Force Times*, Family Supplement (3 November 1971): 10-16+.

Schweitzer, Theodore, ed. *Iceland Defense Force 5 May 1951- 5 May 1952*. Reykjavik: Steindorsprent H.F., 1952.

Sparring, Ashe. "Iceland, Europe and NATO." *The World Today* 28 (September 1972): 393-403.

Stefansson, Unnstein. "The Icelanders and the Sea." *The UNESCO Courier* (February 1974): 26-30.

Svetlov, B. "British-Icelandic Conflict." *New Times* (Moscow), No. 22 (June 1973): 24.

U.S. Department of State. *Defense Agreement Pursuant to the North Atlantic Treaty Between the United States of America and the Republic of Iceland*. Washington, D.C.: GPO, 1951.

ITALY

Are, Giusseppe. "Italy's Communists: Foreign and Defense Policies." *Survival* 18 (September/October 1976): 210-216.

Basagni, Fabio and Flynn, Gregory A. "Italy, Europe and Western Security." *Survival* 20 (May/June 1977): 98-106.

Colonna, Guido. "The State of the Alliance: An Italian View." *Atlantic Community Quarterly* 2 (Fall 1964): 397-407.

Grindrod, Muriel. *The Rebuilding of Italy*. London: Royal Institute of International Affairs, 1955.

Hildebrand, George H. "The Postwar Italian Economy: Achievements, Problems and Prospects." *World Politics* 8 (October 1955): 46-70.

Jacoviello, Alberto. "The Italian Situation and NATO." *Survival* 18 (July/August 1976): 166-167.

Kogan, Norman. *A Political History of Post-War Italy: From the Old to the New Center Left*. New York: Praeger, 1981.

Merlini, Cesare. "Italy in the Atlantic Community and the Atlantic Alliance." *The World Today* 31 (April 1975): 160-166.

Mettimano, (Gen.) Alessandro. "The Italian Air Force." *NATO's Fifteen Nations* Special Issue No. 2 (1979): 63+.

Sassoon, Donald. *The Strategy of the Italian Communist Party: From the Resistance to the Historic Compromise*. New York: St. Martin's, 1981.

Silvestri, Stefano, and Aliboni, Roberto. "Italy's Mediterranean Role." *International Journal* 27 (Autumn 1972): 499-510.

Taylor, Paul. "The Future of East-West Relations: Italy and NATO." *Millennium* 5 (Winter 1976-1977): 303-311.

Vanicelli, Primo. *Italy, NATO and the European Community: The Interplay of Foreign Policy and Domestic Politics*. Cambridge, MA: Center for International Affairs, Harvard University, 1974.

NETHERLANDS

Furlong, R.D.M. "Dutch Defense Policy for the '80s." *International Defense Review* 21 (No. 3, 1979): 319-322.

"The Future of Dutch Defense: Report by the Commission of Civilian and Military Experts." *Survival* 14 (November/December 1972): 293-300.

Griffiths, Richard T., ed. *The Economy and Politics of the Netherlands Since 1945*. Nijhoff: Martinus, 1980.

Neuman, H.J. "The Dutch Defense Reforms." *Survival* 17 (January/February 1975): 2-8.

van Campen, S.I.P. *The Quest for Security: Some Aspects of Netherlands Foreign Policy 1945-1950*. The Hague: Martinus Nijhoff for the Netherlands Institute of International Affairs; London: Batsford, 1958.

Vlekke, B.H.M. "A Dutch View of the World Situation." *International Affairs* 28 (October 1952): 413-421.

Vuren, A.T. van. "The Royal Netherlands Army Today." *Military Review* 62 (April 1982): 13-28.

Weers, (Col., Ret.) Mozes W.A. "The Nuclear Debate in the Netherlands." *Strategic Review* 9 (Spring 1981): 67-77.

NORWAY

Andren, Nils. "Prospects for the Nordic Security Pattern." *Cooperation and Conflict* 4 (1978): 180-192.

———. "The Nordic Balance: An Overview." *The Washington Quarterly* 3 (Summer 1979): 49-62.

Berg, John. "Norway's Vital Defense Changes." *Armed Forces Journal International* 118 (December 1980): 49-50+.

Bertram, Christoph, and Holst, Johan. *New Strategic Factors in the North Atlantic.* Oslo: IPC Science and Technology Press, 1977.

Bruntland, Arne Olav. "Norwegian Foreign Policy." *Cooperation and Conflict* 3 (1968): 169-183.

Burgess, Philip M. *Elite Images and Foreign Policy Outcomes: A Study of Norway.* Columbus: Ohio State University Press, 1968.

East, Maurice A., and Lei, Helge Salomonsen. "Adapting Foreign Policy-making to Interdependence: A Proposal and Some Evidence from Norway." March 1981 (NUPI Notation No. 217). Norsk Utenrikspolitik Institutt, Postbors 8159, Oslo Dep., Oslo 1, Norway.

Frankel, Joseph. "Comparing Foreign Policies: The Case of Norway." *International Affairs* 44 (July 1968): 482-491.

Greve, Tim. *Norway and NATO.* Oslo: Press Department, Royal Ministry of Foreign Affairs, 1968.

Hansen, Guttorm. "Norway and NATO." *Atlantic Community Quarterly* 7 (Summer 1969): 235-240.

Herlofson, Ch. O. "The Royal Norwegian Navy--Its Present State, Future Development and Role Within NATO." *Navy International* 84 (April 1979): 5-11.

Holst, Johan J. "Norwegian Security Policy." *Cooperation and Conflict* 1 (1966): 64-79.

———. "A Norwegian Looks Into the Early Seventies." *International Journal* 24 (Spring 1969): 356-366.

———. "Norwegian Security Policy and Peace in Nordic Europe." *World Today* (London) 37 (January 1981): 22-28.

———. "Norway's Search for a Nordpolitik." *Foreign Affairs* 60 (Fall 1981): 63-86.

Holst, Johan J. and Urban, G.R. *Norway in the Evolving Process of European Security.* Oslo: Norsk Utenrikspolitik Institutt, 1974.

Kerry, Richard J. "Norway and Collective Defense Organization." *International Organization* 17 (Autumn 1963): 860-871.

Krosby, H. Peter. "Norway in NATO: A Partial Commitment?" *International Journal* 20 (Winter 1964): 68-78.

Lochen, Einar. *Norway in European and Atlantic Cooperation.* Oslo: Universitetsforlaget, 1964.

MacCaskill, (Lt. Col.) Douglas C. "Norway's Strategic Importance." *Marine Corps Gazette* 65 (February 1981): 28-33.

Narvhus (Maj. Gen.) Ingar T. "The Royal Norwegian Air Force." *NATO's Fifteen Nations* Special Issue Number 22 (1979): 72ff.

PORTUGAL

Broga de Macedo, Jorge and Serfaty, Simon. *Portugal Since the Revolution: Economic and Political Perspectives.* Boulder, CO: Westview Press, 1981.

Chilcote, Robert H. "Politics in Portugal and Her Empire." *The World Today* 17 (September 1961): 376-387.

Crollen, Luc. *Portugal, the U.S. and NATO.* Louvain: Louvain University Press, 1973.

Ferraira, (Lt. Gen.) Jose Lemos. "The Portuguese Air Force and NATO." *NATO's Fifteen Nations* Special Issue Number 2 (1979): 28ff.

Ferreira, Jose Medeiros. "Portugal and NATO." *Survival* 18 (September/October 1976): 230-232.

Grayson, George W. "Portugal and the Armed Forces Movement." *Orbis* 19 (Summer 1975): 335-378.

Griswold, Lawrence. "The Iberian Quandary--Spain, Portugal, and NATO: Turmoil and Trouble." *Sea Power*, February 1975, pp. 24-30.

Libby, Ruthven E. "Portugal: A Setback for NATO." *Strategic Review* 3 (Spring 1975): 25-29.

Marshall, Andrew. "Portugal: A Determined Empire." *The World Today* 17 (March 1961): 95-101.

Salazar, Dr. Antonio de Oliveira. "Realities and Trends of Portugal's Policies." *International Affairs* 39 (April 1963): 169-183.

Story, Jonathan. "Portugal's Revolution of Carnations: Patterns of Change and Continuity." *International Affairs* 52 (July 1976): 417-433.

SPAIN

Carothers, Thomas. "Spain, NATO and Democracy." *World Today* (London) 37 (July/August 1981): 298-303.

Fusi Aizpurva, Juan, Pablo. *Spain: Dictatorship to Democracy*, 2nd Ed. London: George Allen and Unwin Ltd., 1981.

Myers, William. "Spanish Foreign Policy: Between North and South." *Europe* (New York) 1 (September 1981): 36-40.

TURKEY

Akmandor, Neset. "Turkish and European Security--the Role of Eurogroup." *NATO Review* (August 1979): 7-10.

Birgi, Nuri. "The Unfolding Alliance." *Atlantic Community Quarterly* 2 (Fall 1964): 408-412.

Boll, Michael M. "Turkey New National Security Concept: What It Means for NATO." *Orbis* 23 (Fall 1979): 609-631.

Bonnart, Frederick. "The Situation in Greece and Turkey." *NATO's Fifteen Nations* (Dec.-Jan. 1978-79): 28.

Butler, Francis P. "Reassessing Turkey: A Faithful Ally Disillusioned and in Trouble." *Parameters* 10 (March 1980): 24-32.

Christopher, Warren. "Europe: Additional Assistance for Turkey." *Department of State Bulletin* (August 1979): 44-45.

Fay, James R. "Terrorism in Turkey: Threat to NATO's Troubled Ally [and Implications of the Military Coup, September 1980]." *Military Review* 61 (April 1961): 16-26.

Grigoryev, K. "Effects of Turkey's Militarization." *International Affairs* (Moscow) 1 (1960): 73-79.

Harris, George S. *Troubled Alliance: Turkish-American Problems in Historical Perspective 1945-1971.* Washington, D.C.: American Enterprise Institute for Public Policy Research, 1972.

Kiep, Walther Leisler. "Strengthening Our Turkish Partner: Germany Spearheading the Effort." *NATO's Fifteen Nations* 24 (June-July 1979): 18-19.

Lewis, Geoffrey. "Turkey: The Thorny Road to Democracy." *The World Today* 18 (May 1962): 182-191.

MacKenzie, Kenneth. "Turkey at the Crossroads." *World Survey* (May 1974): 16.

McGhee, George C. "Turkey Joins the West." *Foreign Affairs* 32 (July 1954): 617-630.

Milton, Theodore Ross. "The American Presence in Turkey." *NATO's Fifteen Nations* 24 (June-July 1979): 21-24.

Okyar, Osman. "The North-South Dialogue and Turkey." *NATO Review* 27 (April 1979): 18-21.

Rustow, Dankwart A. "Turkey Travails." *Foreign Affairs* 58 (Fall 1979): 82-102.

Sadak, Necmeddin. "Turkey Faces the Soviets." *Foreign Affairs* 27 (April 1949): 449-461.

Sahinkaya, (Gen.) Tahsin. "The Turkish Air Force and Its Progress." *NATO's Fifteen Nations* Special Issue Number 2 (1979): 78-79.

Steinbach, Udo. "Turkey--Diversification of Foreign Policy." *Aussenpolitik* (Winter 1973): 439-449.

United States Library of Congress. *Greece and Turkey: Some Military Implications Related to NATO and the Middle East.* Prepared for the Special Subcommittee on Investigations, of the Committee on Foreign Affairs, by the Congressional Research Service, Library of Congress. Washington, D.C.: Government Printing Office, 1975.

Vali, Ferenc. A. *Bridge Across the Bosphorous: The Foreign Policy of Turkey.* Baltimore, MD: Johns Hopkins Press; Toronto: Capp Clark, 1971.

―――. *The Turkish Straits and NATO.* Stanford: Hoover Institution Press, 1972.

Yalcin, Aydin. "Turkey: Emerging Democracy." *Foreign Affairs* 45 (July 1967): 706-714.

―――. "View from Ankara." *NATO's Fifteen Nations* 23 (December 1978-January 1979): 34-35.

WEST GERMANY

Abs, Hermann J. "Germany and the London and Paris Agreements." (September and October 1954). *International Affairs* 31 (April 1955): 167-173.

Adenauer, Konrad. "Germany and the Problem of Our Times." *International Affairs* 28 (April 1952): 156-161.

———. "Germany and Europe." *Foreign Affairs* 31 (April 1953): 361-366.

———. "German Reunion and the Future of Europe." *International Journal* 9 (Summer 1954): 173-176.

———. "Germany, the New Partner." *Foreign Affairs* 33 (January 1955): 177-183.

———. "The German Problem, a World Problem." *Foreign Affairs* 41 (October 1962): 59-65.

———. *Memoirs 1945-1953*. Chicago: H. Regnery, 1966.

Albert, E.H. "Bonn's Moscow Treaty and Its Implications." *International Affairs* 47 (April 1971): 316-326.

———. "The Brandt Doctrine of Two States in Germany." *International Affairs* 46 (April 1970): 293-303.

Allemann, F.R. "Adenauer's Eastern Policy." *Survey* No. 44/45 (October 1962), pp. 29-36.

Almond, Gabriel A. "The Political Attitudes of German Business." *World Politics* 8 (January 1956): 157-186.

Alves, Dora. "The Federal German Navy: Linchpin of the Northern Flank." *U.S. Naval Institute* June 1981: 100-104.

Amme, Carl H., Jr. "National Strategies Within the Alliance: West Germany." *NATO's Fifteen Nations* 17 (August-September 1972); 76.

Anderson, Evelyn. "Germany in the Cold War." *Survey*, No. 58 (January 1966), pp. 177-186.

Apel, Hans. "Federal Republic of Germany--25 Years in NATO." *NATO's Fifteen Nations* 25 (August-September 1980): 18+.

Bahr, Egon. "German Ostpolitik and Super-Power Relations." *Survival* 15 (November/December 1973): 296-300.

Bailey, George. "Germany Between Two Alliances." *Survival* 8 (December 1966): 386-391.

Barnhart, (Maj.) William C. *The Future of Europe and NATO: Ostpolitik Implications*. (Research Study.) Maxwell AFB, AL: Air Command and Staff College, 1973.

Bathurst, M.E., and Simpson, J.L. *Germany and the North Atlantic Community: A Legal Survey*. New York: Praeger, 1956.

Baudissin, Count Wolf. "The New German Army." *Foreign Affairs* 34 (October 1955): 1-13.

Bender, Peter. ———. "In Search of a New Policy." *Survey*, No. 61 (October 1966): 80-92.

———. "The Special Relationship of the Two German States." *The World Today* 29 (September 1973): 389-397.

Bertram, Christoph. "West German Perspectives on European Security: Continuity and Change." *The World Today* 27 (March 1971): 115-123.

———. "European Security and the German Problem." *International Security* 4 (Winter 1979/1980): 105-116.

Birnbaum, Immanuel. "German Eastern Policy: Yesterday and Tomorrow." *International Affairs* 31 (October 1955): 427-434.

Birnbaum, Karl E. *East and West Germany: A Modus Vivendi*. Lexington, MA: Lexington Books, D.C. Heath, 1973.

Birrenbach, Kurt. "Partnership and Consultation in NATO." *Atlantic Community Quarterly* 2 (March 1964): 62-71.

Bleek, Wilhelm. "From Cold War to Ostpolitik: Two Germanies in Search of Separate Identities." *World Politics* 29 (October 1976): 114-129.

Bluhm, Georg R. *Detente and Military Relaxation in Europe: A German View*. Adelphi Paper, No. 40, September 1967. London: I.S.S.

Bolling, Klaus. *Republic in Suspense: Politics, Parties and Personalities in Post-War Germany*. New York: Praeger, 1964.

"Bonn and a Peace Treaty." *International Affairs* (Moscow, No. 2) (1960), pp. 64-68.

Brandt, Willy. "The Means Short of War." *Foreign Affairs* 39 (January 1961): 196-207.

———. "German Policy Toward the East." *Foreign Affairs* 46 (April 1968): 476-486.

———. "German Foreign Policy." *Survival* No. 11 (December 1969), pp. 370-372.

———. "Germany's 'Westpolitik.'" *Foreign Affairs* 50 (April 1972): 416-426.

Bronska-Pampuch, Wanda. "Russia in German Eyes: 1964." *Survey*, No. 51 (April 1964), pp. 93-101.

Cipra, (Lt. Col.) Donald J. "Ostpolitik: Its Influence on the Malaise in NATO Solidarity." (Professional Study.) Maxwell AFB, AL: Air War College, 1974.

Clay, (General) Lucius D. *Decision in Germany (1945-1949)*. Garden City, NY: Doubleday, 1950.

———. *Germany and the Fight for Freedom*. Cambridge, MA: Harvard University Press, 1950.

Cornides, Wilhelm. "German Unification and the Power Balance." *Survey*, No. 58 (January 1966), pp. 140-148.

Craig, Gordon A. *The Germans*. New York: Putnam, 1982.

Croan, Melvin. "Reality and Illusion in Soviet-German Relations." *Survey*, Nos. 44/45 (October 1962), pp. 12-28.

———. "Bonn and Pankow: Intra-German Politics." *Survey*, No. 67 (April 1965), pp. 77-89.

Dahrendorf, Ralf. "Bonn After 20 Years: Are Germany's Problems Any Nearer Solution?" *The World Today* 25 (April 1969): 158-171.

Davidson, Eugene. *The Death and Life of Germany*. New York: Knopf, 1959.

Dean, Robert W. "Bonn-Prague Relations: The Politics of Reconciliation." *The World Today* 29 (April 1973): 149-159.

———. *West German Trade with the East: The Political Dimension*. New York: Praeger, 1974.

Dernburg, H.J. "Rearmament and the German Economy." *Foreign Affairs* 33 (July 1955): 648-662.

Dethleffsen, Erich. "The Chimera of German Neutrality." *Foreign Affairs* 30 (April 1952): 361-375.

Deutsch, Karl W., and Edinger, Lewis J. *Germany Rejoins the Powers*. Stanford: Stanford University Press, 1959; London: Oxford University Press, 1960.

Donhoff, Marion. "Germany Puts Freedom Before Unity." *Foreign Affairs* 28 (April 1950): 398-411.

Dulles, Eleanor Lansing. *One Germany or Two*. Stanford: Hoover Institution, Stanford University Press, 1970.

———. *One Germany or Two: The Struggle at the Heart of Europe*. Stanford: Hoover Institution Press, 1970.

Erhard, Ludwig. "German Policy Today." *Atlantic Community Quarterly* 1 (Winter 1963-64): 501-511.

Erler, Fritz. "The Struggle for German Reunification." *Foreign Affairs* 34 (April 1956): 380-393.

———. "The Reunification of Germany and Security for Europe." *World Politics* 10 (April 1958): 366-377.

———. "Germany and Nassau." *Survival* 5 (May/June 1963): 102-106.

———. *Democracy in Germany*. Cambridge, MA: Harvard University Press, 1965.

———. "The Alliance and the Future of Germany." *Foreign Affairs* 43 (April 1965): 436-446.

———. *West Germany and the European Community*. New York: Praeger, 1981.

Feld, Werner J. *Reunification and West German-Soviet Relations 1949-1957*. The Hague: Nijhoff, 1963.

"The Four Powers and Germany: The Reunification Issues." *The World Today* 11 (November 1955): 471-483.

Freund, Gerald. "Adenauer and the Future of Germany." *International Journal* 18 (Autumn 1963): 458-467.

———. *Germany Between Two Worlds*. New York: Harcourt, Brace and Co., 1961.

Full Committee Briefing on German Offset Agreement. Washington, D.C.: U.S. Government Printing Office, 14 June 1974, 19pp.

Future West German Politico-Military Developments and Alternative Foreign and Defense Policy Strategies. McLean, VA: Research Analysis Corp., July 1970.

Genscher, Hans-Dietrich. "The Federal Republic of Germany's Alliance Policy." *NATO Review* 22 (December 1974): 3-5.

"A German Peace Treaty:--The Demand of the Hour." *International Affairs* (Moscow), No. 2 (1959), pp. 71-75.

Goodman, Elliot R. "NATO and German Reunification." *Survey*, No. 76 (Summer 1970), pp. 30-40.

Gorgey, Lazslo. *Bonn's Eastern Policy 1964-1971: Evolution and Limitations*. (International Relations Series, No. 3). Hamden, CT: Archon for the Institute of International Studies, University of South Carolina, 1972.

Griffith, William E. "The German Problem and American Policy." *Survey*, No. 61 (October 1966), pp. 105-117.

―――. "Bonn and Washington: From Deterioration to Crisis." *Orbis* 26 (Spring 1982): 117-133.

Grosser, Alfred. *Germany in Our Time: A Political History of the Post-War Years*. New York: Praeger, 1971.

Hahn, Walter F. "The Germans and the West." *Orbis* 1 (Summer 1957): 184-198.

Hallstein, Walter. "Germany's Dual Aim: Unity and Integration." *Foreign Affairs* 31 (October 1952): 58-66.

Hanreider, Wolfram F. *West German Foreign Policy 1949-1963*. Stanford: Stanford University Press, 1967.

Hartmann, Frederick H. *Germany Between East and West*. Englewood Cliffs, NJ: Prentice-Hall, 1965.

Hassner, Pierre. "German and European Reunification; Two Problems or One?" *Survey*, No. 61 (October 1966), pp. 14-37.

Heathcote, Nina. "Brandt's Ostpolitik and Western Institutions." *The World Today* 26 (August 1970): 334-343.

Herz, John H. "German Officialdom Revisited: Political Views and Attitudes of the West German Civil Service." *World Politics* 7 (October 1954): 63-83.

Hiscocks, Richard. *The Adenauer Era*. Philadelphia: Lippincott, 1966.

Jacobi, Claus. "Germany's Great Old Man." *Foreign Affairs* 33 (January 1955): 239-249.

―――. "German Paradoxes." *Foreign Affairs* 35 (April 1957): 432-440.

Jaspers, Karl. "The Political Vacuum in Germany." *Foreign Affairs* 32 (July 1954): 595-607.

―――. *The Future of Germany*. Chicago: University of Chicago Press, 1967.

Kaiser, Karl. *German Foreign Policy in Transition: Bonn Between East and West*. New York: Oxford University Press for the Royal Institute of International Affairs, 1968.

―――. "Prospects for West Germany After the Berlin Agreement." *The World Today* 28 (January 1972): 30-35.

Kaltefleiter, Werner. "German Divisions (West German Attitudes Toward the North Atlantic Treaty Organization)." *Policy Review* (Fall 1981): 41-49.

Kielmansegg, (Gen.) J.A. Graf. "A German View of Western Defense." *RUSI Journal* 119 (March 1974): 11-17.

Kohl, Wilfrid L. and Basevi, Giorgio, eds. *West Germany: A European and Global Power*. Lexington, MA: Lexington Books, 1980.

Korbel, Josef. "German-Soviet Relations: The Past and Prospects." *Orbis* 10 (Winter 1967): 1046-1060.

Kressler, Diane A. "Germany, NATO and Europe." *Orbis* 10 (Spring 1966): 223-239.

Krippendorff, Ekkehart. "Beyond the Oder-Neisse: A Critique of Bonn's Ostpolitik." *Survey*, No. 61 (October 1966), pp. 47-55.

Landauer, Carl. *Germany: Illusions and Dilemmas*. New York: Harcourt, Brace and World, 1969.

Legters, Lyman. "A 'Successful' Partition: The Case of Germany." *Intellect* 103 (February 1975): 294-296.

Lewis, Flora. "The Unstable States of Germany." *Foreign Affairs* 38 (July 1960): 588-597.

Lippmann, Heinz. *Honecker and the New Politics of Europe*. London: Angus and Robertson, 1973.

Lowenthal, Richard. "Germany's Role in East-West Relations." *The World Today* 23 (June 1967): 240-248.

Lower, Arthur. "The West and Western Germany." *International Journal* 6 (Autumn 1951): 300-307.

Ludz, Peter Christian. *Two Germanys in One World*. (Atlantic Papers 1973. No. 3). Paris: Atlantic Institute for International Affairs, 1973.

Magathan, Wallace C., Jr. "West German Defense Policy." *Orbis* 8 (Summer 1964): 292-315.

Majonica, Ernst. *East-West Relations: A German View*. New York: Praeger, 1969.

McInnis, Edgar. "Adenauer's Germany: Some Post-Election Impressions." *International Journal* 9 (Winter 1954): 1-7.

McInnis, Edgar S., ed. *The Shaping of Post-War Germany*. London: Dent, 1960.

Merkl, Peter H. *German Foreign Policies, West and East: On the Threshold of a New European Era*. Santa Barbara: American Bibliographical Center-Clio Press, 1974.

Mettler, Erich. "Whose Success?" *Survival* 12 (October 1970): 325-326.

Morgan, Roger. "Washington and Bonn: A Case Study in Alliance Politics." *International Affairs* 47 (July 1971): 489-502.

―――. *The United States and West Germany 1945-1973: A Study in Alliance Politics*. London: Oxford University Press for Royal Institute of International Affairs and Harvard Center for International Affairs, 1974.

Morgenthau, Hans J., ed. *Germany and the Future of Europe*. Chicago: University of Chicago Press, 1951.

Muhlen, Norbert. "The New Army of a New Germany." *Orbis* 1 (Fall 1957): 278-290.

―――. "Post-War Germany: Miracle or Mirage?" *Orbis* 3 (Fall 1959): 351-353.

Neal, Fred Warner. *War and Peace and Germany*. New York: W.W. Norton and Co., 1962.

Nelson, Harold I. "The German Problem, 1955." *International Journal* 10 (Summer 1955): 183-191.

Nettl, J.P. *The Eastern Zone and Soviet Policy in Germany, 1945-50*. New York: Oxford University Press, 1951.

Nettl, Peter. "Economic Checks on German Unity." *Foreign Affairs* 30 (July 1952): 554-563.

Novoseltsev, Y. "Bonn's Excessive Ambitions." *International Affairs*, No. 2 (1966), pp. 29-36.

Obleser, (Lt. Gen.) F. "The Luftwaffe." *NATO's Fifteen Nations* Special Issue No. 1 (1979): 56-58ff.

Onslow, C.G.D. "West German Rearmament." *World Politics* 3 (July 1951): 450-485.

Oppermann, Thomas. "German Unity and Peace." *Survival* 13 (July 1971): 239-243.

Paterson, W.E. "Foreign Policy and Stability in West Germany." *International Affairs* 49 (July 1973): 413-430.

Pickert, General. "The Value of Numbers in the Nuclear Age: A German View." *Survival* 3 (September/October 1961): 229-232.

Planck, Charles R. *The Changing Status of German Reunification in Western Diplomacy, 1955-1966*. Baltimore: Johns Hopkins Press, 1967.

Polyanov, N. "Bonn's Challenge to Europe." *International Affairs* (Moscow), No. 1 (1969), pp. 21-28.

Pritt, D.N. *Unrepentant Aggressors: An Examination of West German Policies*. London: Lawrence and Wishart, 1969.

Prittie, Terence. *Germany Divided: The Legacy of the Nazi Era*. Boston: Atlantic (Little, Brown), 1960.

Pross, Harry. "West Germany: Unfinished Democracy." *Orbis* 2 (Fall 1958): 356-370.

Richardson, James. "Germany's Eastern Policy: Problems and Prospects." *The World Today* 24 (September 1968): 375-386.

Richardson, James L. *Germany and the Atlantic Alliance: The Interaction of Strategy and Politics*. Cambridge, MA: Harvard University Press, 1966.

Ruhle, Hans. "The Theater Nuclear Issue in German Politics." *Strategic Review* 9 (Spring 1981): 54-60.

Ruhm von Oppen, Beate. "The End of the Adenauer Era." *The World Today* 19 (August 1963): 343-351.

Saeter, Martin. "Change of Course in German Foreign Policy." *Cooperation and Conflict* 2 (1967): 82-101.

Schlamm, William S. *Germany and the East-West Crisis: The Decisive Challenge to American Policy*. New York: David McKay, 1959.

Schmid, Carlo. "Germany and Europe." *International Affairs* 27 (July 1951): 306-311.

———. "Germany and Europe: The German Social Democratic Program." *Foreign Affairs* 30 (July 1952): 531-544.

Schmidt, Helmut. "The Defense Debate in Germany: The Opposition View." *Survival* 3 (July/August 1961): 178-181.

———. "Germany in the Era of Negotiations." *Foreign Affairs* 49 (October 1970): 40-50.

———. "Federal Republic of Germany, A Partnership for Security." *Vital Speeches of the Day* (1 August 1979): pp. 610-615.

———. "A Policy of Reliable Partnership." *Foreign Affairs* 59 (Spring 1981): 743-755.

Schroder, Gerhard. "Germany Looks at Eastern Europe." *Foreign Affairs* 44 (October 1965): 15-25.

———. "Integrated Defense." *Atlantic Community Quarterly* 4 (Summer 1966): 226-228.

Schultz, Heinz. "The Dilemma of German Rearmament After the Second World War (Events from 1945-55)." *Army Quarterly* 110 (April 1980): 189-204.

Schutz, Wilhelm Wolfgang. "German Foreign Policy: Foundations in the West, Aims in the East." *International Affairs* 35 (July 1959): 310-315.

——————. *Rethinking German Policy: New Approaches to Reunification.* New York: Frederick A. Praeger, 1967.

Schweigler, Gebhard. "A New Political Giant? West German Foreign Policy in the 1970's." *The World Today* 31 (April 1975): 134-141.

The Security of the Federal Republic of Germany and the Development of the Federal Armed Forces. (Defense White Paper 1975/1976). Bonn: Federal Ministry of Defense, 1976.

Shears, David. *The Ugly Frontier.* New York: Knopf, 1970.

Siegler, Heinrich von. *The Reunification and Security of Germany: A Documentary Basis for Discussion.* Bonn: Siegler and Co., K.G., 1957.

Sommer, Theo. "Bonn Changes Course." *Foreign Affairs* 45 (April 1967): 477-491.

Speier, Hans. "German Rearmament and the Old Military Elite." *World Politics* 6 (January 1954): 147-168.

——————. *German Rearmament and Atomic War: The Views of the German Military and Political Leaders.* Evanston, IL; White Plains, New York: Row, Peterson, 1957.

——————. "The Hallstein Doctrine." *Survey*, No. 61 (October 1966), pp. 93-104.

Speier, Hans and Davison, W. Phillips. *West German Leadership and Foreign Policy.* Evanston, IL; White Plains, New York: Row, Peterson, 1957.

Spencer, Robert A. "Germany and the 'Long Haul.'" *International Journal* 11 (Winter 1955/56): 16-24.

Stahl, Walter. *The Politics of Post-War Germany.* New York: Praeger for Atlantik-Bruecke, 1963.

Stehle, Hansjakob. "The Federal Republic and Eastern Europe." *Survey*, No. 61 (October 1966), pp. 70-79.

Stent, Angela. *From Embargo to Ostpolitik: The Political Economy of West German-Soviet Relations, 1955-1980.* Cambridge, England: Cambridge University Press, 1981.

——————. "The USSR and Germany." *Problems of Communism* 30 (September/October 1981): 1-24.

Stenzl, Otto. "Germany's Eastern Frontier." *Survey*, No. 51 (April 1964), pp. 118-130.

Stewart-Smith, Geoffrey, ed. *Brandt and the Destruction of NATO.* New York: International Publication Service, 1973.

—————— and Davison, W. Phillips. *West German Leadership*

Strang, Lord. "Germany Between East and West." *Foreign Affairs* 33 (April 1955): 387-401.

Strauss, Franz Josef. "Soviet Aims and German Unity." *Foreign Affairs* 37 (April 1959): 366-377.

―――. "The Defense Debate in Germany: The Government View." *Survival* 3 (July/August 1961): 176-178.

―――. "Europe, America and NATO: A German View." *Survival* 4 (January/February 1962): 5-8.

―――. *The Grand Design: A European Solution to German Reunification*. New York: Praeger, 1966.

Strausz-Hupe, Robert. "Will West Germany Stay in Step?" *Policy Review* (Winter 1980): 37-49.

Stewart-Smith, Geoffrey, ed. *Brandt and the Destruction of NATO*. New York: International Publication Service, 1973.

Szaz, Zoltan Michael. *Germany's Eastern Frontiers: The Problem of the Oder-Neisse Line*. Chicago: Regnery, 1960.

Thompson, (Lt. Col.) James E. "West Germany and the NATO Strategy of Flexible Response." (Research Study). Maxwell AFB, AL: Air Command and Staff College, 1970.

Vali, Ferenc A. *The Quest for a United Germany*. Baltimore: Johns Hopkins Press, 1967.

Vigers, (Colonel) T.W. "The German People and Rearmament." *International Affairs* 27 (April 1951): 151-155.

von Brentano, H. *Germany and Europe: Reflections on German Foreign Policy*. New York: Praeger, 1964.

von dem Bussche, Axel. "German Rearmament: Hopes and Fears." *Foreign Affairs* 32 (October 1953): 68-79.

von Herwarth, Hans. "Anglo-German Relations: A German View." *International Affairs* 39 (October 1963): 511-520.

von Kielmansegg, (Gen.) J.A. Graf. "A German View of Western Defense." *Military Review* 54 (November 1974): 43-53.

Wagner, Wolfgang. "European Security: Foreign Policy After the Change." *Survival* 12 (February 1970): 46-50.

Wagner, Wolfgang. "Towards a New Political Order: German Ostpolitik and the East-West Realignment." *International Journal* 27 (Winter 1971): 18-31.

Watts, Anthony J. "The Federal German Navy--Its Role in NATO Naval Strategy." *Navy International* 84 (April 1979): 28-32.

"West Germany and NATO." *International Affairs* (Moscow), No. 9 (1956), pp. 127-129.

Weymar, Paul. *Adenauer, His Authorized Biography.* New York: Dutton, 1957.

Whetten, Lawrence L. "Appraising the Ostpolitik." *Orbis* 15 (Fall 1971): 856-878.

―――. *Germany's Ostpolitik: Relations Between the Federal Republic and the Warsaw Pact Countries.* London: Oxford University Press for Royal Institute of International Affairs, 1971.

―――. "Scope, Nature, and Change in Inner-German Relations." *International Affairs* (London) 57 (Winter '80/81): 60-78.

Wighton, Charles. *Adenauer, Democratic Dictator; A Critical Biography.* London: Muller, 1963.

Williams, J. Emlyn. "The German Federal Republic Today." *International Affairs* 28 (October 1952): 422-431.

―――. "Western Germany Before the Summit." *The World Today* 16 (February 1960): 63-70.

Windsor, Philip. *German Reunification.* London: Elek, 1969.

―――. *Germany and the Management of Detente.* London: Chatto and Windus for the Institute for Strategic Studies, 1971.

Winzer, Otto. "Some Features of West German Foreign Policy." *International Affairs* (Moscow), No. 8 (1956), pp. 50-60.

Wiskemann, Elizabeth. *Germany's Eastern Neighbours: Problem Relating to the Oder-Neisse Line and the Czech Frontier Regions.* London: Oxford University Press for the Royal Institute of International Affairs, 1956.

Wolfe, James H. *Indivisible Germany: Illusion or Reality?* The Hague: Nijhoff, 1963.

Worner, Manfred. "The 'Peace Movement' and NATO: An Alternative View from Bonn." *Strategic Review* 10 (Winter 1982): 15-21.

ISSUES IN NATO

BERLIN

Allemann, F.R. "Berlin in Search of a Purpose." *Survey* 61 (October 1969): 129-138.

Anon. "The Berlin Crisis." *The World Today* 17 (August 1961): 319-322.

Augstein, Rudolf. "The Spur of Berlin." *Survival* 7 (November 1965): 296-297.

Bark, Dennis L. *Agreement on Berlin: A Study of the 1970-1972 Quadripartite Negotiations.* Washington, D.C.: American Enterprise Institute for Public Policy Research, 1974.

―――――. *The Dilemmas of Detente: Negotiation and Agreement on Berlin 1970-1972.* Washington: American Enterprise Institute for Public Policy Research, 1974.

Barker, Elisabeth. "The Berlin Crisis, 1958-1962." *International Affairs* 39 (January 1963): 59-73.

Brandt, Willy. "The East-West Problem as Seen from Berlin." *International Affairs* 34 (July 1958): 297-304.

Clay, (General) Lucius D. "Berlin." *Foreign Affairs* 41 (October 1962): 47-58.

Collier, David S., and Glaser, Kurt, eds. *Berlin and the Future of Eastern Europe.* Chicago: Regnery, 1963.

Davison, W. Phillips. *The Berlin Blockade: A Study in Cold War Politics.* Princeton: Princeton University Press; London: Oxford University Press, 1958.

Deutsch, Harold C. *New Crisis on Berlin.* Toronto: Canadian Institute of International Affairs, 1959. (*Behind the Headlines.* Vol. 14. No. 2).

Dulles, Eleanor Lansing. *Berlin: The Wall Is Not Forever.* Chapel Hill: University of North Carolina Press, 1967.

Franklin, William M. "Zonal Boundaries and Access to Berlin." *World Politics* 16 (October 1963): 1-31.

Frei, Otto. "The Barrier Across Berlin and Its Consequences." *The World Today* 17 (November 1961): 459-470.

Haffner, Sebastian. "The Berlin Crisis (1958-1962)." *Survey* 44/45 (October 1962): 37-44.

Hillenbrand, Martin L., ed. *The Future of Berlin.* Montclair, NY: Allanheld, Osmun & Company for the Atlantic Institute, 1980.

Legien, R. *The Four Power Agreements on Berlin: Alternative Solutions to the Status Quo?* Berlin: Carl Heymanns Verlag, 1960.

Mahncke, Dieter. "In Search of a Modus Vivendi for Berlin: Prospects for Four-Power Talks." *The World Today* 26 (April 1970): 137-146.

───────. "The Berlin Agreement: Balance and Prospects." *The World Today* 27 (December 1971): 511-521.

Mander, John. *Berlin: The Eagle and the Bear.* London: Barrie and Radcliff, 1959.

───────. *Berlin: Hostage for the West.* Harmondsworth: Penguin, 1962.

Morgan, Roger and Bray, Caroline. "Berlin in the Post-Detente Era [Effect of the Worsening East-West Situation in the 1980's in the International Situation of Berlin]." *World Today (London)* 38 (March 1982): 81-89.

Morris, Eric. *Blockade: Berlin and the Cold War.* New York: Stein and Day, 1973.

On the Situation in Berlin 1948. London: Soviet News, 1948.

Pounds, Norman J.G. *Dividend Germany and Berlin.* Princeton: Van Nostrand, 1962.

"The Powers and Berlin." *The World Today* 14 (December 1958): 507-510.

The Problem of West Berlin and Solutions Proposed by the Government of the German Democratic Republic. Berlin: Ministry of Foreign Affairs of the German Democratic Republic, 1961.

Robson, Charles B. *Berlin--Pivot of German Destiny.* Chapel Hill: The University of North Carolina Press; London: Oxford University Press, 1960.

Schick, Jack M. "The Berlin Crisis of 1961 and U.S. Military Strategy." *Orbis* 8 (Winter 1965): 816-831.

———. *The Berlin Crisis 1958-1962*. Philadelphia: University of Pennsylvania Press, 1971.

Schutz, Klaus. "Berlin in the Age of Detente." *The World Today* 31 (January 1975): 29-35.

Shell, Kurt L. "Berlin and the German Problem." *World Politics* 16 (October 1963): 137-146.

Slusser, Robert M. *The Berlin Crisis of 1961: Soviet-American Relations and the Struggle for Power in the Kremlin, June-November 1961*. Baltimore: Johns Hopkins Press, 1973.

Smith, Jean Edward. *The Defence of Berlin*. Baltimore: Johns Hopkins Press; London: Oxford University Press, 1963.

Spencer, Robert. "Berlin, the Blockade and the Cold War." *International Journal* 23 (Summer 1968): 383-407.

Stanger, Roland J., ed. *West Berlin: The Legal Context*. Columbus: Ohio State University Press, 1966.

Whetten, Lawrence L. "The Problem of Berlin." *The World Today* 27 (May 1971): 222-227.

Windsor, Philip. *City on Leave: A History of Berlin 1945-1962*. New York: Praeger, 1963.

Wiskemann, Elizabeth. "Berlin Between East and West." *The World Today* 16 (November 1960): 463-471.

ECONOMICS AND SCIENTIFIC COOPERATION

Alder-Karlsson, Gunnar. *Western Economic Warfare 1947-1967*. Stockholm: Alquist and Wiksell, 1968.

Art, Robert J. "Why We Overspend and Underaccomplish." *Foreign Policy* 6 (Spring 1972): 95-114.

Aspin, Les. "NATO Surcharge: The Three Percent Misunderstanding." *Nation* 228 (21 April 1979): 430-432.

———. "The Three Percent Solution: NATO and the U.S. Defense Budget." *Challenge* 22 (May-June 1979): 22-29.

Atlantic Council Energy Policy Committee. *U.S. Energy Policy and U.S. Foreign Policy in the 1980's; Report, Foreword by Kenneth Rush*. Cambridge, MA: Balliger Publishing Company, 1981.

Bare, C. Gordon. "Burden-Sharing in NATO: The Economics of Alliances." *Orbis* 20 (Summer 1976): 417-436.

"The Battle over Sharing NATO's Costs." *Congressional Quarterly Weekly Report* 37 (30 June 1979): 1306.

Bergquist, Mats. "Trade and Security in the Nordic Area." *Co-operation and Conflict* 4 (1969): 237-246.

Binkin, Martin. *Support Costs in the Defense Budget: The Submerged One-Third.* Washington, D.C.: The Brookings Institution, 1972.

Blechman, Barry M., and Kuzmack, Arnold M. "Oil and National Security." *Naval War College Review* (May-June 1974): 8-25.

"Budgets and Theater Nuclear Forces." *Defense and Foreign Affairs Digest* 7 (1979): 40-41.

Burnham, T. "AGARD--What It Is and What It Does." *NATO's Fifteen Nations* 25 (August-September 1980): 57-58.

Burrell, R.M., and Cottrell, Alvin J. *Politics, Oil and the Western Mediterranean.* Washington, D.C.: Center for Strategic and International Studies, 1973: 88.

Callaghan, Thomas A., Jr. "A Common Market for Atlantic Defense." *Survival* 17 (May/June 1975): 129-132. *Atlantic Community Quarterly* 13 (Summer 1975): 161-167.

Clark, Wilson and Page, Jack. *Energy Vulnerability and War: Alternatives for America.* New York: W.W. Norton and Company, Inc., 1981.

Clayton, James L. *The Economic Impact of the Cold War: Sources and Readings.* New York: Harcourt, Brace and World, Inc., 1970.

Cohen, Stephen D. *The Making of United States International Economic Policy: Principles, Problems and Proposals for Reform; Foreword by C. Fred Bergsten,* 2nd Ed. New York: Praeger Publishers, Inc., 1981.

Collins, (V. Adm.) D.A. "NATO Common-funded Intrastructure Projects (Address to AFCEA NATO Brussels Symposium, October, 1980)." *Signal* 35 (December 1980): 35-38.

Conant, Melvin A. *The Oil Factor in U.S. Foreign Policy; 1980-1990.* Lexington, MA: Lexington Books for the Council on Foreign Relations, 1982.

Cooper, Richard N. *The Economics of Interdependence: Economic Policy in the Atlantic Community.* New York: McGraw-Hill for the Council on Foreign Relations, 1968.

Currie, Malcolm R. "Economics of Standardization Analyzed." *Aviation Week and Space Technology* (1 January 1979): 56-57.

Day, A.C.L. "The Cost of Defense." *Survival* 2 (March/April 1960): 81-85.

"Defense Expenditures of NATO Countries 1949-1978." *NATO Review* 27 (February 1979): 30-31.

DeWeerd, H.A. "The Cost of Detente: No Rest for the Wary." *Army* 24 (May 1974): 17-20.

Diebold, William, Jr. "The Changed Economic Position of Western Europe: Some Implications for United States Policy and International Organization." *International Organization* 14 (Winter 1960): 1-19.

———. "Economic Aspects of an Atlantic Community." *International Organization* 17 (Summer 1963): 663-682.

Douglas-Home, Charles. "British Defense Cuts (1968)." *Survival* 10 (March 1968): 70-78.

Drummond, Dennis M. "Getting Traffic Moving on NATO's Two-Way Street." *Air University Review* 30 (September-October 1979): 26-34.

Edmonds, Martin, ed. *International Arms Procurement*. Elmsford, NY: Pergamon Press, 1981.

Fieleke, Norman S. "Rising Oil Prices and the Industrial Countries." (Address). *New England Economic Review* (January/February 1981): 17-28.

"Financial and Economic Data Relating to NATO Defense." *NATO's Fifteen Nations* 24 (1979): 196-197.

Fostervoll, Alv Jakob. "European Defense and the Euro-Group." *NATO Review* 22 (June 1974): 8-11.

Franks, Lord. "Co-operation Is Not Enough." *Foreign Affairs* 41 (October 1962): 24-35.

Friedland, Edward. *The Great Detente Disaster; Oil and the Decline of American Foreign Policy*. New York: Basic Books, Inc., 1975.

Furlong, R.D.M. "Can NATO Afford AWACS?" *International Defence Review* 7 (October 1975): 667-676.

Gail, Bridget. "The FY80 Defense Budget." *Armed Forces Journal International* (March 1979): 26.

Goldberg, Edward D., ed. *North Sea Science: Papers Presented at the NATO Science Committee Conference*. Cambridge, MA: MIT Press, 1973.

Golden, James R. *NATO Burden Sharing*, Washington Paper No. 96. New York: Praeger Press, 1983.

———. *The Dynamics of Change in NATO: A Burden-Sharing Perspective.* New York: Praeger Press, 1983.

Gordon, Colin. "The WEU and European Defense Community." *Orbis* 17 (Spring 1973): 247-257.

Gordon, Lincoln. "Economic Aspects of Coalition Diplomacy: The NATO Experience." *International Organization* 10 (Autumn 1956): 529-543.

Griswold, Lawrence. "North Sea Oil: NATO's Refuge or Ruin?" *Air Force Magazine* 58 (February 1975): 49-54.

Gundersen, H.F. Zeiner. "The Balance of Force and Economic Problems." *NATO Review* 27 (October 1979): 3-7.

Haig, Alexander M., Jr. "Relationship of Foreign Aid and Defense Policies." *Department of State Bulletin* 81 (September 1981): 16-18.

Hall, David K. "Economic Stresses in the NATO Alliance." *AEI Foreign Policy and Defense Review* 2, Number 5 (1980): 11-14.

Hardt, John P. *The Cold War Economic Gap: The Increasing Threat to American Security.* New York: Praeger, 1961.

Harnwell, Gaylord P. "Science, Technology and the North Atlantic Community." *Orbis* 2 (Summer 1958): 209-220.

Harvey, David. "NATO and the U.S. Budget." *Defense and Foreign Affairs Digest* (February 1979): 34.

Harvey, Mose L. *East-West Trade and United States Policy.* New York: National Association of Manufacturers, 1966.

Hitch, Charles J., and McKean, Roland N. *The Economics of Defence in the Nuclear Age.* Santa Monica, CA: Rand Corporation, 1960.

Hoag, Malcolm W. "On NATO Pooling." *World Politics* 10 (April 1958): 475-483.

Hoeffding, Oleg. "Strategy and Economics: A Soviet View." *World Politics* 2 (January 1959): 316-324.

Holzman, Franklyn D., and Legvold, Robert. "The Economics and Politics of East-West Relations." *International Organization* 29 (Winter 1975): 275-320.

Jenner, Peter. "Allied Co-operation Saves on Cost of Maintenance and Supply; Fifteen Years of NAMSO." *NATO Review* 21 (No. 2, 1973): 18-22.

Johnston, Ernest B., Jr. "Soviet Energy Development and the Western Alliance." *Department of State Bulletin* 82 (April 1982): 62-64.

Jordan, Amos A. "Military Assistance and National Policy." *Orbis* 2 (Summer 1958): 236-253.

Kahn, Herman, and Schneider, Ernest. "Globaloney 2000" (Critical of report entitled "The Global 2000 Report to the President" by U.S. Department of State and Council on Environmental Quality.) *Policy Review* (Spring 1981): 129-47. For "Global 2000" report see: hearing September 4, 1980, '80iii+57p (96th Cong., 2nd Session) (Joint Economic Committee).

Kanter, Hershel. "The Reagan Defense Program in Early Outline." *Strategic Review* 9 (Summer 1981): 27-38.

———. "The Reagan Defense Program: Can It Hold Up?" *Strategic Review* 10 (Winter 1982): 19-34.

Kennedy, Gavin. *The Economics of Defense.* Totowa, NJ: Rowan and Littlefield, 1975.

———. *Burden Sharing in NATO.* New York: Holmes and Meier Publishers, Inc., 1979.

Keyserling, Leon H. "International Implications of U.S. Economic Performance and National Policies." *Atlantic Economic Journal* 9 (December 1981): 27-33.

King, Wilfred. "Fair Shares on Teeth and Tanks." *Foreign Affairs* 29 (July 1951): 608-624.

Kirby, Stephen. "The Independent European Programme Group: The Failure of Low-Profile High-Politics." *Journal of Common Market Studies* 18 (December 1979): 175-96.

Korb, Lawrence J. "The FY 1981-1985 Defense Program: Issues and Trends." *Foreign Policy and Defense Review* 2 (No. 2, 1980): 2-63.

Kozicharow, Eugene. "Modernization to Hike NATO Budget." *Aviation Week and Space Technology* 110 (11 June 1979): 109-112.

Krause, Lawrence B. *European Economic Integration and the United States.* Washington: Brookings Institution, 1968.

Krell, Gert. "Capitalism and Armaments: Business Cycles and Defense Spending in the United States, 1945-1979." *Journal of Peace Research* 18 (No. 3, 1981): 221-240.

"The Lashing of Public Enemy Number One." *OPEC Bulletin* 11 (October 1980): 77-85.

Legere, Lawrence J. "A Presidential Perspective." *Foreign Policy* 6 (Spring 1972): 84-94.

Leitenberg, Milton. "Efforts at Reducing Defense Expenditure in the United States, 1960-1978." *Public Policy* 28 (No. 3, 1981): 437-441.

Lettau, Ulrich H. "COBs (Collected Operating Bases) in Europe." *Air Force Engineering and Services Quarterly* 22 (Summer 1981): 19-22.

Lippmann, Walter. *Western Unity and the Common Market.* Boston, MA: Atlantic (Little, Brown), 1962.

Maddison, Angus. *Economic Growth in the West: Comparative Experience in Europe and North America.* New York: Twentieth Century Fund, 1964.

Marriott, John. "The Defense of North Sea Oil and Gas." *NATO's Fifteen Nations* 19 (October-November 1974): 73-77.

Maurischat, G. "Economic Preparation for War in West Germany." *International Affairs* (Moscow) 7 (1961): 59-60.

Meeker, Thomas A. *The Military-Industrial Complex: A Source Guide to the Issues of Defence Spending and Policy Control.* (Political Issues Series, Center for the Study of Armament and Disarmament). Los Angeles, CA: California State University, 1973.

Mendershausen, H. *October in Western Europe.* Santa Monica, CA: Rand Corp., (November 1974): 14.

Morgenstern, Oskar. *The Question of National Defence.* New York: Random House, 1959.

"NATO Defense Spending." *Defense and Foreign Affairs Daily* (13 March 1979): 1.

"The North Sea Oil Scramble: Scores of American Suppliers Are Competing for a Wealth of Business." *Dun's* 100 (December 1972): 108+.

Oakeshott, Robert. "The Strategic Embargo: An Obstacle to East-West Trade." *The World Today* 19 (June 1963): 240-247.

Occupation Costs: Are They a Defence Contribution? Tubingen: J.C.B. Mohr, 1951.

Olvey, Lee D.; Golden, James R.; and Kelly, Robert C. *Economics of National Security.* Wayne, NJ: Avery Publishing Group, 1983.

Ott, George. "The Con Against NATO: Europe Can Afford to Defend Itself." *Washington Monthly* 12 (December 1980): 34-36.

Ozdas, Nimet. "Transatlantic Science--A Unique Programme." *NATO's Fifteen Nations* 24 (1979): 181-182+.

Parker, (Lt. Col.) Glynn E. "NATO and Rationalization, Standardization, and Interoperability." *Army Logistician* 12 (March-April 1980): 24-27.

Perry, William J. "NATO Two-Way Street Called Essential." *Aviation Week* 110 (February 1979): 49-51.

"Perspectives on the Military Budget." *Defense Monitor* 8 (May 1979): 2+.

Pfaltzgraff, Robert L., Jr. "European-American Defense Burden-Sharing." *Atlantic Community Quarterly* 12 (Summer 1974): 197-204.

Pierre, Andrew J. "Arms Sales: The New Diplomacy." *Foreign Affairs* 60 (Winter 1981/1982): 266-286. Princeton, NJ: Princeton University Press, 1982.

――――. *The Global Politics of Arms Sales*. Princeton, NJ: Princeton University Press, 1982.

Pisar, Samuel. *Co-Existence and Commerce: Guidelines for Transactions Between East and West*. New York: McGraw-Hill, 1970.

Rannestad, Andreas. "Scientific Co-operation in NATO." *NATO Review* 21 (No. 2, 1973): 23-26.

Rashish, Myer. "Approaches to Foreign Economic Issues [Statement before the Joint Economic Committee, U.S. Congress, July 14, 1981]." *Department of State Bulletin* 81 (October 1981): 40-46.

Ravenal, Earl C. *Regan's 1983 Defense Budget: An Analysis and an Alternative*. San Francisco, CA: Cato Institute, 1982.

Ritchie, Ronald S. *NATO: The Economics of an Alliance*. Toronto: The Ryerson Press for the Canadian Institute of International Affairs, 1956.

Rowan, Sir Leslie. *Arms and Economics: The Changing Challenge*. (The Lees Knowles Lecture 1960). Cambridge, MA: Cambridge University Press, 1960.

Rupp, Rainer W. "Defense Related Economic Co-operation and Assistance Within the Alliance." *NATO's Fifteen Nations* 25 (June-July 1980): 61-62+.

Rusk, Dean. "Tensions in International Trade and Foreign Policy Facing President Reagan." *St. Louis University Public Law Forum* 1 (1981): 1-10.

Schemmer, Benjamin F. "Carter's FY80 Defense Budget Meets NATO's 3% Real Growth Commitment." *Armed Forces Journal International* (February 1979): 18-19.

Schmidt, Helmut. "Shrinking Defense Resources in the West and the World Balance." *Atlantic Community Quarterly* 11 (Winter 1973-74): 422-437.

Schultze, Charles L. "Do More Dollars Mean Better Defense?" *Challenge* 24 (January/February 1982): 30-35.

"Should 3.1-Percent Increase in President Carter's Military Spending Budget Be Pegged to NATO's Recommendations?" *Congressional Record* 125 (March 5, 1979): E851-E856.

Spaulding, Harry S. "NAMSA: The NATO Maintenance and Supply Agency--Its Role in International Logistics." *NATO's Fifteen Nations* 24 (December 1979-January 1980): 54+.

Speth, Gus. "The Global 2000 Report to the President: Entering the Twenty-First Century." *Boston College Environmental Affairs Law Review* 8 (No. 4, 1980): 695-703.

Stanley, Timothy W. "The Political Economics of Defense: Burden-Sharing." *Atlantic Community Quarterly* 9 (Winter 1971-72): 442-450.

Stent, Angela E. *Soviet and Western Europe.* Foreword by Robert F. Byrnes. New York: Praeger Publishers, Inc., 1982.

Sullivan, Leonard, Jr. "The Real Long-range Defense Dilemma: Burden Sharing." *Armed Forces Journal International* 119 (October 1981): 56-58+.

Sweet, William. "Defense Spending Debate." *Editorial Research Reports* (April 16, 1982): 275-292.

Taylor, Phillip. "Weapons Standardization in NATO: Collaborative Security or Economic Competition?" *International Organization* 36 (Winter 1982): 95-112.

Timbrell, Robert W. "Aclant Mobile Logistics a Requirement for Standardization." *NATO's Fifteen Nations* 17 (February-March 1972): 82-84+.

Towell, Pat. "Fiscal 1979 Budget: Carter Continues NATO Buildup; Navy Plans Slowed." *Congressional Quarterly Weekly Report* 36 (January 28, 1978): 167+.

———. "Pentagon Fund Backlog Target for Cuts." *Congressional Quarterly Weekly Report* (17 February 1979): 304.

Tsambiras, Sotirios. "NATO and Industrial Property." *NATO Review* 22 (No. 1, 1974): 19-21.

Tucker, Gardiner. *Towards Rationalizing Allied Weapons Production.* With the Assistance of Fabio Basagni. Atlantic Institute of International Affairs, October 1976.

Tuthill, John W. "Economic Slowdown and NATO." *Survival* 14 (March/April 1972): 58-61.

"The U.S. Arms Debate [five articles reprinted from various sources]." *World Press Review* 29 (May 1982): 37-42.

U.S. Congress, House of Representatives. *Military Construction Appropriations for 1974. Hearings Before a Sub-Committee on Appropriations, House of Representatives, Ninety-Third Congress, First Session.* Washington, D.C.: U.S. Government Printing Office, 1973.

United States Congress. Joint Economic Committee. *The Ottawa Summit and U.S. International Economic Policy: Hearings, July 14 and 16, 1981.* Washington, D.C.: Superintendent of Documents, 1981.

United States Congress. Joint Economic Committee. *U.S. International Economic Policy in the 1980's: Selected Essays.* Washington, D.C.: Superintendent of Documents, 1982.

United States. House. Committee on Foreign Affairs. *NATO Mutual Support Act of 1979.* Hearing and Markup, November 14 and 27, 1979, before the Sub-Committee on International Security and Scientific Affairs and on Europe and the Middle East, on HR. 5580. 1979 iii-44p (96th Congress, 1st Session) Washington, D.C. 20515.

United States. House. Committee on Foreign Affairs. Subcommittee on International Economic Policy and Trade. *U.S. International Economic Influence: Agenda for the Future: Hearing, February 24, 1981.* 97th Congress, 2nd Session. Washington, D.C.: Government Printing Office, 1981.

United States Senate. *U.S. Security Issues in Europe: Burden Sharing and Offset, MBFR and Nuclear Weapons, September 1973. A Staff Report Prepared for the Use of the Subcommittee on U.S. Security Agreements and Commitments Abroad of the Committee on Foreign Relations, United States Senate.* Washington, D.C.: U.S. Government Printing Office, 1973.

Vandevanter, E., Jr. *Common Funding in NATO.* (Memorandum RM-5282 PR). Santa Monica: Rand Corporation, 1967.

Vernon, Raymond. "Foreign Trade and National Defense." *Foreign Affairs* 34 (October 1955): 77-88.

Warburton, Anne, and Wood, John. *Paying for NATO.* London: Friends of Atlantic Union, 1956.

Weintraub, Sydney, ed. *Economic Coercion and U.S. Foreign Policy: Implications of Case Studies from the Johnson Administration.* Boulder, CO: Westview Press, Inc., 1982.

Wellershoff, (F. Adm.) Dieter. "NATO Naval Armaments and Cooperation." *NATO's Fifteen Nations* 24 (December 1979-January 1980): 39-40+.

Wilcox, John G. "Military Implications of the Global 2000 Report." *Military Review* 61 (August 1981): 30-38.

Wolf, Charles, Jr. *'Offsets,' Standardization and Trade Liberalization in NATO.* (Rand Paper, p-5779). Santa Monica: Rand Corporation, October 1976.

Yudin, Y. "'Pay More!' The U.S.A. Tells Its NATO Allies." *International Affairs* (Moscow) (1961): 32-40.

SALT

Aaron, David. "Salt: A New Concept." *Foreign Policy*, No. 17 (Winter 1974-75): 157-165.

Beavers, (Cmdr.) Roy L., Jr. "Salt I." *United States Naval Institute Proceedings* 100 (May 1974): 204-219.

Biden, Joseph R., Jr. "Salt and NATO Allies." *Congressional Record* 125 (October 12, 1979): S14525-S14538.

Booth, Kenneth. "The Strategic Arms Limitation Talks: A Stock-taking." *World Survey*, No. 73 (January 1975): 18+.

Bull, Hedley. *The Moscow Agreements and Strategic Arms Limitation.* Canberra: Australian National University Press, 1973.

Burt, Richard. "Salt II and Offensive Force Levels." *Orbis* 18 (Summer 1974): 465-481.

———. "Soviet Sea-Based Forces and Salt." *Survival* 17 (January/February 1975): 9-13.

Caldwell, Lawrence T. *Soviet Attitudes to SALT.* (Adelphi Paper No. 75). London: International Institute for Strategic Studies, 1971.

Calogero, Francesco. "A Scenario for Effective Salt Negotiations." *Bulletin of the Atomic Scientists* 29 (June 1973): 16-22.

Carter, Luther J. "Beyond Vladivostok: The Feasibility and the Politics of Arms Reduction." *Science Magazine*, 11 April 1975.

Coffey, J.I. "Strategic Arms Limitations and European Security." *International Affairs* 47 (October 1971): 692-707.

———. "The Savor of Salt." *Bulletin of the Atomic Scientists* 29 (May 1973): 9-15.

Cohen, Stuart A. "SALT Verification: The Evolution of Soviet Views and Their Meaning for the Future." *Orbis* 24 (Fall 1980): 657-83.

Cutler, Lloyd N. and Molander, Roger C. "Is There Life After Death for Salt?" *International Security* 6 (Fall 1981): 3-20.

"Diplomacy at Home and Abroad: Paul Warnke on Negotiating SALT." *Arms Control Today* 9 (May 1979): 3-8.

Freedman, Lawrence. "S.A.L.T. and N.A.T.O." *Ditchley Journal* 6 (Autumn 1979): 36-43.

Gray, Colin S. and Payne, Kenneth B. *SALT: Deep Force Level Reductions; Final Report*. Prepared for the SALT/Arms Control Support Group, United States Office of the Assistant to the Secretary of Defense (Atomic Energy). Croton-on-Hudson, NY: Hudson Institute, 1981.

———. "SALT II and the NATO Alliance." *International Security Review* 4 (Summer 1979): 178-206.

Haig, Alexander M., Jr. "Arms Control and Strategic Nuclear Forces." *Department of State Bulletin* 81 (December 1981): 22-24.

Hoffman, Hubertus and Steinrucke, Rolf. "Participation of the European States in the SALT III Negotiations." *NATO's Fifteen Nations* 24 (June-July 1979): 78-86.

Jackson, Henry M. "SALT: An Analysis and a Proposal." *Vital Speeches of the Day* 40 (1 January 1974): 169-172.

Kaplan, Morton A., ed. *SALT: Problems and Prospects*. Morristown, NJ: General Learning Press, 1973.

Kintner, William R., and Pfaltzgraff, Robert L., Jr. "Assessing the Moscow Salt Agreements." *Orbis* 16 (Summer 1972): 341-360.

———, eds. *SALT: Implications for Arms Control in the 1970's*. Pittsburgh: University of Pittsburgh Press, 1973.

Kissinger, Henry A. "Press Statement by Secretary of State Dr. Kissinger on the Soviet-American Statement on Strategic Arms Limitation. (November 1974)." *Survival* 17 (January/February 1975): 33-34.

Kozicharow, Eugene. "NATO Members Urge SALT III Parleys." *Aviation Week & Space Technology* 110 (21 May 1979): 17-18.

Kruzel, Joseph. "SALT II: The Search for Follow-on Agreement." *Orbis* 17 (Summer 1973): 334-363.

Lehman, John F. and Weiss, Seymour. *Beyond the SALT II Failure.* New York: Praeger Publishers, Inc., 1981.

Menaul, Stewart. "SALT II: The Eurostrategic Imbalance." *Conflict Studies* 104 (February 1979): 1-17.

Metcalf, Arthur G.B. "SALT II--Some Principles." *Strategic Review* 1 (Summer 1973): 6-17.

Murovchik, Joshua. "Expectations of SALT I: Lessons for SALT III." *World Affairs* 143 (Winter 1980/81): 278-97.

Newhouse, John. *Cold Dawn: The Story of SALT.* New York: Holt, Rinehart and Winston, 1973.

Nitze, Paul H. "The Vladivostok Accord and SALT II." *The Review of Politics* 37 (April 1975): 147-160.

Pierre, Andrew J. "The SALT Agreement and Europe." *The World Today* 28 (July 1972): 281-288.

Potter, (Maj.) G.A. "SALT I: A Military Evaluation." *Canadian Defence Quarterly* 3 (Summer 1973): 29-30ff.

"President Nixon and Dr. Henry Kissinger Discuss SALT Agreements." *NATO Review* 20 (July/August 1972): 5-12.

"Prospects for Strategic Arms Limitation." *Survival* 16 (March/April 1974): 54-74.

Resor, Stanley R. "The Limitations of Armaments and Arms Control: SALT and NATO Security." *Vital Speeches of the Day* 45 (April 15, 1979): 397-402.

Rose, Francois de. "The Future of SALT and Western Security in Europe." *Foreign Affairs* 57 (Summer 1979): 1065-1074.

Scoville, Herbert Jr. "Beyond SALT 1." *Foreign Affairs* 50 (April 1972): 488-500.

———. "Strategic Forum: The SALT Agreements." *Survival* 14 (September/October 1972): 210-216.

Sharp, Jane M.O. "Restructuring the SALT Dialogue." *International Security* 6 (Winter 1981/1982): 144-176.

Sjaastad, Anders C. "SALT II: Consequences for Europe and the Nordic Region." *Co-operation and Conflict* 15 (No. 4, 1980): 237-48.

Slominski, (Col.) Martin J. "SALT Facets." *Military Review* 54 (January 1974): 82-88.

Smart, Ian. "The Strategic Arms Limitation Talks." *The World Today* 26 (July 1970): 296-304.

Stone, Jeremy. "When and How to Use SALT." *Foreign Affairs* 48 (January 1970): 262-273.

"Strategic Arms Limitation (Joint Soviet-American Statement of Strategic Arms Limitation, 24 November 1974)." *Survival* 17 (January/February 1975): 32-34.

Szulc, Tad. "Soviet Violations of the SALT Deal. Have We Been Had?" *New Republic* 172 (June 7, 1975): 11-15.

Tammen, Ronald L. *Mirv and the Arms Race: An Interpretation of Defense Strategy.* New York: Praeger, 1973.

United States Congress. *Fiscal Year 1983 Arms Control Impact Statements: Statements Submitted to the Congress by the President Pursuant to Section 36 of the Arms Control and Disarmament Act.* 97th Congress, 2nd Session. Washington, D.C.: Superintendent of Documents, 1982.

United States. Senate Committee on Foreign Relations. Subcommittee on European Affairs. *SALT and the NATO Allies: A Staff Report, October 1979.* '79 x +57p tables (96th Congress, 1st Session) (Com. print).

Vance, Cyrus R. "Where We Stand with SALT." *Department of State Bulletin* 79 (November 1979): 36-43.

Warnke, Paul C. "SALT II and NATO Security." *NATO Review* (August 1979): 3.

Williams, Phil. "SALT, Strategy and Atlantic Relations." *Royal United Services Institute for Defence Studies* 124 (March 1979): 50-54.

Willrich, Mason, and Rhinelander, John B., eds. *SALT: The Moscow Agreements and Beyond.* New York: Free Press, 1974.

Winne, (Col.) Clinton H., Jr. "SALT and the Blue-Water Strategy." *Air University Review* 25 (September-October 1974): 25-35.

Wyle, Frederick S. *U.S., Europe, SALT and Strategy.* Chicago: Center for Policy Study, University of Chicago Press, 1971.

Yost, David S. *European Security and the SALT Process.* Foreword by Uwe Nerlich. Beverley Hills, CA: Sage Publications (published for the Center for Strategic and International Studies, Georgetown University), 1981.

GENERAL DISARMAMENT AND FORCE REDUCTIONS

Amme, Carl H. Jr. "Arms Control Concepts and the Military Balance in Europe." *Orbis* 8 (Winter 1965): 832-853.

Bar-Levov, Doron. "Vladivostok Arms Race." *The Nation* 220 (12 April 1975): 424-425.

Barton, John H. *The Politics of Peace: An Evolution of Arms Control*. Stanford, CA: Stanford University Press, 1981.

Bechhoeffer, Bernhard G. *Post-War Negotiations for Arms Control*. Washington, D.C.: Brookings Institution, 1961.

Bell, Coral. *Negotiation from Strength*. London: Chatto and Windus, 1962.

Bernard, Stephen. "Some Political and Technical Implications of Disarmament." *World Politics* 8 (October 1955): 71-90.

Bertram, Christoph, ed. "Arms Control and Military Force." *Adelphi Library* 3, published for International Institute for Strategic Studies. Totowa, NJ: Allenheld, Osman and Co., Publishers, Inc., 1980.

―――. *Mutual Force Reductions in Europe: The Political Aspects*. London: The International Institute for Strategic Studies, 1972.

―――. "The Politics of MBFR." *The World Today* 29 (January 1973): 1-7.

Bethe, Hans A. "Disarmament and Strategy." *Survival* 4 (November/December 1962): 267-276.

Blaisdell, (Maj.) Allan C. *NATO and the Warsaw Pact--The Challenge of Mutual and Balanced Force Reductions*. (Research Study). Maxwell AFB, AL: Air Command and Staff College, 1972.

Blechman, Barry M. "Do Negotiated Arms Limitations Have a Future?" *Foreign Affairs* 59 (Fall 1980): 102-25.

"The Bomb: Beyond Control." (five articles--various sources). *World Press Review* 2 (August 1981): 37-42.

Borawski, John. "East-West Bargaining on Theater Nuclear Forces." *Parameters* 11 (September 1981): 31-38.

"Both Sides Table Proposals at MBFR Negotiations." *NATO Review* 23 (January 1975): 18-19.

Boyd, (Maj.) Alfred A. *The Effects of MBFR on NATO Strategy*. (Research Study). Maxwell AFB, AL: Air Command and Staff College, 1974.

Borawski, John. "East-West Bargaining on Theater Nuclear Forces." *Parameters* 11 (September 1981): 31-38.

Brady, Linda P. "Negotiating European Security." *International Security Review* 6 (Summer 1981): 189-208.

Brennan, Donald G. "Some Fundamental Problems of Arms Control and National Security." *Orbis* 15 (Spring 1977): 218-231.

Brzezinski, Zbigniev. "Moscow and the M.F.F.: Hostility and Ambivalence." *Foreign Affairs* 43 (October 1964): 126-134.

Bull, Hedley. *Soviet-American Relations and World Order: Arms Limitations and Policy*. (Adelphi Paper No. 65). London: International Institute for Strategic Studies, February 1970.

Bundy, McGeorge. "To Cap the Volcano." *Foreign Affairs* 48 (October 1969): 1-20.

Buntinx, Henry M.V. "Symmetrical Force Reductions Versus European Collective Security." *NATO's Fifteen Nations* 15 (October-November 1970): 29-33.

Burt, Richard. "The Relevance of Arms Control in the 1980's." *Daedalus* 110 (Winter 1981): 159-77.

Caldwell, Lawrence T. "The Soviet Union and Arms Control." *Current History* 67 (October 1974): 150-152.

Chester, Conrad V., and Wigner, Eugene P. "Population Vulnerability: The Neglected Issue in Arms Limitation and the Strategic Balance." *Orbis* 18 (Fall 1974): 763-769.

Clemens, Walter C., Jr. "Mutual Balanced Force Reductions." *Military Review* 15 (October 1971): 3-11.

―――. *The Superpowers and Arms Control: From Cold War to Interdependence*. Lexington, MA: Lexington Books, 1973.

Coffey, J.I. *New Approaches to Arms Reduction in Europe*. (Adelphi Paper No. 105). London: International Institute for Strategic Studies, 1974.

―――. "Arms Control and the Military Balance in Europe." *Orbis* 17 (Spring 1973): 132-154.

Coleman, Herbert J. "NATO Divided on Arms Talks." *Aviation Week & Space Technology* 99 (12 November 1973): 12-13.

Cook, Don. "The European Security Conference." *Atlantic Monthly* (October 1973): 6-12.

Deutsch, Karl W. *Arms Control and the Atlantic Alliance*. London and New York: John Wiley, 1967.

Dewey, (Lt. Col.) Arthur E. "Who's Afraid of a European Security Conference?" *Military Review* 53 (July 1973): 5-16.

Dougherty, James E. "Key to Security: Disarmament or Arms Stability." *Orbis* 4 (Fall 1960): 261-283.

―――. "Zonal Arms Limitation in Europe." *Orbis* 7 (Fall 1963): 478-517.

―――. "Arms Control in the 1970's." *Orbis* 15 (Spring 1977): 194-217.

Engle, Kenneth W. "European Arms Control Negotiations: Prospects for a 'Window' in the 1980's." *Air University Review* 32 (October 1981): 31-39.

Erickson, John. "MBFR: Force Levels and Security Requirements." *Strategic Review* 1 (Summer 1973): 28-43.

European Security, Disarmament and Other Problems. Anlanko, Finland: Pugwash Conference, 1973.

"European Security." *Survival* 15 (September/October 1973): 236-242.

Foster, William C. "Ban All Nuclear Testing." *Atlantic Community Quarterly* 9 (Summer 1971): 174-183.

Gittings, John, and Gott, Richard. *NATO's Final Decade*. London: Campaign for Nuclear Disarmament, 1964.

Gollancz, Victor. *The Deveil's Repertoire, or, Nuclear Bombing and the Life of Man*. Garden City, NY: Doubleday, 1959.

Gray, Colin S. "Of Bargaining Chips and Building Blocks: Arms Control and Defense Policy." *International Journal* 28 (Spring 1973): 266-296.

Greenwood, Ted. *Reconnaissance, Surveillance and Arms Control*. (Adelphi Paper No. 88). London: International Institute for Strategic Studies, June 1972.

Gutteridge, William. *European Security, Nuclear Weapons and Public Confidence*. New York: St. Martin's, 1982.

Haig, Alexander M., Jr. "Arms Control for the 1980's: An American Policy." *Department of State Bulletin* 81 (August 1981): 31-34.

Harrison, Stanley L. "Congress and President: NATO Troop-Reduction Conflict." *Military Review* 21 (September 1971): 13-24.

Healey, Denis. *A Neutral Belt in Europe?* London: Fabian Society, 1958.

Hill, R.J. "Mutual and Balanced Forced Reductions: The State of a Key Alliance Policy." *NATO Review* 19 (September/October 1971): 17-20.

―――. "MBFR." *International Journal* 29 (Spring 1974): 242-255.

Holst, Johan Jorgen. "Arms Limiting and Force Adjusting in the Northern Cap Area." *Conciliation and Conflict* 2 (1972): 113-120.

―――, and Melander, Karen Alette. "European Security and Confidence Building Measures." *Survival* 19 (July/August 1977): 146-154.

Israelyan, V. "International Detente and Disarmament." *International Affairs* (Moscow) 5 (1974): 24-29.

―――. "New Soviet Initiative on Disarmament." *International Affairs* (Moscow) 11 (November 1974): 19-25.

Johnson, U. Alexis. "Arms Control and the Gray Area Weapons Systems." *Atlantic Community Quarterly* 17 (Spring 1979): 89-100.

Keliher, John G. *The Negotiation on Mutual and Balanced Force Reductions: The Search for Arms Control in Central Europe.* Washington, D.C.: Published in cooperation with the U.S. National Defense University by Pergamon Publishers, 1980.

Khlestov, O. "Mutual Force Reduction in Europe." *Survival* 16 (November/December 1974): 293-298.

Klaiber, Wolfgang. *Era of Negotiations: European Security and Force Reductions.* Lexington, MA: Lexington Books, 1973.

Kozicharow, Eugene. "NATO Rejects Brezhnev's Bid to Forego Arms Update." *Aviation Week* 11 (October 15, 1979): 18-19.

Lachs, Manfred. "An Atom-Free Zone in Central Europe." *International Affairs* (Moscow) 8 (1959): 19-23.

Larson, Thomas B. *Disarmament and Soviet Policy, 1964-1968.* Englewood Cliffs, NJ: Prentice-Hall, 1969.

Lloyd, Trevor. "Open Skies in the Arctic." *International Journal* 14 (Winter 1958/59): 42-49.

Luns, Joseph M.A.H. "NATO View of Security Conferences." *Atlantic Community Quarterly* 11 (Spring 1973): 55-64.

Macdonald, Hugh. "NATO's Dilemma: Defense, Security and Arms Control." *Millennium* 9 (Autumn 1980): 147-160.

Major, (Wing Comdr.) Douglas H. *The Dilemma of Mutual and Balanced Force Reductions.* (Professional Study). Maxwell AFB, AL: Air War College, 1973.

Matteson, Robert E. "The Disarmament Dilemma." *Orbis* 2 (Fall 1958): 285-299.

McKenney, (Lt.) Edward A. "Mutually Balanced Force Reductions: The Complex Problem." *Naval War College Review* 24 (June 1972): 29-41.

Minter (Vice Adm.) Charles S., Jr. "NATO Forces--Prospects for MBFR." *RUSI Journal* 119 (September 1974): 3-8.

Multan, W., and Towpik, A. "Western Arms Control Policies in Europe Seen from the East." *Survival* 16 (May/June 1974): 127-132.

"NATO Arms Control Group Proposed." *Aviation Week & Space Technology* 110 (16 April 1979): 18.

"The Next Step: Disarmament and Nuclear War." *Survival* 1 (September/October 1959): 119-122.

Nitze, Paul H. "The Strategic Balance Between Hope and Skepticism." *Foreign Policy* 17 (Winter 1974-75): 136-156.

Norstad, Lauris. "The Control of Nuclear Weapons." *Survival* 6 (November/December 1964): 278-279.

Nutting, Anthony. "Disarmament, Europe and Security." *International Affairs* 36 (January 1960): 1-6.

Palmer, Michael, and Thomas, David. "Arms Control and the Mediterranean." *The World Today* 27 (November 1971): 495-502.

Payne, Kenneth B. "Deterrence, Arms Control, and U.S. Strategic Doctrine." *Orbis* 25 (Fall 1981): 747-769.

Pierre, Andrew J. "Limiting Soviet and American Conventional Forces." *Survival* 15 (March/April 1973): 59-64.

Plants, (Maj.) Louis B. *Considerations for the Reduction of U.S. Forces in NATO.* (Research Study). Maxwell AFB, AL: Air Command Staff College, 1974.

Polk, (Gen.) James H. "Force Reduction Options in Central Europe." *Military Review* 53 (October 1973): 36-42.

Povolny, Mojmir. "The Soviet Union and the European Security Conference." *Orbis* 18 (Spring 1974): 201-230.

Prospects of Mutual Reductions in Europe. Stockholm: Ministry of Defense, 1976.

Pugh, George E. "Strategy and Arms Control." *Survival* 5 (November/December 1963): 273-281.

Ranger, Robin. "Arms Control Negotiations: Progress and Prospects." *Canadian Defense Quarterly* 4 (Winter 1974): 16-25.

―――. "An Alternative Future for MBFR: A European Arms Control Conference." *Survival* (July-August 1979): 164.

―――. "MBFR: Political or Technical Arms Control?" *The World Today* 30 (October 1974): 411-417.

General Disarmament and Force Reductions 133

Reagan, Ronald. "Arms Reduction and Nuclear Weapons." *Weekly Compilation of Presidential Documents* 17 (November 23, 1981): 1273-1278.

Reppert, (Capt.) John C. "The Soviet Military and Force Reductions." *Military Review* 54 (October 1974): 24-49.

Roberts, Chalmers M. "The ABC's of FBS and SALT and MBER and CES (ESC)." *Survival* 13 (September 1971): 303-306.

Rosenthal, Benjamin S. "America's Move." *Foreign Affairs* 51 (January 1973): 380-391.

Rostow, Eugene V. "Policy Problems of Arms Control." *Department of State Bulletin* 81 (October 1981): 30-34.

―――. "America's Blueprint for Controlling Nuclear Weapons." *Department of State Bulletin* 81 (August 1981): 59-64.

Rush, Kenneth. "United States Troop Levels in Europe: A Balance Force Reduction." *Vital Speeches of the Day* 39 (August 1, 1973): 631-635.

Russett, Bruce M., and Cooper, Caroline C. *Arms Control in Europe: Proposals and Political Constraints*. Denver, CO: University of Denver, 1966.

"SALT and MBFR: The Next Phase: Report of a Trilateral Conference." *Survival* 17 (January/February 1975): 14-24.

Sandstrom, Anders. "MBFR: A Non-Starter or a Slow Starter?" *Conciliation and Conflict* 1 (1976): 71-94.

Sattler, James F. *MBFR: Its Origins and Perspectives*. Paris: Atlantic Treaty Association, 1974.

Smart, Ian. *MBFR Assailed: A Critical View on the Proposed Negotiations*. Ithaca: Cornell University Peace Studies Program, 1972.

Stanley, Timothy W. "Mutual Force Reductions." *Survival* 12 (May 1970): 152-160.

Stockholm International Peace Research Institute (SIPRI). *World Armaments and Disarmaments: SIPRI Yearbook, 1981*. London: Taylor and Francis Ltd., 1981.

Stone, Jeremy J. "Bomber Disarmament." *World Politics* 17 (October 1964): 13-39.

Sukovic, Olga. *Force Reductions in Europe*. Stockholm: Stockholm International Peace Research Institute, 1974.

Szaz, A. Michael, ed. *Mutual Balanced Force Reductions at the Crossroads*. Washington, D.C.: American Institute on Problems of European Unity, Inc., 1974.

Terchek, Ronald J. *The Making of a Test-Ban Treaty*. The Hague: Nijhoff, 1970.

Thompson, (Brig.) W.F.K. "NATO in the Development of Mutually Acceptable Security Arrangements Between East and West." *NATO's Fifteen Nations* 15 (December 1970-January 1971): 87-90.

United States. Senate. Committee on Foreign Relations. *Strategic Weapons Proposals: Hearings: Parts 1-2, November 3-13, 1981, on the Foreign Policy and Arms Control Implications of President Reagan's Strategic Weapons Proposals*. 97th Congress, 1st Session, 1981. Washington, D.C.: U.S. Government Printing Office, 1981.

Verrier, Anthony. "Test-Ban Treaty: Aftermath in NATO." *The World Today* 19 (September 1963): 369-371.

Vidyasova, L. "The Conference on Security and Cooperation in Europe: A Successful Beginning." *International Affairs* (Moscow) 9 (1973): 11-17.

Wheeler, Tim. "Growing Challenge to Nuclear Peril." *Political Affairs* 61 (May 1982): 9-14.

Wieck, Hans-Georg. "Perspectives of MBFR in Europe." *Aussen Politik* 1 (1972): 36-40.

Williams, Phil. "Whatever Happened to the Mansfield Resolution?" *Survival* 18 (July/August 1976): 146-153.

Willot, Albert. "Mutual and Balanced Force Reductions in Europe." *NATO Review* 21 (No. 1, 1973): 5-9.

Wyle, Frederick S. "European Security: Beating the Numbers Game." *Foreign Policy* 10 (Spring 1973): 41-54.

Yochelson, John. "MBFR: The Search for an American Approach." *Orbis* 17 (Spring 1973): 155-175.

―――――. "Mutual Force Reductions in Europe." *Survival* 15 (November/December 1973): 275-283.

Yost, David S., ed. *NATO's Strategic Options: Arms Control and Defense*. Elmsford, NY: Pergamon, 1981.

Yuriev, N. "The Foundations of Peace and Security in Europe." *International Affairs* (Moscow) 10 (1973): 15-22.

Zimmerman, Peter D. "Future of Arms Control: Quota Testing." *Foreign Policy* (Fall 1981): 82-93.

NATIONAL NUCLEAR STRIKE FORCES AND NUCLEAR SPREAD IN NATO

Ailleret, (Gen.) C. "Flexible Response: A French View." *Survival* 6 (November/December 1964): 258-265.

Bader, W.B. "Nuclear Weapons Sharing and 'The German Problem.'" *Foreign Affairs* 44 (July 1966): 693-700.

Baker, Steven. *Italy and the Nuclear Option*. Santa Monica: Seminar on Arms Control and Foreign Policy, 1974.

Baylis, John. *Anglo-American Defence Relations, 1939-1980*. New York: St. Martin's, 1981.

Beaton, Leonard. *Must the Bomb Spread?* Middlesex, England: Penguin, 1966.

Berry, John A. "Force De Frappe." *Atlantic Community Quarterly* 5 (Winter 1967-68): 569-577.

Blackett, P.M.S. *Military and Political Consequences of Atomic Energy*. London: Turnstile Press, 1948.

Brenner, Michael J. *Nuclear Power and Non-Proliferation: The Remaking of U.S. Policy*. New York: Cambridge University Press, 1981.

Bridge, T.D. "Britain Decides Upon Trident." *Army Quarterly* 110 (July 1980): 280-284.

"The British Nuclear Deterrent: Resolution and Report of a Working Group." London: S.C.M. Press, 1963.

Brown, Neville. "Britain's Strategic Weapons I: The Manned Bomber." *The World Today* 20 (July 1964): 293-297.

———. "Britain's Strategic Weapons II: The Polaris A-3." *The World Today* 20 (August 1964): 358-364.

———. "Anglo-French Nuclear Collaboration?" *The World Today* 25 (August 1969): 351-356.

Carey, Roger. "British Thinking on Tactical Nuclear Deterrence in Europe." *The World Today* 25 (April 1969): 172-177.

Chirac, Jacques. "The Purpose of Pluton." *Survival* 17 (September/October 1975): 241-243.

de Carmoy, Guy. "Force De Frappe: A Triple Debate." *Atlantic Community Quarterly* 2 (Summer 1964): 278-284.

de Gaulle, Charles. "Views on the Nassau Agreement, the Atlantic Alliance and a National Nuclear Forces." *Survival* 5 (March/April 1963): 58-59.

Eayrs, James. "Canada, NATO and Nuclear Weapons." *Survival* 3 (March/April 1961): 76-83.

Erler, Fritz. "Partners in Strategy." *Atlantic Community Quarterly* 2 (Summer 1964): 292-302.

Freedman, Lawrence. "Limited War Unlimited Protest [West European Opposition to United States and North Atlantic Treaty Organization Limited Nuclear War Strategies]." *Orbis* 26 (Spring 1982): 89-103.

———. "Britain: The First Ex-Nuclear Power?" *International Security* 6 (Fall 1981): 80-104.

Gallois, (Gen.) Pierre M. *The Balance of Terror: Strategy for the Missile Age.* Boston: Houghton-Mifflin, 1961.

———. "U.S. Strategy and the Defense of Europe." *Orbis* 7 (Summer 1963): 226-249.

Goldberg, Alfred. "The Military Origins of the British Nuclear Deterrent." *International Affairs* 40 (October 1964): 600-619.

Gott, Richard. "The Evolution of the Independent British Deterrent." *International Affairs* 39 (April 1963): 238-252.

Halperin, Morton H. "NATO and the TNF Controversy: Threats to the Alliance." *Orbis* 26 (Spring 1982): 105-116.

Hartley, Anthony. "The British Bomb." *Survival* 6 (July/August 1964): 170-81.

Hoag, Malcolm W. "Nuclear Policy and French Intransigence." *Foreign Affairs* 41 (January 1963): 286-298.

Hoffman, Stanley. "NATO and Nuclear Weapons: Reasons and Unreason.." *Foreign Affairs* 60 (Winter 1981/1982): 327-346.

Ignatieff, George. "NATO, Nuclear Weapons and Canada's Interests." *International Perspectives* (Canada) (November/December 1978), pp. 3-9.

Janosik, Edward G. "The Nuclear Deterrent as an Issue in British Politics." *Orbis* 10 (Summer 1966): 588-604.

Johnson, Christopher. "France's Deterrent." *Survival* 5 (March/April 1964): 60-62.

Kelly, George A. "The Political Background of the French A-Bomb." *Orbis* 4 (Fall 1960): 248-306.

Kemp, Geoffrey. *Nuclear Forces for Medium Powers: Part I: Targets and Weapons Systems.* (Adelphi Paper No. 106). London: The International Institute for Strategic Studies, 1974.

———. *Nuclear Forces for Medium Powers: Parts II and III: Strategic Requirements and Options.* (Adelphi Paper No. 107). London: The International Institute for Strategic Studies, 1974.

Knorr, Klaus. "Nuclear Weapons: 'Haves' and 'Have-Nots.'" *Foreign Affairs* 36 (October 1957): 167-178.

Kohl, Wilfrid L. *French Nuclear Diplomacy.* Princeton, NJ: Princeton University Press, 1972.

Kolodziej, Edward A. "French Strategy Emergent: General Andre Beaufre--A Critique." *World Politics* 19 (April 1967): 417-442.

Legault, Albert. "Atomic Weapons for Germany." *International Journal* 21 (Autumn 1966): 447-469.

Leitenberg, Milton. "The Stranded USSR Submarine in Sweden and the Question of a Nordic Nuclear-Free Zone." *Cooperation and Conflict* 17 (No. 1, 1982): 17-28.

Lieber, Robert J. "The French Nuclear Force: A Strategic and Political Evaluation." *International Affairs* 42 (July 1966): 421-431.

Lovins, Amory B., et al. "Nuclear Power and Nuclear Bombs." *Foreign Affairs* 58 (Summer 1980): 1137-1177.

Marshall, D. Bruce. "The Evolving French Strategic Debate." *Strategic Review* 8 (Spring 1980): 59-77.

Menaul, (Adm.) Stewart W.B., Ret. "Great Britain and NATO Theater Nuclear Forces." *Strategic Review* 9 (Spring 1981): 61-66.

Mendl, Wolf. "The Background of French Nuclear Policy." *International Affairs* 41 (January 1965): 22-36.

———. *Deterrence and Persuasion: French Nuclear Armaments in the Context of National Policy 1945-1969.* New York: Praeger; London: Faber and Faber, 1970.

Messmer, Pierre. "French Nuclear Forces: An Interview with the French Minister of Defense." *Survival* 4 (November/December 1962): 277-281.

Mulley, Frederick W. "A European Nuclear Deterrent." *Survival* 2 (January/February 1960): 34-36.

———. "Nuclear Weapons: Challenge to National Security." *Orbis* 7 (Spring 1963): 32-40.

Mumford, (Lt. Col.) Jay C. "Problems of Nuclear Free Zones--the Nordic Example." *Military Review* (March 1976): 3-10.

Pierre, Andrew J. *Nuclear Politics: The British Experience with an Independent Strategic Force 1939-1970.* London: Oxford University Press, 1972.

Pigasse, Jean-Paul. "The Case for a European Defense of Europe." *Strategic Review* 8 (Fall 1980): 29-39.

"Polaris Successor. (Report of a Seminar Held at Royal United Services Institute, April 30, 1980)." *RUSI Journal for Defence Studies* 125 (September 1980): 16-26.

Pym, Francis. "The Nuclear Element for British Defense Policy." *RUSI Journal for Defence Studies* 126 (June 1981): 3-9.

Rosecrance, R.N. *Defense of the Realm: British Strategy in the Nuclear Epoch.* New York: Columbia University Press, 1968.

Ruhl, Luthar. "The European Nuclear Balance--A German View." *NATO's Fifteen Nations* 26 (October-November 1981): 46-48+.

Ruhle, Hans. "The Theater Nuclear Issue in German Politics." *Strategic Review* 9 (Spring 1981): 54-60.

Scheinman, Lawrence. *Atomic Energy Policy in France Under the Fourth Republic.* Princeton: Princeton University Press, 1965.

Slessor, Sir John. "Nuclear Power and Britain's Defense." *Survival* 4 (November/December 1962): 250-254.

Sommer, Theo. "How Many Fingers on How Many Triggers?" *Atlantic Community Quarterly* 1 (Winter 1963-64): 556-560.

Stares, Paul. "The Future of the French Strategic Nuclear Force." *International Security Review* 5 (Summer 1980): 231-257.

―――. "The Modernization of the French Strategic Nuclear Force." *RUSI Journal for Defence Studies* 125 (December 1981): 34-41.

Symms, Steven D. and Snow, Edward D., Jr. "Soviet Propaganda and the Neutron Bomb Decision." *Political Communication and Persuasion* 1 (No. 3, 1981): 257-268.

Thumborg, Anders I. "The UN Study on Nuclear Weapons 1980." *Disarmament* (UN) 3 (November 1980): 29-35.

Toynbee, Philip, et al. *The Fearful Choice.* Detroit: Wayne State University Press, 1959.

"The Ultimate Arm." *Survival* 12 (September 1970): 290-292.

United States. Senate. Committee on Foreign Relations. *Interim Report on Nuclear Weapons in Europe, December 1981.* 97th Congress, 1st Session, 1981. Washington, D.C.: U.S. Government Printing Office, 1981.

Weers, (Col.) Mozas W.A., Ret. "The Nuclear Debate in the Netherlands." *Strategic Review* 9 (Spring 1981): 67-77.

Winkler, Theodor H. "Nuclear Proliferation in the Third World--Problems and Prospects for the 1980's." *International Defense Review* 13 (No. 2, 1980): 198-204.

Wohlstetter, Albert. "Nuclear Sharing: NATO and the N + 1 Country." *Foreign Affairs* 39 (April 1961): 355-387.

DOCTRINES, STRATEGIES AND MILITARY ISSUES

MILITARY DOCTRINE

Ailleret, (Gen.) Charles. "The Strategic Theory of 'Flexible Response.'" *Atlantic Community Quarterly* 2 (Fall 1964): 413-428.

Albrecht-Carrie, Rene. "The North Sea Triangle." *Orbis* 17 (Winter 1974): 1306-1325.

Amme, Carl H. *NATO Without France: A Strategic Reappraisal.* Stanford: The Hoover Institution, 1967.

Anderson, David K. "The Counter-mobility Potential in the NATO Context." *Strategic Review* 7 (Winter 1979): 67-75.

Andren, Nils. "Nordic Integration." *Co-operation and Conflict* 2 (1967): 1-25.

──────. "In Search of Security." *Co-operation and Conflict* 3 (1968): 217-239.

Ball, Robert A. "A Decision That Will Shape NATO's Future." *Fortune* 100 (December 17, 1979): 82-89.

Bambini, Adrian P., Jr. "Chemical Warfare and the NATO Alliance." *Military Review* 61 (April 1981): 27-33.

Baylis, John, ed. *Contemporary Strategy, Theories and Policies.* London: Croom Helm, 1975.

──────. *Anglo-American Defense Relations, 1939-1980.* New York: St. Martin's Press, 1981.

Beaton, Leonard. "Transatlantic Alienation." *Survival* 11 (August 1969): 246-247.

──────. "The Strategic and Political Issues Facing America, Britain and Canada." *Atlantic Community Quarterly* 9 (Winter 1971-72): 476-492.

Beaufre, (Gen.) Andre. *An Introduction to Strategy.* New York: Frederick A. Praeger, 1965.

———. *Deterrence and Strategy.* New York: Frederick A. Praeger, 1966.

———. *The Strategy of Action.* New York: Praeger, 1967.

———. *Strategy for Tomorrow.* New York: Crane, Russak, 1974.

Bertram, Christoph, and Holst, Johan Jorgen, eds. *New Strategic Factors in the North Atlantic.* Guilford, Surrey: IPC Science and Technology Press; Oslo: Universitetsforlaget, 1977.

Betts, Richard K. "Surprise Attack: NATO's Political Vulnerability." *International Security* 5 (Spring 1981): 117-149.

Blades, (Cdr.) Todd, Ret. "How to Best Defend NATO." *Armed Forces Journal International* 118 (July 1981): 62-63+.

Borcier, Paul. *Eight Years Work for European Defense: A Political Survey.* Paris: Western European Union, 1964.

Borden, Donald F. "Inflexibility in NATO's Flexible Response." *Military Review* 52 (January 1976): 26-41.

Boyd, (Maj.) Darwin D. "Need for an Improved Non-Nuclear Force Within NATO." (Sesearch Study 0240-71). Maxwell AFB, AL: Air Command and Staff College, 1971.

Bracken, Paul. "Urban Sprawl and NATO Defense." *Survival* 18 (November/December 1976): 254-260.

Brodie, Bernard. *A Guide to Naval Strategy.* Princeton, NJ: Princeton University Press, 1944.

———. "The Possibility of Total War." *Survival* 4 (November-December 1962): 242-249.

———. "Conventional Capabilities in Europe." *Survival* 5 (July/August 1963): 148-155.

———. "Why Were We So Strategically Wrong?" *Foreign Policy* 5 (Winter 1971-72): 151-161.

Bruntland, Arne Olav. "The Nordic Balance: Past and Present." *Co-operation and Conflict* 1 (1966): 30-63.

Buchan, Alastair, ed. *Europe's Futures: Europe's Choices: Models of Western Europe in the 1970's.* New York: Columbia University Press, 1969.

———. *Europe and America, From Alliance to Coalition.* Farnburough, England: Saxon House for the Atlantic Institute for International Affairs, 1973.

Burbank, Lyman B. "Scandinavian Integration and Western Defense." *Foreign Affairs* 35 (October 1956): 144-150.

Burrows, Bernard, and Irwin, Christopher. *The Security of Western Europe: Towards a Common Defense Policy.* London: Charles Knight, 1972.

Buzzard, (Rear Adm.) Anthony. *The Possibilities of Conventional Defense.* (Adelphi Paper No. 6). London: The International Institute for Strategic Studies, 1965.

Cameron, Air Vice Marshal Robert. "Options Make Good Propaganda but Poor Defense for NATO." *NATO's Fifteen Nations* 15 (June-July 1970): 20-23.

Canby, Steven. "NATO Strategy: Political-Military Problems or Divergent Interests and Operational Concepts." *Military Review* 59 (April 1979): 50-58.

---------. "U.S. Defense Policy: The Problem Is Not More Money." *AEI Foreign Policy and Defense Review* 1 (No. 3, 1979): 23-26.

Carter, Barry. "Flexible Strategic Options: No Need for New Strategy." *Survival* 17 (January/February 1975): 25-31.

Clarke, Bruce C. "Problems of Defending NATO in Case of a Conventional Warsaw Pact Forces Attack." *Officer Review* 19 (November 1979): 17-18.

Clemens, Walter C., Jr. "NATO and the Warsaw Pact: Comparisons and Contrasts." *Parameters* 4 (No. 2, 1974): 13-22.

Cleveland, Harlan. "NATO After the Invasion." *Foreign Affairs* 47 (January 1969): 251-265.

Coffey, J.L. "Strategy, Alliance Policy and Nuclear Proliferation." *Orbis* 11 (Winter 1968): 975-995.

Coffey, Kenneth J. "Defending Europe Against a Conventional Attack: The Increasing Gap Between the Army's Capabilities and NATO Commitments and What to Do About It." *Air University Review* 31 (January/February 1980): 47-59.

Coggi, Igino. "If There's a Threat at All It's on the Southern Flank." *Defense Today* 14 (June 1979): 292-296.

Colbert, (Adm.) Richard G. "Defending NATO's Southern Flank." *NATO's Fifteen Nations* 18 (August-September 1973): 20-40.

Connell (Maj.) George M. "NATO's Land and Sea Strategies-- Are They Compatible?" *Marine Corps Gazette* 64 (June 1980): 41-46.

The Control of Western Strategy. (Adelphi Paper No. 3). London: The International Institute of Strategic Studies, 1963.

Critchley, Julian. "A Community Policy for Armaments." *NATO Review* (February 1979): 10-14.

Curl, Richard L. "Strategic Doctrine in the Nuclear Age." *Strategic Review* 3 (Winter 1975): 46-56.

Cutler, (Capt.) Katie. "Tackling Tactics Together." *Airman* 24 (December 1980): 43-48.

Dewey, Arthur E. "The Nordic Balance." *Strategic Review* 4 (Fall 1976): 49-60.

Dodd, Norman L. "NATO in Disarray." *Army Quarterly* 111 (July 1981): 288-297.

Dupuy, (Col.) T.N., Ret. "The Problem of NATO Forward Defense." *Armed Forces Journal International* 118 (July 1981): 64-67.

Engleberdt, Stanley L. *Strategic Defenses.* New York: Crowell, 1966.

Enthoven, Alain C. "U.S. Forces in Europe: How Many? Doing What?" *Foreign Affairs* 53 (April 1975): 513-532.

Even-Tov, Ori. "The NATO Conventional Defense: Back to Reality." *Orbis* 23 (Spring 1979): 35-49.

Fallows, James. *National Defense.* New York: Random House, Inc., 1981.

Fowler, (Col.) Delbert M. "How Many Divisions? A NATO-Warsaw Pact Assessment." *Military Review* 52 (November 1972): 76-88.

Fullerton, John. "European Military Report." *Defense and Foreign Affairs Digest* 7 (March 1979): 42-44.

Furlong, R.D.M. "The Strategic Situation in Northern Europe--Improvements Vital for NATO." *International Defense Review* (June 1979): 899.

――――. "Closing the Credibility Gap--A Top-priority Problem for NATO." *International Defence Review* 14 (No. 11, 1981): 1418-1420.

Gail, Bridget. "NATO, Kissinger and the Future of Strategic Deterrence." *Armed Forces Journal* 117 (November 1979): 58-59.

Gallois, (Gen.) Pierre. "Collective Defense." *Survival* 1 (May/June 1959): 49.

Gans, (Col., Ret.) Daniel. "Fight Outnumbered and Win ... Against What Odds?" *Military Review* pt 1 60 (December 1980): 31-46.

Garnett, John C., ed. *The Defense of Western Europe*. New York: St. Martin's Press, 1974.

Gasteyger, Curt. "Modern Warfare and Soviet Strategy." *Survey* 57 (October 1965): 46-59.

Geneste, Marc E. "The City Walls: A Credible Defense Doctrine for the West." *Orbis* 19 (Summer 1975): 477-496.

George, Alexander L. and Smoke, Richard. *Deterrence in American Foreign Policy: Theory and Practice*. New York: Columbia University Press, 1974.

Gesienheyner, Stefan. "NATO's Northern Flank--Vital but Increasingly Vulnerable." *Air Force Magazine* 54 (July 1971): 56-61.

--------. "A Defensive Mix for Europe: Pandora, Medusa, Dragon Seed." *Survival* 13 (September 1971): 307-309.

Ginsburgh, (Col.) Robert N. *U.S. Military Strategy in the Sixties*. New York: Norton, 1965.

Glazov, (Col.) V. "What Is Local War?" *Survival* 3 (September/October 1961): 226-228.

Goldmann, Kjell. "Strategic Doctrines and the Future of NATO: Some Reflections." *Co-operation and Conflict* 1 (1966): 1-10.

Gole, (Lt. Col.) Henry G. "Siren Call to Disaster: The Emerging Campaign for U.S. Troop Reductions in Europe." *Parameters* 11 (September 1981): 22-30.

--------. "Through European Eyes: Should NATO Strategy Be Changed?" *Parameters* 11 (December 1981): 14-23.

Goodpaster, (Gen.) Andrew J. "NATO and U.S. Forces: Challenges and Prospects." *Strategic Review* 2 (Winter 1974): 6-17.

--------. "NATO Strategy and Requirements 1975-1985." *Survival* 17 (September/October 1975): 210-216.

Gray, Colin S. *Strategic Studies: A Critical Assessment*. Westport, CT: Greenwood Press, Inc., 1982.

Gray, Norman. "The NATO Long-Term Defense Program." *Signal* 33 (April 1979): 29-30.

Griffin, (Maj.) Donald K. "If the Soviets *Don't* Mass." *Military Review* (February 1979): 2-13.

Grosser, Alfred. "France and Germany in the Atlantic Community." *International Organization* 17 (Summer 1963): 55-573.

―――. "France and Germany: Divergent Outlooks." *Foreign Affairs* 44 (October 1965): 26-36.

Hackel, Erwin. *Military Manpower and Political Purpose.* (Adelphi Paper No. 72). London: The International Institute for Strategic Studies, 1970.

Hahn, Walter F., and Neff, John C. *American Strategy for the Nuclear Age.* New York: Doubleday Anchor, 1960.

Haig, Alexander. "NATO--An Agenda for the Future." *NATO Review* 27 (June 1979): 3-5.

―――. "An Interview." *Trialogue* 21 (Fall 1979): 8-11.

Harnig, (Lt. Col., Ret.) Norbert. "The Defense of Western Europe with Conventional Weapons." *International Defense Review* 14 (No. 11, 1981): 1439-1443.

Hartig, G. Hans-Chr. "NATO Force Planning Data Base." *Soldat und Technik* 1 (January 1979): 3-5.

Head, (Brig.) A.H. "European Defense." *International Affairs* 27 (January 1951): 1-9.

Healey, Denis. "The Sputnik and Western Defense." *International Affairs* 34 (April 1958): 145-156.

―――. "On European Defense." *Survival* 11 (April 1969): 110-115.

Heilbrunn, Otto. *Conventional Warfare in the Nuclear Age.* London: Allen and Unwin; New York: Praeger, 1965.

Herbert, (Wing Cmdr.) Clive A. *West European Defense.* (Professional Study). Maxwell AFB, AL: Air War College, 1974.

Hessman, James D. "NATO South: The Forgotten Flank." *Sea Power* 22 (September 1979): 17-22.

Heyerdahl, (Col.) L.R. "The Western Fringe of Scandinavia: Guarding the Northern Gates to the Atlantic--Allied Forces Northern Europe." *NATO's Fifteen Nations* 18 (February-March 1973): 24-30.

Hinterhoff, (Maj.) E. "The Complex Problems of the Southern NATO Flank." *NATO's Fifteen Nations* 17 (April-May 1972): 32-39.

Holst, Johan J., ed. "The Soviet Union and Nordic Security." *Conciliation and Conflict*, nos. 3-4 (1971): 137-146.

―――, ed. *Five Roads to Nordic Security.* Oslo: Universitetsforlaget, 1973.

Hoopes, Townsend. "Overseas Bases in American Strategy." *Foreign Affairs* 37 (October 1958): 69-82.

Howell, (Cpt.) Phillip D. "Divergent Doctrines Snarl Nuclear Face-off." *Army* 31 (December 1981): 18-23.

Hunt, (Cmdr.) Herman L. "Policy and Posture of NATO on the Northern Flank: An Appraisal." (Unpublished Thesis). Newport, RI: U.S. Naval War College, 1972.

Hunter, Robert E. "The Politics of U.S. Defense 1963: Manned Bombers Versus Missiles." *The World Today* 19 (March 1963): 98-107.

Ikle, Fred Charles. "The Reagan Defense Program: A Focus on the Strategic Imperatives." *Strategic Review* 10 (Spring 1982): 11-18.

International Institute for Strategic Studies. "The East-West Conventional Balance in Europe." *Air Force Magazine* 64 (December 1981): 114-117.

Jablonsky, David. "NATO's Long-term Defense Planning: Will It Work?" *Parameters* 11 (June 1981): 75-82.

Jaquet, Louis G.M. "Strong Express." *NATO's Fifteen Nations* 17 (December 1972-January 1973): 90-96.

----------. "The Role of NATO Military Forces as Part of the Alliances Overall Objectives." *NATO Review* 22 (December 1974): 6-13.

Johansen, (Capt.) Erik B. "On NATO's Northern Flank." *Military Review* 51 (August 1971): 63-69.

Jones, (Lt. Col.) L.M. "Professional Views on Tactical Weapons: An American View." *Survival* 4 (September/October 1962): 214-216.

Kahan, J.H. "Stable Deterrence: A Strategic Policy for the 1970's." *Orbis* 15 (Summer 1971): 528-543.

Kaplan, Morton A., ed. *NATO and Dissuasion*. Chicago: Center for Policy Study, University of Chicago, 1974.

Kaufmann, William W. *Military Policy and National Security*. Princeton, N.J.: Princeton University Press, 1956.

Kaysen, Carl. "Keeping the Strategic Balance." *Foreign Affairs* 46 (July 1968): 665-675.

----------. "American Military Policy." *Survival* 11 (February 1969): 51-56.

Kennedy, William. East vs. West: The Balance of Military Power. (January 1981).

Kielmansegg, J.A. Graf. "Europe's Heightened Role in Global Strategy." *Atlantic Community Quarterly* 17 (Summer 1979): 145-154.

King-Hall, Stephen. *Defense in the Nuclear Age.* London: Gollancz, 1958.

Kingston-McCloughry, (Air Vice-Marshal) E.J. *Defense: Policy and Strategy.* New York: Praeger, 1960.

Kissinger, Henry A. *Nuclear Weapons and Foreign Policy.* New York: Harper for the Council on Foreign Relations, 1957.

―――. "Limited War: Nuclear or Conventional?" *Survival* 3 (January/February 1961): 2-11.

Klenberg, Jan. *The Cape and the Straits: Problems of Nordic Security.* (Papers in International Affairs [18]). Cambridge, MA: Center for International Affairs, Harvard University (February 1968).

Knorr, Klaus. *On the Uses of Military Power in the Nuclear Age.* Princeton, NJ: Princeton University Press, 1966.

―――. *Europe and America in the 1970's: II: Society and Power.* (Adelphi Paper No. 71). London: The International Institute for Strategic Studies, November 1970.

Knorr, Klaus and Read, Thornton, eds. *Limited Strategic War.* New York: Praeger, 1962.

Komer, R.W. "Treating NATO's Self-Inflicted Wound." *Foreign Policy* 13 (Winter 1973-74): 34-48.

Kozicharow, Eugene. "NATO Leaders Optimistic Despite Major Problems." *Aviation Week* 110 (12 March 1979): 55-58.

Kristol, Irving. "NATO's Moment of Truth." *Wall Street Journal* (24 September 1979): 30.

Kupperman, Robert H.; Behr, Robert M.; and Jones, Thomas P., Jr. "The Deterrence Continuum." *Orbis* 18 (Fall 1974): 728-749.

Lange, Christian, and Goldmann, Kjell. "A Nordic Defense Alliance 1949-1965." *Co-operation and Conflict* 1 (1966): 46-63.

Lauder, John A. "Lessons of the Strategic Bombing Survey for Contemporary Defense Policy." *Orbis* 18 (Fall 1974): 770-790.

Lemnitzer, (Gen.) Lyman L. "Forward Strategy Reappraised." *Survival* 3 (January/February 1961): 22-25.

―――. "Collective Defense--The Basis of Military Security." *Atlantic Community Quarterly* 6 (Summer 1968): 238-244.

Levin, Viktor A. *Collective Security in Europe.* Moscow: Novosti Press Agency, 1967.

Lider, Julian. "Towards a Modern Concept of Strategy." *Cooperation and Conflict* 16 (No. 4, 1981): 217-235.

Maconochie, Alexander K. "Across or Along: Soviet Amphibious Options in Northwestern Europe." *U.S. Naval Institute Proceedings* 106 (April 1980): 46-50.

Malmgren, H.B. "A Forward-Pause Defense for Europe." *Orbis* 8 (Fall 1964): 595-606.

Malone, (Col.) Daniel K. "Current NATO Observations." *National Defense* 66 (July-August 1981): 64-67.

Mansfield, (Sen.) Mike. "And Now Another View." *Atlantic Community Quarterly* 8 (Spring 1970): 13-16.

──────. "Exercise Strong Express." *NATO's Fifteen Nations* 18 (February-March 1973): 74-80.

Martin, Laurence W. *Arms and Strategy: The World Power Structure Today.* New York: David McKay, 1973.

──────. "Changes in American Strategic Doctrine--An Initial Interpretation." *Survival* 16 (July/August 1974): 154-164.

Martin, Thomas L., and Laham, Donald C. *Strategy for Survival.* Tucson, AZ: University of Arizona Press, 1964.

Maxwell, Stephen. *Rationality in Deterrence.* (Adelphi Paper No. 50). London: The International Institute for Strategic Studies, 1968.

McNamara, Robert S. "The Ann Arbor Speech 16 June 1962." *Survival* 4 (September/October 1962): 194-200.

McQuade, Lawrence C. "NATO's Non-Nuclear Needs." *International Affairs* 40 (January 1964): 11-21.

Melton, T.R. "NATO's Troubled Southern Flank." *Strategic Review* 3 (Fall 1975): 27-31.

Mendershausen, H. *Territorial Defense in NATO and Non-NATO Europe.* Santa Monica, CA: Rand Corp., February 1973.

Middleton, Drew. *The Defense of Western Europe.* New York: Appleton-Century-Crofts, 1952.

Miller, (Lt. Col.) D.M.O. "Strategic Factors Affecting the Defense by NATO of Western Europe: A Reappraisal." *RUSI Journal for Defense Studies* 125 (September 1980): 37-43.

Miller, Lynn H. "The Contemporary Significance of the Doctrine of the Just War." *World Politics* 16 (January 1964): 254-286.

Milton, (Gen.) T.R. "Can NATO Mend Its Fences--and Defenses?" *Air Force Magazine* 57 (October 1974): 49.

Minich, Cecil M. "The Ultimate Deterrent." *Military Review* (January 1979): 64-66.

Moulton, Harland B. "The McNamara General War Strategy." *Orbis* 8 (Summer 1964): 238-254.

Moulton, (Maj. Gen.) J.L. "The Defense of Northwest Europe and the North Sea." *United States Naval Institute Proceedings* 97 (May 1971): 80-97.

──────. "Seaborne and Airborne Mobility in Europe." *United States Naval Institute Proceedings* 100 (May 1974): 122-143.

"NATO Force Sufficiency Study--1970: Executive Summary." Menlo Park, CA: Stanford Research Institute, September 1970.

"NATO and the Far North." *NATO's Fifteen Nations* 15 (February-March 1970): 18-19.

"NATO's Northern Flank." *The Royal Air Force Quarterly* 10 (Summer 1970): 133-143.

"NATO Plans Continued Force Update." *Aviation Week* 111 (December 17, 1979): 16-17.

Newhouse, John. *U.S. Troops in Europe: Issues, Costs and Choices.* Washington: The Brookings Institution, 1971.

Nicholls, David. "Long Term Defense Planning." *NATO's Fifteen Nations* 26 (April-May 1981): 26-27+.

Nitze, Paul H. "Atoms, Strategy and Policy." *Foreign Affairs* 34 (January 1956): 187-198.

──────. "Political Aspects of a National Strategy." *Survival* 2 (November/December 1960): 219-226.

Norstad, (Gen.) Lauris. "The Defense of Europe: Speech to the NATO Parliamentarians, 21 November 1960." *Survival* 3 (January/February 1961): 26-30.

──────. "Saceur's Views--1961: Speech to the NATO Parliamentarians, 13 November 1961." *Survival* 4 (January/February 1962): 13-14.

Nunn, (Sen.) Sam. "NATO Strategy." *Survival* 19 (January/February 1977): 30-38.

Oliphant, M.L. *The Atomic Age.* London: Allen and Unwin, 1949.

O'Neil, Robert and Horwer, D.M., eds. *New Directions in Strategic Thinking.* London: Allen and Unwin, 1981.

Oppenheimer, J. Robert. "Atomic Weapons and American Policy." *Foreign Affairs* 31 (July 1953): 525-535.

Orvik, Nils. "Base Policy--Theory and Practice." *Co-operation and Conflict* 2 (1967): 188-204.

──────. "Scandinavian Security in Transition: The Two-Dimensional Threat." *Orbis* 16 (Fall 1972): 720-742.

Orvik, Nils and Haagerup, Niels J. *The Scandinavian Members of NATO*. (Adelphi Paper No. 23). London: The International Institute for Strategic Studies, December 1965.

Osgood, Robert E. *Limited War: The Challenge to American Strategy*. Chicago: University of Chicago Press, 1957.

──────. "Kinds of Counterforce." *Survival* 5 (January/February 1963): 23-26.

──────. *Limited War Revisited*. Boulder, CO: Westview Press, 1979.

Owen, J.I., ed. *Infantry Weapons of the NATO Armies*. 2nd Edition. 1980.

Ozarne, (Maj.) E.H. "NATO's Flexible Response." *Army in Europe* (October 1973): 10-13.

Palit, (Maj. Gen.) D.K. *War in the Deterrent Age*. South Brunswick, NJ: A.S. Barnes, 1966.

Panofsky, Wolfgang K.H. "The Mutual-Hostage Relationship Between America and Russia." *Foreign Affairs* 52 (October 1973): 109-118.

Peeters, Paul. *Massive Retaliation: The Policy and Its Critics*. Chicago: H. Regenery, Co., 1959.

Quanbeck, Alton H., and Blechman, Barry M. *Strategic Forces: Issue for the Mid-Seventies*. Washington: Brookings Institution, 1973.

Rasiulis, Andrew P. *On the Utility of War in the Nuclear Age*. Toronto: Canadian Institute of International Affairs, 1981.

Rathjens, George W., Jr. "Notes on the Military Problems of Europe." *World Politics* 10 (January 1958): 182-201.

──────. "Flexible Response Options." *Orbis* 18 (Fall 1974): 677-688.

"Reality of a Common Defense System Validity of a Jointly-Defined Policy." *NATO Review* 20 (September/October 1972): 7-11.

"Red Signals Flash on NATO's Forgotten Front; the Vulnerable Southeast." *To the Point* 8 (April 13, 1979): 8-11.

"The Reinforcement of Europe." *NATO's Fifteen Nations* 4 (August-September 1979): 24.

Reinhardt, (Col.) George C. *American Strategy in the Atomic Age.* Norman, OK: University of Oklahoma Press, 1955.

Richardson, Elliot L. [and Mansfield, (Sen.) Mike]. "American Force in Europe--The Pros and Cons." *Atlantic Community Quarterly* 8 (Spring 1970): 5-13.

Richardson, R.C. "Can NATO Fashion a New Strategy?" *Orbis* 17 (Summer 1973): 415-438.

Robinson, Clarence A., Jr. "Gen. Haig Warns of Tenuous Strategic Position." *Aviation Week* 11 (July 2, 1979): 24-25.

Robison, David. "A European Co-ordinated Force." *Orbis* 9 (Fall 1965): 655-676.

Rogers, (Gen.) Bernard W. "Toe to Toe with the Soviet Buildup: The Warsaw Pact Ahead in Numbers Is Now Making Impressive Gains in Qualtiy." *Defense 81* (June 1981): 11-19.

Rose, Francois de. "Inflexible Response." *Foreign Affairs* 61 (No. 1, Fall 1982): 136-150.

Russett, Bruce M. "Counter-Combatant Deterrence: A Proposal." *Survival* 16 (May/June 1974): 135-140.

Samuel, (Lt. Col.) Wolfgang W.E. "The Impossible Task--Defense Without Relevant Strategy." *Air University Review* 31 (March-April 1980): 15-28.

Sanders, John S. "Health Is Not Valued Till Sickness Comes: A Report on NATO." *Defense and Foreign Affairs* 9 (February 1981): 6-9+.

Santilli, (Lt. Col.) Joseph, Jr. "NATO Strategy Updated: A First Use Policy." *Military Review* 54 (March 1974): 3-20.

Schelling, Thomas C. *Arms and Influence.* New Haven, CT: Yale University Press, 1966.

Schlesinger, James R. "Flexible Strategic Options and Deterrence." *Survival* 16 (March/April 1974): 86-90.

Schmuckle, Gerd. "Mobility as a Strategic Element." *NATO's Fifteen Nations* 24 (August-September 1979): 104-106.

Schopflin, George. "NATO and the Nordic Balance." *The World Today* 22 (March 1966): 114-122.

Schwarz, Urs. *American Strategy: A New Perspective.* Garden City, KS: Doubleday, 1966.

Seagrave, Sterling. *Yellow Rain: A Journey Through the Terror of Chemical Warfare.* New York: M. Evans, 1981.

"Second Exercise of Mediterranean On-Call Force." *NATO Review* 19 (July/August 1971): 13.

Seybold, Calvin. "But Who Is Guarding the Rear?" *Military Review* (January 1979): 23-28.

Slessor, Sir John. *Strategy for the West*. New York: William Morrow, 1954.

―――. "Western Strategy in the Nuclear Age." *Orbis* 1 (Fall 1957): 357-364.

―――. "Sword and Shield." *Survival* 3 (January/Fenruary 1961): 12-15.

Slocombe, Walter. *The Political Implications of Strategic Parity*. (Adelphi Paper No. 77). London: International Institute for Strategic Studies, May 1971.

Smith, Sydney E. "NATO and the Challenge of the Missile Age." *International Journal* 13 (Summer 1958): 165-174.

Smith, (Gen.) W.Y. "Reinforcing NATO--Rapidly." *Defense* 80 (August 1980): 2-7.

Smyth, J.G., ed. *The Western Defenses*. London: Wingate, 1951.

Snyder, Jed. "Strengthening the NATO Alliance: Toward a Strategy for the 1980's." *Naval War College Review* 34 (March-April 1981): 18-37.

Speier, Hans. "Soviet Atomic Blackmail and the North Atlantic Alliance." *World Politics* 9 (April 1957): 307-328.

Stanley, Timothy W. "NATO's Strategic Doctrine." *Survival* 11 (November 1969): 342-349.

Staudenmaier, (Col.) William O. "Strategic Concepts for the 1980's." *Military Review* 62 (March 1982): 36-50; (April 1982): 38-59.

―――. "Some Strategic Implications of Fighting Outnumbered in the NATO Battlefield." *Military Review* 60 (May 1980): 38-50.

Steeves, Thomas W., and Dietrich, E. Handt. "NATO Forces Under Test." *NATO's Fifteen Nations* 24 (August-September 1979): 46-47.

Stehlin, (Gen.) Paul. "The Evolution of Western Defense." *Foreign Affairs* 42 (October 1963): 70-83.

Steinbruner, John. "Beyond Rational Deterrence: The Struggle for New Conceptions." *World Politics* 28 (January 1976): 223-245.

Steinhoff, (Gen.) Johannes. "NATO Crisis: A Military View." *Survival* 8 (November 1966): 365-371.

———. "Strategy and Stability." *NATO's Fifteen Nations* (April-May 1967): 27.

———. "NATO's Current Military Problems: An Address Before the NATO Defense College." *NATO's Fifteen Nations* 18 (December 1973-January 1974): 20-22.

Stone, Thomas R. "Modern Warfare: Flexible Forces for the 1980's." *Military Review* 61 (December 1981): 57-66.

Tanmen, Ronald L. *MIRV and the Arms Race: An Interpretation of Defense Strategy*. New York: Praeger, 1973.

Tilsen, John C.F., IV. "The Forward Defense of Europe." *Military Review* 61 (May 1981): 66-76.

Towell, Pat. "House Panel Skeptical of Arms Cooperation Policy with NATO Allies." *Congressional Quarterly Weekly Report* 37 (24 February 1979): 323.

Turner, Stansfield (Adm.) and Thibault, George (Capt.). "Preparing for the Unexpected: The Need for a New Military Strategy." *Foreign Affairs* 61 (No. 1, Fall 1982): 122-135.

Ulsamer, Edgar. "New Critical Defense Needs." *Air Force Magazine* (February 1979): 26-31.

———. "No Substitute for Military Preparedness." *Air Force Magazine* 62 (May 1979): 44-48.

Ulstein, Egil. *Nordic Security*. (Adelphi Paper No. 81). London: The International Institute for Strategic Studies, 1971.

———. "The Nordic Countries in a Changing Europe." *Military Review* 52 (September 1972): 50-63.

Underwood, (LCDR.) G.L. "Soviet Threat to the Atlantic Sea Lines of Communications: Lessons Learned from the German Capture of Norway in 1940." *Naval War College Review* 34 (May-June 1981): 43-47.

United States. Congress. Committee on Foreign Relations. Delegation Report on *Perspectives on NATO's Southern Flank: April 3-13, 1980*. 96th Congress, 2nd Session, 1980.

Vascencelos, Alvaro. "Allied Defense and Portugal--The Atlantic Dimension." *NATO's Fifteen Nations* 26 (June-July 1981): 50+.

Vincent, R.J. *Military Power and Political Influence*. (Adelphi Paper No. 119). London: International Institute for Strategic Studies, 1975.

von Cleave, William R., and Barnett, Roger W. "Strategic Adaptability." *Orbis* 18 (Fall 1974): 655-676.

von Weizsacker, Carl-Fredrich. *Problems of Modern Strategy, Part II.* (Adelphi Paper No. 55). London: International Institute for Strategic Studies, 1969.

Waites, Neville. "Britain and France: Towards a Stable Relationship." *The World Today* 32 (December 1976): 451-458.

Walker, (Gen.) Walter. "Problems of the Defense of NATO's Northern Flank." *RUSI Journal* 115 (September 1970): 13-23.

———. "The Defense of the Northern Flank." *RUSI Journal* 118 (September 1973): 21-30.

Wall, Patrick. "The Importance of NATO's Northern Flank." *Defense* 10 (January 1979): 9-14.

———. "Peace or War? A View from Europe." *Sea Power* 24 January 1981): 41-43.

Ward, Chester C. "The 'New Myths' and 'Old Realities' of Nuclear War." *Orbis* 8 (Summer 1964): 255-291.

Warnke, Paul C. and Woolsey, James. *Keeping America Safe: Studies in Strategic Military Policy.* Washington, D.C.: Center for National Policy, 1982.

Weinstein, Adalbert. "Harmonious Strategy--The Case for Increased Conventional Forces." *Survival* 1 (September/October 1959): 117-118.

Whitely, Peter. "The Reinforcement of Europe." *NATO's Fifteen Nations* 24 (August-September 1979): 20-26.

Wilmot, Chester. "If NATO Had to Fight." *Foreign Affairs* 31 (January 1953): 200-214.

Yost, David S., ed. *NATO's Strategic Options: Arms Control & Defense.* Elmsford, NY: Pergamon Press, 1981.

MILITARY TECHNOLOGIES

"Agard (Advisory Group for Aerospace Research and Development." *NATO's Fifteen Nations* 17 (December 1972-January 1973): 39-44.

"Air Forces of the World--Part I: European NATO Members." *Interavia* 28 (September 1973): 1003-1007.

"Allied Command Atlantic's Anti-Submarine Warfare Research Center." *NATO's Fifteen Nations* 17 (February-March 1972): 70-75.

Amaduzzi, (Comdr.) Francesco. "The Future of NATO Communications." *NATO Review* 22 (No. 1, 1974): 14-18.

Anderson, Frederic M. "Weapons Procurement Collaboration: A New Era for NATO?" *Orbis* 20 (Winter 1977): 965-990.

Anderson, John. "The Evolution of NATO's New Integrated Communications Systems." *NATO's Fifteen Nations* Special Issue Number 2 (1980): 26-28+.

Ashcroft, Geoffrey. *Military Logistic Systems in NATO: The Goal of Integration, Part I: Economic Aspects*. (Adelphi Paper No. 62). London: The Institute for Strategic Studies, 1969.

―――. *Military Logistic Systems in NATO: The Goal of Integration, Part II: Military Aspects*. (Adelphi Paper No. 68). London: The Institute for Strategic Studies, 1969.

"Assault Breaker: A Plethora of Options." *Defense and Foreign Affairs Digest* 7 (1979): 38-39.

Bailly-Cowell, G.M. "Belgium Holds NATO Army Display." *NATO's Fifteen Nations* 19 (April-May 1974): 87-88.

Bambini, (Maj.) Adrian P. "Chemical Warfare and the NATO Alliance." *Military Review* 61 (April 1981): 27-33.

Basiuk, Victor. "Technology, Western Europe's Alternative Futures, and American Policy." *Orbis* 15 (Summer 1971): 485-506.

Betts, Richard K., ed. *Cruise Missiles: Technology, Strategy Politics*. Washington, D.C.: Brookings, 1981.

Blanchard, George S. "CENTAG/USAREUR Interoperability: A Total Program: From the Bottom Up." *Strategic Review* 5 (Winter 1977): 7-13.

Borklund, C.W. "C^3I in Defense: Why Interoperability Shakes Organizations." *Government Executive* (June 1979): 12.

―――. "Perry's NATO Triad: How Pentagon Thinks Armament 'Co-op' Will Work." *Government Executive* 11 (March 1979): 16+.

Boy, Siegfried. "AWACS--A Significant Step Towards Improved Air Defense." *NATO Review* 27 (April 1979): 9-13.

―――. "AWACS: In Defense of Peace." *NATO's Fifteen Nations* 24 (June-July 1979): 96-98.

Boyle, Dan. "The NATO Identification System." *Interavia* 35 (March 1980): 201-205.

Brocken, Paul. "Command and Control for a Long War." *Air Force Magazine* 63 (April 1980): 50-54.

Brown, Peter V. "NATO's Role in Promoting Co-operation on Aircraft Projects." *NATO Review* 19 (September/October 1971): 13-16.

Burt, Richard. "New Weapons Technologies and European Security." *Orbis* 19 (Summer 1975): 514-532.

———. *New Weapons Technologies: Debate and Directions.* (Adelphi Paper No. 126). London: The International Institute for Strategic Studies, 1976.

———. "The SS-20 and the Eurostrategic Balance." *The World Today* 33 (February 1977): 43-51.

Callaghan, Thomas A., Jr. "Standardisation: A Plan for US/Europe Co-operation." *Atlantic Community Quarterly* 13 (Winter 1975-76): 477-485.

———. "The Inoperability of Interoperability?" *Armed Forces Journal* 116 (April 1979): 36.

Carruthers, James F. "The Automatic Data Link Plotting System (ADLIPS)." *Naval Engineers Journal* 91 (April 1979): 185-191.

Christopher, Warren. "Armaments Cooperation in NATO." *Department of State Bulletin* 78 (December 1978): 36-39.

Clarke, John L. "NATO Standardization: Panacea or Plague?" *Military Review* 59 (April 1979): 59-65.

Cliffe, Trevor. *Military Technology and the European Balance.* (Adelphi Paper No. 89). London: The International Institute for Strategic Studies, 1972.

Cornell, Alexander H. *International Collaboration in Weapons and Equipment Development and Production by the NATO Allies: Ten Years Later and Beyond.* Hingham, MA: Kluwer/Nyhoff Publishing, 1981.

Critchley, Julian. "A Community Policy for Armaments." *NATO Review*, February 1979, p. 10.

Dean, Robert W. "The Future of Collaborative Weapons Acquisition." *Survival* (July-August 1979): 155.

"Details of Tanks in Service in NATO and the Warsaw Pact." *NATO's Fifteen Nations* 20 (February-March 1975): 47-56.

Digby, James F. *Precision-Guided Weapons*. (Adelphi Paper No. 118). London: The International Institute for Strategic Studies, 1975.

Edmonds, Martin. "International Collaboration in Weapons Procurement: The Implications of the Anglo-French Case." *International Affairs* 43 (April 1967): 252-264.

Eekelen, W.F. "Equipment Procurement--Need for Longer Term NATO Planning." *NATO Review* 27 (June 1979): 6-9.

"Electronics for Defense." *NATO's Fifteen Nations* Special Issue No. 2 (1980): entire issue.

"European Armaments Procurement Cooperation." *NATO's Fifteen Nations* 24 (April-May 1979): 113-114.

Facer, Roger. *The Alliance and Europe: Part III: Weapons Procurement in Europe--Capabilities and Choices*. London: The International Institute for Strategic Studies, 1975.

Felder, Wilson N., and Skarlatos, Paul. "Implications of Communications Sophistication for NATO Naval C^2." *Signal* 33 (April 1979): 51-54.

Finlay, Patrick. *Jane's Freight Containers*. London: Jane's Yearbooks, 1973.

Foreign Military Sales and Military Assistance Facts. Washington, D.C.: Department of Defense, Security Assistance Agency, April 1974.

Franks, H. George. "New Eyes and Ears for NATO Forces." *NATO's Fifteen Nations* 17 (August-September 1972): 87-92.

Friederich, J.S. "Fourth Symposium on NATO Codification of Equipment, 15-19 September 1969." *NATO's Fifteen Nations* 15 (February-March 1970): 42-47.

Gangler, Jacques S. "Can the Defense Industry Respond to the Reagan Initiatives?" *International Security* 6 (Spring 1982): 102-121.

Gellner, John, and Jackson, James. "Modern Weapons and the Small Power." *International Journal* 13 (Spring 1958): 87-99.

Gregg, (Lt. Col.) William R. "Troposcatter and Radio Delay." *NATO's Fifteen Nations*, Special Issue Number 2 (1980): 92-94ff.

Haddock, (Lt. Col.) Clovis C. *Cooperative Research, Development and Procurement Within NATO*. (Professional Study). Maxwell AFB, AL: Air War College, 1974.

Hartman, Richard. "NATO Needs and Plans Revealed." *Defense Electronics* 12 (February 1980): 35-36.

Hoeberg, (Brig.) Kjell T. "Architectural Design Study for ACE (Allied Command Europe) Automated C^2 Information System." *Signal* 36 (December 1981): 35-40.

Horowitz, S., and Shisko, R. *A Model for Evaluating VSTOL Versus CTOL Combat Aircraft Systems.* Santa Monica, CA: Rand Corporation, March 1971.

Howard, (Major-Gen.) G.B. "United States Defense Procurement in Canada." *International Journal* 5 (Autumn 1950): 315-324.

International R & D Trends and Policies: An Analysis of Implications for the U.S. Washington, D.C.: Aerospace Industries Association of America, 1973.

"International Report." *Electronic Warfare/Defense Electronics* 11 (March 1979): 19+.

Karas, Thomas H. *Implications of Space Technology for Strategic Nuclear Competition.* Mascatine, IA: Stanley Foundation, 1981.

Karber, Philip A. "The Soviet Anti-Tank Debate." *Survival* 18 (May/June 1976): 105-111.

Kennedy, Robert. "New Weapons Technologies: Implications for Defense Policy." *Parameters* 9 (June 1979): 64-75.

―――. "Precision ATGMs and NATO Defense." *Orbis* (Winter 1979): 897.

Klippenberg, Erik. "Updating Command and Control Systems in NATO." *Signal* 35 (December 1980): 31-33.

Krivinyi, Nikolaus, ed. *World Military Aviation: Aircraft, Airforces and Weaponry.* New York: Arco Publishing Co., 1973.

Kurth, James R. "Why We Buy the Weapons We Do." *Foreign Policy* 11 (Summer 1973): 33-56.

Kyle, Deborah M. "NATO's Chemical Warfare Defense: Improving but Inadequate." *Armed Forces Journal International* 118 (November 1980): 33.

―――., and Schemmer, Benjamin F. "C3/CW in Europe--Can NATO Get Its Electrons Together?" *Armed Forces Journal* 118 (September 1980): 24-25.

Latour, Charles. "Aircraft, Ships, and Weapons in NATO's Northern Command." *NATO's Fifteen Nations* 18 (February-March 1973): 62-65.

―――. "Electronic Warfare." *NATO's Fifteen Nations* 19 (April-May 1974): 72-79.

―――. "Highlights of the (Second) Royal Navy Equipment Exhibition (Greenwich, England, September 17 to 24)." *NATO's Fifteen Nations* 18 (December 1973-January 1974): 64+.

―――. "Small Arms." *NATO's Fifteen Nations* 19 (June-July 1974): 62-68.

Loeb, Larry M. "Jupiter Missiles in Europe: A Measure of Presidential Power." *World Affairs* 139 (Summer 1976): 27-39.

Lorell, Mark A. *Multinational Development of Large Aircraft: The European Experience.* Santa Monica, CA: Rand Corporation, 1980.

Mallorie, (AVM) Paul R., Ret. "Modernization of the NATO Command and Control System." *Signal* 36 (December 1981): 31-33.

Mancini, Angelo N., Jr. "NATO Field Trials." *Army R D & A* (May-June 1979): 14.

Marriott, John. "NATO's ASW Potential." *Survival* 12 (September 1970): 298-303.

―――. "The Anti-Tank Problem." *NATO's Fifteen Nations* 17 (April-May 1972): 72-82.

―――. "New Weapons for Defense in Europe." *NATO's Fifteen Nations* 18 (December 1973-January 1974): 54-60.

―――. "Improvements in NATO's Conventional Weapons 1949/74." *NATO's Fifteen Nations* 19 (February-March 1974): 28-36.

―――. "Surface to Surface Artillery." *NATO's Fifteen Nations* 19 (December 1974-January 1975): 68-73.

Meller, R. "Expensive Luxury or Painful Necessity? Europe's New Generation of Combat Aircraft: Part I: The Increasing Threat." *International Defense Review* 2 (April 1975): 175-194.

―――. "Pentagon Endorses Family of Weapons Concept." *International Defense Review* 12 (No. 5, 1979): 702-703.

Morgenstern, John. "C^3 for Tactical Nuclear Forces in Europe." *Signal* 35 (December 1980): 57-58.

Morse, John H. "New Weapons Technologies: Implications for NATO." *Orbis* 19 (Summer 1975): 497-513.

"Nadge, NATO's New Air Defense Net." *Army in Europe* (September 1973): 2-5.

"NATO Arms Control Group Proposed." *Aviation Week* 110 (April 16, 1979): 18.

"NATO Standardization: Price Too High?" *Astronautics & Aeronautics* 17 (February 1979): 16-20.

Nau, Henry R. "A Political Interpretation of the Technology Gap Dispute." *Orbis* 15 (Summer 1971): 507-527.

Neal, Alfred C. "Economic Necessities and Atlantic Communities." *Foreign Affairs* 45 (July 1967): 694-705; *Atlantic Community Quarterly* 5 (Fall 1967): 347-357.

Newing, Anthony. "ADP in Support of Maritime Operations." *NATO's Fifteen Nations* Special Issue Number 2 (1980): 65-66+.

Norman, Floyd. "The Reluctant Dragon: NATO's Fears and the Need for New Nuclear Weapons." *Army* 24 (February 1974): 16-21.

Nouel, Elise. "Nadge: The Last Word in Computerized Air Defense." *NATO Review* 19 (July/August 1971): 8-12.

Owen, J.I., ed. *Infantry Weapons of the NATO Armies*, 2nd Edition, 1980.

Parker, (Lt. Col.) Glynn E. "NATO and Rationalization, Standardization, and Interoperability." *Army Logistician* 12 (March-April 1980): 24-27.

Perrett, Bryan. *NATO Armour.* London: Ian Allen, 1971.

Pfaltzgraff, Robert L., Jr. "The Future of Atlantic Economic Relationships." *Orbis* 10 (Summer 1968): 408-437.

Pocklington, (Lt. Col.) James H. "NATO's Challenge on the Electronic Battlefield." *NATO's Fifteen Nations* 26 (April-May 1981): 65-66.

Port, A. Tyler. "Co-operation on Arms Production: The Task Ahead." *NATO Review* 21 (No. 3, 1973): 13-17.

Richards, W.J. "Out of the Last Ditch: HF Communications." *NATO's Fifteen Nations* Special Issue Number 1 (1980): 98-100f.

Rienzi, Thomas M., and Coleman, David W. "The Transition in NATO Telecommunications." *Signal* 34 (September 1979): 31-35.

Robins, Yves. "AWACS: E-3A Sentry Gains Experience in World-Wide Deployment." *NATO's Fifteen Nations* 24 (June-July 1979): 94-95.

—————. "AWACS: Portrait of a Sentry." *NATO's Fifteen Nations* 24 (June-July 1979): 89-92.

———. "E-3A Sentry Gains Experience in Worldwide Deployment." *Military Technology and Economics* 3 (May/June 1979): 19-21.

Rorholt, Lars. "Satellite Communications." *NATO's Fifteen Nations*, Special Issue Number 2 (1980): 86-88f.

Rudnick, David. "The Case of the Leopard Tank." *International Affairs* 52 (April 1976): 197-207.

"The Saclant Anti-Submarine Warfare Research Centre." *NATO Review* 21 (No. 1, 1973): 20-24.

Sandoff, Lawrence R. "The Future of Standardization in NATO." *Military Review* 62 (February 1981): 47-54.

Schneider, Barry R. "Can a Bullet Stop a Bullet? [Whether the United States Should Develop an Anti-ballistic Missile System]." *Across the Board* 19 (January 1982): 8-19.

Schurkens, H. "Controlling Quality of Allies Defense Equipment." *NATO Review* 20 (March/April 1972): 23-25.

Shohat, Murry. "The 'A's in AMRAAM." *Military Electronics/Countermeasures* (January 1979): 44.

———. "Army Electronics Future Mirrored in Chip Program." *Military Electronics/Countermeasures* (July 1979): 41.

Simmons, Henry T. "NATO Equipment Standardization and Commonality--U.S. Opinions and Proposals." *International Defence Review* 8 (April 1975): 156-157.

Simpson, John and Gregory, Frank. "West European Collaboration in Weapons Procurement." *Orbis* 16 (Summer 1972): 435-461.

———. "Technology and Political Choice in Future NATO Maritime Strategy." *Orbis* 17 (Spring 1973): 258-276.

Smart, Ian. *Advanced Strategic Missiles: A Short Guide*. (Adelphi Paper No. 63). London: International Institute for Strategic Studies, January 1969.

"Special Report: Defense Electronics Exports." *Defense Electronics* 11 (MAy 1979): 58+.

Stoehrmann, (Lt.) Kenneth C. "Toward a Common European Armaments Effort." *Air University Review* 25 (January-February 1974): 22-31.

Stone, John. "Niag Helps Stimulate Allied Research and Development Co-operation." *NATO Review* 20 (January/February 1972): 18-19.

Sundaram, Gowrie S. "NATO Identification System--The U.S. and Europe Were Friends Then Foes." *International Defense Review* 14 (No. 2, 1981): 175-177.

Taylor, John W.R., ed. *Jane's All the World's Aircraft, 1974-75.* London: Jane's Yearbooks, 1974.

Tucker, Gardiner L. "Standardization and the Joint Defense." *NATO Review* 23 (January 1975): 10-14.

————. *Towards Rationalizing Allied Weapons Production.* (Atlantic Paper No. 1). Paris: Atlantic Institute for International Affairs, 1976.

Ulsamer, Edgar. "Soviet Objective: Technological Supremacy." *Air Force Magazine* 57 (June 1974): 22-27.

United States National Defense University. *ROLAND: A Case for or Against NATO Standardization?* Malone, Daniel K. Washington, D.C.: National Defense University Press, 1980.

Valentine, (Col.) D.R. "NATO's Communications Satellite System." *NATO's Fifteen Nations* 15 (October-November 1970): 61-68.

Wall, Patrick. "Can NATO Effect Standardization?" *Defense and Foreign Affairs Digest* 7 (April 1979): 18.

Walsh, Bill. "View from the Top." *Military Electronics/ Countermeasures* 5 (April 1979): 14.

Warwick, Graham. "The A-10 and Europe." *Flight International* 116 (November 1979): 1491-1496.

Watts, Anthony J. "The Nimrod AEW." *Navy International* 84 (May 1979): 14-19.

Wesche, (Rear-Adm.) H.H. "NATO Agency Works for Increased Military Standardization." *NATO Review* 20 (March/April 1972): 21-22.

Wetzel, (Maj. Gen.) Robert J. and Keane, (Maj.) John J., Jr. "Command and Control in the NATO Environment." *Military Review* 61 (November 1981): 10-18.

Whitehead, Bill. "NATO Small Arms Trials." *Sentinel* 15 (1979): 7-9.

Wilson-Brown, (Maj.) M.S. "Tactical Communications--Army." *NATO's Fifteen Nations* Special Issue Number 1 (1980): 55-58.

Woodcock, Michael J. "NATO Standardization." *Military Review* 55 (October 1975): 39-48.

World Armaments and Disarmament: Sipri Yearbook 1982. Stockholm: International Peace Research Institute, 1982.

STRUCTURE OF THE ALLIANCE

"A Look at a New Command in the Central Region." *NATO's Fifteen Nations* 19 (December 1974-January 1975): 58-64.

Atkenson, (Maj. Gen.) Edward B. "When Turfs Overlap: A Study of Intelligence Organizations in Collision." *Army* 30 (November 1980): 33-43.

Barham, (Lt. Col.) Thomas J. "NATO's Ready Force (Southern European Task Force, SETAF) to the South." *Army* 31 (April 1981): 27-30.

Bennecke, (Gen.) J. "The Role and Capability of NATO Forces Central Europe." *RUSI Journal* 118 (June 1973): 17-23.

Birrenbach, Kurt. "The Reorganisation of NATO." *Orbis* 6 (Summer 1962): 244-257.

Bolton, David. "European Defense--Arms and Options." *RUSI Journal for Defence Studies* 120 (March 1975): 38-41.

Bonnart, Frederick. "Autumn Forge 1980." *NATO's Fifteen Nations* 25 (October-November 1980): 81-82.

Boyd, (Maj.) Darwin D. "Need for an Improved Non-Nuclear Force Within NATO." (Research Study 0240-71). Maxwell AFB, AL: Air Command and Staff College, 1971.

Boyle, Dan. "The NATO Identification System." *Interavia* 35 (March 1980): 201-205.

Bracken, Paul. "Urban Sprawl and NATO Defense." *Survival* 18 (November/December 1976): 254-260.

Brodie, Bernard. "Conventional Capabilities in Europe." *Survival* 5 (July/August 1963): 148-155.

Bruber, Frederic J. "Links to the NATO Nations: The National Military Representatives at Shape." *NATO's Fifteen Nations* 15 (June-July 1970): 38-44.

Bruntland, Arne Olav. "The Nordic Balance: Past and Present." *Co-operation and Conflict* 1 (1966): 30-63.

Buchanan, Keith C. "AMF the Ace Mobile Force (Land)." *NATO's Fifteen Nations* 15 (February-March 1970): 49-56.

Burbank, Lyman B. "Scandinavian Integration and Western Defense." *Foreign Affairs* 35 (October 1956): 144-150.

Burgin, Don. "SIXATAF; 20 Years as NATO's Southeastern Air Arms." *NATO's Fifteen Nations* 18 (August-September 1973): 41-48.

Cameron, Air Vice Marshal Robert. "Options Make Good Propaganda but Poor Defense for NATO." *NATO's Fifteen Nations* 15 (June-July 1970): 20-23.

Canby, Steven L. *NATO Military Policy: The Constraints Imposed by an Inappropriate Military Structure.* Santa Monica, CA: Rand Corporation, February 1972.

──────. *NATO Military Policy: Obtaining Conventional Comparability with the Warsaw Pact.* (Rand Report R-1088-ARPA). Santa Monica, CA: Rand Corporation, June 1973.

──────. *Damping Nuclear Counterforce Incentives: Correcting NATO's Inferiority in Conventional Military Strength.* Santa Monica, CA: California Arms Control and Foreign Policy Seminar, August 1974.

──────. "Dumping Nuclear Counterforce Incentives: Correcting NATO's Inferiority in Conventional Military Strength." *Orbis* 19 (Spring 1975): 47-71.

──────. *The Alliance and Europe: Part IV--Military Doctrine and Technology.* (Adelphi Paper No. 109). London: The International Institute for Strategic Studies, 1975.

Carrington, William M. "NATO's Institute for Professional Development." (Professional Study). Maxwell AFB, AL: Air War College, 1973.

Clark, John J. "Is NATO Structured for the 1980's?" *Defense and Foreign Affairs Digest* 7 (April 1979): 36-39.

──────. "Is the NATO Alliance Structure Appropriate for the 1980's?" *Military Review* 59 (April 1979): 25-34.

Cleveland, Harlan. "NATO After the Invasion." *Foreign Affairs* 47 (January 1969): 251-265.

Coggi, Igino. "If There's a Threat at All It's on the Southern Flank." *Defence Today* 14 (June 1979): 292-296.

Colbert, (Adm.) Richard G. "Defending NATO's Southern Flank." *NATO's Fifteen Nations* 18 (August-September 1973): 20-40.

Cromwell, William C. *The Eurogroup and NATO.* Philadelphia: Foreign Policy Research Institute, University of Pennsylvania, 1974.

Cuthbertson, B.C. "The Strategic Significance of the Northern Cap." *Royal United Service Institution Journal* 117 (June 1972): 45-47.

Davison, Michael S. "Portrait of an Army: The U.S. Seventh Army in Europe." *Survival* 14 (September/October 1972): 220-225.

Dawson, Raymond H., and Nicholson, George E., Jr. "NATO and the Shape Technical Center." *International Organization* 21 (Summer 1967): 565-591.

de Marchi, Antonio. "The Eurogroup." *Military Review* 54 (July 1974): 75-77.

de Poix, Vincent Paul. "NATO's Striking Fleet Atlantic." *NATO's Fifteen Nations* 17 (February-March 1972): 38-44.

Dewey, Arthur E. "The Nordic Balance." *Strategic Review* 4 (Fall 1976): 49-60.

Dodd, Norman L. "Cincent's Responsibilities for the Ace Mobile Force." *NATO's Fifteen Nations* 15 (June-July 1970): 60-67.

Dube, F.P. "NATO Electronic Warfare Advisory Committee." *Journal of Electronic Defense* 2 (May/June 1979): 33-34.

Duncan, Charles K. "The Maritime Equation--Saclant in the 1970s." *NATO's Fifteen Nations* 17 (February-March 1972): 28-35.

Eliot, Christian. "The Iberian Atlantic Area Command." *NATO's Fifteen Nations* 24 (October-November 1979): 68-69.

Eliot, George Fielding. "Military Organisation Under the Atlantic Pact." *Foreign Affairs* 27 (July 1949): 640-650.

Eriksen, Bjarne. *The Committee System of the NATO Council.* Oslo: Universitetsforlaget, 1967.

"The Eurogroup." *NATO Review* 20 (November/December 1972): 8-12.

"The Eurogroup." *NATO's Fifteen Nations* 20 (February-March 1975): 19-22.

"The Eurogroup." *Atlantic Community Quarterly* 14 (Spring 1976): 76-88.

"The Eurogroup in NATO: Report by the Planning Staff, West German Ministry of Defense." *Survival* 14 (November/December 1972): 291-293.

"Exercise Report: Autumn Forge." *NATO's Fifteen Nations* 24 (October 1979): 62-64+.

Fox, William T.R., and Schilling, Warner R., eds. *European Security and the Atlantic System.* New York: Columbia University Press, 1973.

Gasteyger, Curt. "Europe Cool to U.S. Suggestions on Revitalized Charter." *Atlantic Community Quarterly* 11 (Fall 1973): 319-321.

Gebel, Wolfgang R. "Centag Southern Germany's Defender." *NATO's Fifteen Nations* 19 (October-November 1974): 54-60.

Goldman, Nancy L. "Women in NATO Armed Forces." *Military Review* 54 (October 1974): 72-82.

Goodpaster, (Gen.) Andrew J. "Strategy and Capabilities of Allied Command Europe." *Naval War College Review* 23 (October 1970): 11-18.

Goodpaster, (Colonel) Andrew J. "The Development of Shape: 1950-1953." *International Organization* 9 (May 1955): 257-262.

Grammuller, Harald, and Murray-Rochard, Alan. "A New Identification System for NATO." *NATO's Fifteen Nations*, Special Issue Number 2 (1980): 104-107.

Haas, Ernst B., and Merkl, Peter H. "Parliamentarians Against Ministers: The Case of Western European Union." *International Organization* 14 (Winter 1960): 37-59.

Harned, Joseph. "Atlantic Assembly--A Genesis." *Atlantic Community Quarterly* 3 (Spring 1965): 43-49.

Hartley, Livingston. "An Atlantic Commission." *Orbis* 7 (Summer 1963): 300-307.

―――. "An Atlantic Commission of 'Wise Men.'" *Atlantic Community Quarterly* 13 (Winter 1964-65): 557-563.

―――. "The North Atlantic Assembly." *Atlantic Community Quarterly* 13 (Winter 1975-76): 486-491.

Hilgers, (Lt. Col.) J.J.W. "Exercise Display Determination 1979." *Marine Corps Gazette* 64 (May 1980): 64-73.

Hill, R.J. *Political Consultation in NATO*. (ORAE Memorandum No. 64). Ottawa: O.R.A.E., Department of National Defense, March 1975.

Hinterhoff, (Maj.) E. "The Complex Problems of the Southern NATO Flank." *NATO's Fifteen Nations* 17 (April-May 1972): 32-39.

Hoag, Malcolm W. "Rationalizing NATO Strategy." *World Politics* 17 (October 1964): 121-142.

Holmes, John W. "Fearful Symmetry: The Dilemmas of Consultation and Coordination in the North Atlantic Treaty Organization." *International Organization* 22 (Winter 1968): 821-840.

Holst, Johan J., ed. "The Soviet Union and Nordic Security." *Conciliation and Conflict*, Nos. 3-4 (1971), pp. 137-146.

Hooson, Emlyn. "The Reform of NATO." *Atlantic Community Quarterly* 3 (Winter 1965-66): 456-463.

Hovey, J. Allan. *The Superparliaments: Interparliamentary Consultation and Atlantic Co-operation.* New York: Praeger, 1966.

Hunt, Kenneth. *The Alliance and Europe: Part II--Defence with Fewer Men.* (Adelphi Papers 98). London: The International Institute for Strategic Studies, 1973.

International Institute for Strategic Studies. "The North Atlantic Treaty." *Air Force Magazine* 64 (December 1981): 66-75.

Jordan, R.S. *The NATO International Staff/Secretariat 1952-57: A Study in International Administration.* London: Oxford University Press, 1967.

Jordan, Robert S., and Newman, Parley W., Jr. "The Secretary-General of NATO and Multinational Political Leadership." *International Journal* 30 (Autumn 1975): 732-757.

Kirgis, Frederic I., Jr. "NATO Consultations as a Component of National Decision-making." *American Journal of International Law* 73 (July 1979): 372-406.

Kissinger, Henry A. "A New Atlantic Charter." *Atlantic Community Quarterly* 11 (Summer 1973): 151-160.

Klenberg, Jan. *The Cape and the Straits: Problems of Nordic Security.* (Papers in International Affairs, No. 18). Cambridge, MA: Center for International Affairs, Harvard University, 1968.

Klepacki, Zbigniew M. *West European International Organizations.* Moscow: Progress Publishers, 1973.

Knorr, Klaus. *Europe and America in the 1970's: II: Society and Power.* (Adelphi Paper No. 71). London: The International Institute for Strategic Studies, November 1970.

Knowlton, William A. "Early Stages in the Organisation of Shape." *International Organization* 13 (Winter 1959): 1-18.

Korkegi, Robert H. "AGARD's Role in NATO." *NATO Review* 27 (June 1979): 25-26.

Kyle, Deborah M. "Autumn Forge 80: NATO's Readiness Gameplan." *Armed Forces Journal* 118 (November 1980): 30+.

Lawrence, R.D., and Record, J. *U.S. Force Structure in NATO: An Alternative.* Washington, D.C.: Brookings Institution, 1974.

Structure of the Alliance

Lettau, (Maj.) Ulrich H. "COB's (Collocated Operating Bases) in Europe." *AF Engineering and Services Quarterly* 22 (Summer 1981): 19-22.

Lockley, Lt. Col. Stanton G. "Implications of PCS Vs Unit Rotation." (Professional Study). Maxwell AFB, AL: Air War College, 1972.

MacCloskey, Brig.-Gen. Monro. *North Atlantic Treaty Organization: Guardian of Peace and Security.* New York: Richards Rosen Press Inc., 1966.

McGee (Senator) Gale. "Atlantic Union Resolution." *Atlantic Community Quarterly* 10 (1972-73): 541-543.

Medearis, Joseph. "Understanding NATO Intrastructure." *NATO's Fifteen Nations* 25 (December 1980-January 1981): 78-80+.

Meehan, Maj. John F. "Allied Forces Northern Europe (AFNORTH)-- NATO's Assailable Flank?" *Military Review* 55 (January 1975): 3-10.

Messmer, Pierre. "French Military Problems." *Atlantic Community Quarterly* 1 (Summer 1963): 185-186.

"NATO Force Sufficiency Study--1970: Executive Summary." Menlo Park, CA: Stanford Research Institute, September 1970.

"NATO: Two Views." *Army* 25 (February 1975): 10-19.

"NATO Uses Three Approaches for Tactical Communications." *Defence Electronics* 13 (May 1981): 86+.

Neff, Richard. "NATO Political Consultation: Fact or Myth?" *NATO Review* 23 (January 1975): 7-9.

Newhouse, John. "U.S. Troops in Europe: Issues and Alternatives." *Atlantic Community Quarterly* 9 (Winter 1971-72): 460-475.

———. *U.S. Troops in Europe: Issues, Costs and Choices.* Washington, D.C.: The Brookings Institution, 1971.

Norstad, (Gen.) Lauris. "The Defense of Europe: Speech to the NATO Parliamentarians, 21 November 1960." *Survival* 3 (January/February 1961): 26-30.

"The North Atlantic Treaty. International Institute for Strategic Studies." *Air Force Magazine* 63 (December 1980): 75-79.

Nunn, (Sen.) Sam. "NATO Strategy." *Survival* 19 (January/February 1977): 30-38.

Orvik, Nils. "Scandinavia, NATO and Northern Security." *International Organization* 20 (Summer 1966): 380-396.

---. "Scandinavian Security in Transition: The Two-Dimensional Threat." *Orbis* 16 (Fall 1972): 720-742.

---, and Haagerup, Nils J. *The Scandinavian Members of NATO*. Adelphi Paper No. 23, December 1965.

Ostendorf, Col. T.H. "Defense of the Northern European Command: The Ways and the Means." *NATO's Fifteen Nations* 18 (February-March 1973): 50-55.

Owen, Henry. "NATO Strategy: What Is Past Is Prologue." *Foreign Affairs* 43 (July 1965): 682-690.

Ozarne, (Maj.) E.H. "NATO's Flexible Response." *Army in Europe*, October 1973, pp. 10-13.

Partlow, Frank A., Jr. "Deterrence in NATO--The Role of the Military Committee." *Military Review* 54 (December 1974): 3-8.

Partlow, (Maj.) Frank A. "The NATO Military Committee and the International Military Staff: Some Rationale and a Proposal for Reorganization." *RUSI Journal* 119 (September 1974): 29-38.

Phillips, J. *Evolution of NATO Defence Strategy*. (Monographs on National Security Affairs). Providence, RI: Brown University, 1974.

Porth, Jacquelyn S. "Training NATO's Pilots: The Dawn of a New Day." *Defense and Foreign Affairs* 9 (February 1981): 10-11.

Rathjens, George W., Jr. "Notes on the Military Problems of Europe." *World Politics* 10 (January 1958): 182-201.

Read, (Brig.) Greg. "Reconnaissance Forces in the Central Region." *NATO's Fifteen Nations* Special Issue No. 1 (1980): 129-130ff.

"Red Signals Flash on NATO's Forgotten Front; The Vulnerable South-East." *To the Point* 8 (April 13, 1979): 8-11.

Rees, David. *Southern Europe: NATO's Crumbling Flank*. (Conflict Studies, No. 60). London: Institute for the Study of Conflict, August 1975.

Robison, David. "A European Co-ordinated Force." *Orbis* 9 (Fall 1965): 655-676.

Rockefeller, Nelson A. "Federal Union of the Free." *Atlantic Community Quarterly* 2 (Winter 1964-65): 564-570.

Romaneski, (Col.) Albert Leo. "Nordic Balance in the 1970s." *United States Naval Institute Proceedings* 99 (August 1973): 32-41.

Ruhl, Lothar. "NATO's Political Limitations." *Atlantic Community Quarterly* 12 (Winter 1974-75): 463-469.

"SACLANT Headquarters Celebrates 20th Anniversary." *NATO Review* 20 (May/June 1972): 8-11.

Schneider, (Maj. Gen.) G. "C3 Interoperability in NATO." *NATO's Fifteen Nations* Special Issue Number 2 (1980): 34+.

Schopflin, George. "NATO and the Nordic Balance." *The World Today* 22 (March 1966): 114-121.

———. "The Nordic Countries in a Changing Europe." *Military Review* 52 (September 1972): 50-63.

Schulze, Franz-Joseph. The Central Region of Allied Command Europe." *NATO's Fifteen Nations* 24 (April-May 1979): 19-25.

Shere, (Adm.) Harold E. "Allied Forces Southern Europe." *NATO's Fifteen Nations* 24 (December 1979-January 1980): 49-52.

Sherman, Ronald L. "An Interview with Commander Allied Air Central Europe." *NATO's Fifteen Nations* 23 (December 1978-January 1979): 82-88.

Sleiter, (Adm., Ret.) Giovanni. "Monitoring the Southern Flank." *Interavia* 36 (January 1980): 42-43.

Smith, (Gen.) W.Y. "Europe: The Current Military Situation." *Air Force Policy Letter for Commanders* (September 1981): 2-8.

Sundaram, Gowrie S. "NATO Identification System--the U.S. and Europe More Friends Than Foes." *International Defense Review* 14 (No. 2, 1981): 175-177.

Thompson, W.F.K. "NATO's Force Posture in Allied Command Europe." *NATO Review* 22 (No. 2, 1974): 7-13.

Tighe, (Maj.) Earl E. "Training American Personnel Assigned to NATO." (Research Study). Maxwell AFB, AL: Air Command and Staff College, 1974.

Timbrell, (Rear Adm.) Robert W. "ACLANT Mobile Logistics a Requirement for Standardization." *NATO's Fifteen Nations* 17 (February-March 1972): 82-84.

U.S. Forces in Europe. Hearings Before the Subcommittee on Arms Control, International Law and Organization, of the Committee on Foreign Relations, United States Senate, Ninety-Third Congress, First Session, July 25 and 27, 1973. Washington, D.C.: Government Printing Office, 1973.

U.S. Forces in NATO. *Hearings Before the Committee on Foreign Affairs and Its Subcommittee on Europe, House of Representatives, Ninety-Third Congress, First Session June 18, 19, 25, 26, July 10-12, 17, 1973.* Washington, D.C.: Government Printing Office, 1973.

"The U.S. Reply to the French Aid-Memoire of March 1966 on the Removal of NATO Facilities in France." *Survival* 8 (June 1966): 186-187.

van Lynden, (Rear Adm.) R.W. "NATO's Silent Service." *NATO Review* 22 (October 1974): 25-29.

Walker, (Gen.) Walter. "The Defense of the Northern Flank." *RUSI Journal* 118 (September 1973): 21-30.

Wall, Patrick. "The Importance of NATO's Northern Flank." *Defence* 10 (January 1979): 9-14.

Whetten, Lawrence L. "Long-Range Planning Factors in the Brosio Exercise." *Military Review* 51 (July 1971): 50-59.

Whiteley, (Gen.) Peter. "The Northern Flank of NATO." *RUSI Journal for Defense Studies* 125 (March 1980): 9-13.

———. "The Reinforcement of Europe." *NATO's Fifteen Nations* 24 (August-September 1979): 20-26.

Wiegele, Thomas C. "Nuclear Consultation Processes in NATO." *Orbis* 16 (Summer 1972): 462-487.

Wilmot, Chester. "If NATO Had to Fight." *Foreign Affairs* 31 (January 1953): 200-214.

Wood, Colonel Robert J. "The First Year of Shape." *International Organization* 6 (May 1952): 175-191.

Yost, David S., ed. *NATO's Strategic Options: Arms Control & Defense.* New York: Pergamon Press, 1981.

Zakheim, Dov S. "Improving NATO Defenses: The Institutional Dimension." *Military Review* 57 (October 1977): 43-55.

Zumwalt, Elmo R. "The Lessons for NATO of Recent Military Experience." *Atlantic Community Quarterly* 12 (Winter 1974-75): 448-462.

AIR

Adler, Konrad. "Air Defense Suppression in a Central European Theatre." *Armada International* 4 (March-April 1980): 60-62+.

"Aircraft Interception in NATO." *Aviation and Marine International* 62 (April 1979): 43-50.

Alberts, (Maj.) Donald J. "Tactical Air Power Within NATO--A Growing Convergence of Views." *Air University Review* 31 (March-April 1980): 59-69.

Allen, (Gen.) Lew, Jr. "The United States Air Force and NATO." *NATO's Fifteen Nations* Special Issue Number 2 (1979): 84+.

Armitage, (Air Vice Marshal) M.J. "Air Power in the Central Region." *Royal United Services Institute Journal for Defense Studies* 124 (December 1979): 33-38.

Barzaghi, Antonio. "AWACS: NATO's Far-Seeing Eye." *Aviation & Marine International* 61 (March 1969): 51-64.

Boyle, Dan. "Airborne Early Warning--Two Major Systems for Europe." *Interavia* 35 (August 1980): 695-701.

Brett, (Lt. Gen.) Devol. "The Winged Lion (Allied Air Southern Europe)." *NATO's Fifteen Nations* Special Issue No. 2 (1979): 34-36.

Brodie, Bernard. "Some Notes on the Evolution of Air Doctrine." *World Politics* 7 (April 1955): 349-370.

Brooks, Tony. "RAF Strike Command: A Vital Force for NATO." *NATO's Fifteen Nations* 18 (June-July 1973): 49-56.

Brown, David A. "A-10 Crews Sharpen Air Support Skills." *Aviation Week* 110 (April 2, 1979): 37-38+.

Brown, Neville. "The Tactical Air Balance in Europe." *The World Today* 28 (September 1972): 385-392.

Canby, Steven L. "Tactical Air Power in Armored Warfare: The Divergence Within NATO." *Air University Review* 30 (May-June 1979): 2-20.

Chopping, Douglas. "NATO's Maritime Air Defenses: Countering the Increasing Soviet Maritime Threat." *Interavia* 35 (January 1980): 27-29.

Chubbuck, (Maj.) R.M. "USAFE's Role in NATO Defense." *NATO's Fifteen Nations* 18 (April-May 1973): 58-64.

Conwell, (Lt. Col.) Leslie C. *NATO Air Defense: Is the U.S. Fighter Contribution Appropriate?* (Professional Study). Maxwell AFB, AL: Air War College, 1974.

Day, Bonner. "AWACS in Operation." *Air Force Magazine* 62 (June 1979): 52-56.

Desmond, P. "Allied Air Forces Central Europe: Tactical Leadership Programme." *Air Clues* 33 (February 1979): 44-46.

Doty, Laurence. "NATO Reshaping Tactical Air Posture." *Aviation Week & Space Technology* 102 (3 March 1975): 12-13.

Fiddler, (Maj.) John F. *USAF Posture in Europe After the Yom Kippur War of 1973.* Maxwell AFB, AL: Air Command and Staff College, 1974.

Fox, (Maj.) Charles L., and Lorenzini, (Lt. Col.) Dino A. "How Much Is Not Enough? The Non-nuclear Air Battle in NATO's Central Region." *Naval War College Review* 33 (March-April 1980): 58-78.

Gijzen, (Air Commodore) Johannes A., and Facey, David A. "Planning for the Air Command and Control System--Views from SHAPE and NATO." *Signal* 36 (December 1981): 13-14+.

Gunderson, (Gen.) H.F. and others. "The Air Forces of NATO." *NATO's Fifteen Nations*, Special Issue No. 2 (1979): entire issue.

Huebner, (Lt. Col.) Gerhard. "Tactical Communications--Air Force." *NATO's Fifteen Nations* Special Issue Number 2 (1980): 49-51.

Huyser, Robert E. "The Military Airlift Command: Air Reinforcement for NATO." *NATO's Fifteen Nations* 24 (August-September 1979): 29-31.

Kyle, Deborah M. "Enhanced Readiness Goals Spark NATO Jet Pilot Training Program." *Armed Forces Journal International* (April 1981): 118-78.

Lambert, Mark. "In NATO's Front Line--U.S. Air Defense in Germany." *Interavia* 35 (October 1980): 915-919.

Latour, Charles. "Defense Against Low Level Air Attack." *NATO's Fifteen Nations* 19 (August-September 1974): 44-51.

Lisle, Alan G., Jr. "The Sixth Allied Tactical Air Force." *NATO's Fifteen Nations* 15 (April-May 1970): 58-64.

Loy, (Maj.) Noah E. *USAFE and Specialized Tactical Fighter Wings.* (Research Study No. 1215-71). Maxwell AFB, AL: Air Command and Staff College, 1971.

Marriott, John. "The Air Defense of Europe." *NATO's Fifteen Nations* 18 (October-November 1973): 37-68.

Milton, T.R. "Tethering the Team Captain." *Air Force* 62 (September 1979): 129.

"NATO Plans Civil Reserve Air Fleet." *Flight International* 115 (May 1979): 1717.

Nicholls, (Air Marshal) John. "Air Power--Dominant in NATO Strategy." *Hawk* 40 (February 1980): 13-18.

O'Rourke, (Maj.) Robert J. "Marine Air Operations in Northern Europe." *U.S. Naval Institute Proceedings* 106 (November 1980): 53-59.

Structure of the Alliance

Pauly, (Gen.) John W. "NATO Air Operations in the Central Region: Can We Meet the Threat?" *NATO's Fifteen Nations* Special Issue Number 2 (1979): 28ff.

Philipp, Udo. "Defense of the North Sea and Baltic." *Interavia* 35 (January 1980): 40-41.

Possony, Stefan T. *Strategic Air Power.* Washington, Infantry Journal Press, 1949.

Robinson, Clarence A., Jr. "NATO Weighs U.S. Actions on Missiles." *Aviation Week & Space Technology* 110 (June 11, 1979): 86-100.

Sack, (Maj.) Thomas L. "The Melting Pot of Pilot Instruction. (Euro-NATO Joint Jet Pilot Training (ENJJPT)." *Air Force Magazine* 64 (June 1981): 40-42.

"United States Air Force Europe." *NATO's Fifteen Nations* 15 (February-March 1970): 66-69.

Vershinin, (Chief Air Marshal) K. "Aviation in Modern War." *Survival* 5 (March/April 1963): 83-85.

Walker, Rudolf F. "A10 Close Support Operations in Europe." *Air Force Magazine* (August 1979): 73-77.

Wheeler, Barry C. "Luftwaffe in Europe's Front Line." *Flight International* (September 1979): 33.

White, William D. *U.S. Tactical Air Power: Missions, Forces and Costs.* Washington, D.C.: The Brookings Institution, 1974.

LAND

Barham, (Lt. Col.) Thomas J. "NATO's Ready Force (Southern European Task Force, SETAF) to the South." *Army* 31 (April 1981): 27-30.

Bennecke, (Gen.) Jurgen. "Allied Land Forces in NATO's European Central Region." *NATO's Fifteen Nations* 17 (June-July 1972): 50-56.

Bragmann, (Brig. Gen.) G. and others. "The Employment of Non-Mechanized Infantry (Report of a Symposium Jointly Sponsored by RUSI and the Commander ACE Mobile Force (Land), Hamburg, April 18, 1980)." *RUSI Journal for Defense Studies* 125 (December 1980): 56-59.

Brown, James. "Challenges and Uncertainty: NATO's Southern Flank." *Air University Review* 3 (May-June 1980): 3-16.

Bragmann, (Brig. Gen.) G. and others. "The Employment of Non-Mechanized Infantry (Report of a Symposium Jointly Sponsored by RUSI and the Commander ACE Mobile Force (Land), Hamburg, April 18, 1980)." *RUSI Journal for Defense Studies* 125 (December 1980): 56-59.

Callaghan, Thomas A., Jr. "The Conventional Force Balance CAN Be Redressed." *NATO's Fifteen Nations* 24 (April-May 1979): 113-114.

Copley, Gregory. "NATO: The Lost Battalions." *Defense and Foreign Affairs* 8 (No. 2, 1980): 6-9.

Davison, (Gen.) Michael S. "U.S. Army Europe: Ready, Disciplined, Professional." *Army* 24 (October 1974): 20-30.

Deerin, James B. "NATO and the National Guard." *National Guard* 33 (February 1979): 6-11.

Fischer, Robert Lucas. *Defending the Central Front: The Balance of Forces.* (Adelphi Paper No. 127). London: International Institute for Strategic Studies, 1976.

Fowler, (Col.) Delbert M. "How Many Divisions? A NATO-Warsaw Pact Assessment." *Military Review* 52 (November 1972): 76-88.

Gans, (Col.) Daniel. "Fight Outnumbered and Win--Against What Odds?" *Military Review* 60 (December 1980): 31-46.

Garnett, John C. "BOAR and NATO." *International Affairs* (Great Britain) 4 (October 1970): 670-681.

Grover, Major General J. "The Ace Mobile Force (Land) Today: A Force for Tomorrow." *NATO's Fifteen Nations* 18 (October-November 1973): 69-76.

Hoffman, Fred S. "NATO's Mobile Forces." *Atlantic Community Quarterly* 4 (Summer 1966): 242-248.

Karber, Phillip A. "The Growing Armor/Anti-Armor Imbalance in Central Europe." *Armed Forces Journal International* 118 (July 1981): 37-40+.

Kroesen, (Gen.) Frederick J. "U.S. Army, Europe, Modernizes While Keeping the NATO Vigil." *Army* 31 (October 1981): 48-51+.

Liddell Hart, B.H. "Shield Forces for NATO." *Survival* 2 (May/June 1960): 108-110.

Marriott, John. "The Anti-Tank Problem." *NATO's Fifteen Nations* 17 (April-May 1972): 72-82.

---. "Anti-Tank Warfare." *NATO's Fifteen Nations* 24 (April-May 1979): 60-68.

McGlasson, W.D. "POMCUS (Prepositioning of Material Configured in Unit Sets): The Most Affordable Alternative." *National Defense* 65 (December 1981): 28-35.

Merritt, Jack N. "On the Move." *Field Artillery Journal* (Jan.-Feb. 1979): 2.

Structure of the Alliance 177

United States. House. Committee on Armed Services. Military Personnel and Compensation Subcommittee. *Defense Manpower Policies and Problems Among Member Countries of NATO: Presentation by Members of the Subcommittee on Manpower and Personnel of North Atlantic Assembly.* 97th Congress, 1st Session, 1982. Washington, D.C.: Government Printing Office, 1982.

SEA

Alexander, (Lt. Col.) Joseph H. "Combined Amphibious Operations in Northern Europe." *U.S. Naval Institute Proceedings* 106 (November 1980): 26-32.

Allen, Raymond W. "Standing Naval Force Atlantic." *NATO's Fifteen Nations* 17 (February-March 1972): 46-52.

Alves, Dora. "The Federal German Navy: Linchpin of the Northern Flank." *U.S. Naval Institute Proceedings* 107 (June 1981): 100-104.

Bagley, Worth H. "The State of the American Navy in Free World Defense and Its Implications." *Navy International* (June 1979): 6.

Bennett, (Vice Adm.) Fred G. "The Silent Threat." *NATO's Fifteen Nations* 17 (February-March 1972): 102-108.

Booth, Ken. "Law and Strategy in Northern Waters." *Naval War College Review* 34 (July-August 1981): 3-21.

Bruhns, (Cmdr.) Uwe. "Tactical Communications--Navy." *NATO's Fifteen Nations* Special Issue Number 2 (1980): 60ff.

Buchan, Alastair. *Power at Sea: Part I: The New Environment.* (Adelphi Paper No. 122). London: The International Institute for Strategic Studies, 1976.

Cancian, Mark F. "NATO: Obsession to the Corps." *Marine Corps Gazette* 63 (June 1979): 24.

Case, (Col.) Frank B. "Time to Secure the Seas." *United States Naval Institute Proceedings* 99 (August 1973): 24-31.

"The Changing Seascape: Its Implications for the Alliance." *NATO Review* 21 (No. 5, 1973): 7-9.

"The Channel Command." *NATO's Fifteen Nations* 18 (June-July 1973): 22-48.

Chopping, Douglas. "NATO's Maritime Air Defenses: Countering the Increasing Soviet Maritime Threat." *Interavia* 35 (January 1980): 27-29.

Clark, (Adm.) Joseph J. and Barnes, (Capt.) Dwight H. *Sea Power and Its Meaning*. New York: Watts, 1966.

Colbert, (Adm.) Richard G. "Sea Power in the Mediterranean--The New Balance." *NATO's Fifteen Nations* 17 (October-November 1972): 42-48.

--------. "The Shifting Balance of Power at Sea." *Atlantic Community Quarterly* 10 (Winter 1972-73): 470-479.

Dennison, (Adm.) Robert Lee. "Allied Command Atlantic." *NATO's Fifteen Nations* 17 (February-March 1972): 16-19.

Drischler, Alvin Paul. "Standing Naval Forces for NATO: A Proposal." *Survival* 14 (September/October 1972): 226-230.

Ellis, G.M.W. "Mine Countermeasures: The British Go It Alone (Again)." *U.S. Naval Institute Proceedings* 105 (July 1979): 102-105.

Fama, Joseph. "NATO's Navy." *Defense & Foreign Affairs Digest* 3 (February 1975): 21-24.

Fisher, (Lt. Comdr.) M.J. "An Appraisal of the Standing Naval Force Atlantic." *U.S. Navy Institute Proceedings* 106 (November 1980): 107-108.

Fredholm, (Capt.) Christer. "The North Atlantic: The Norwegian Sea, A Scandinavian Security Problem." *Naval War College Review* 24 (June 1972): 56-64.

Gretton, (Vice-Adm.) Sir Peter. *Maritime Strategy: A Study of Defense Problems*. New York: Praeger, 1965.

Heck, Robert. "NATO--Frigate Programme Review." *Armada International* 3 (1979): 14.

Hessman, James D. "NATO Overview." *Sea Power* 11 (October 1979): 31-35.

Holst, Johan J. *Power at Sea: Part II: Super Powers and Navies*. (Adelphi Paper No. 123). London: The International Institute for Strategic Studies, 1976.

Howard, Michael. *Power at Sea: Part III: Competition and Conflict*. (Adelphi Paper No. 124). London: The International Institute for Strategic Studies, 1976.

"Iberian Atlantic Area Command." *NATO's Fifteen Nations* 17 (February-March 1972): 90-92.

Jenner, Peter. "Iberian Atlantic Command Watches Over Crossroads of the Seas." *NATO Review* 19 (May/June 1971): 6-10.

Jungius, James. "The Balance of Power at Sea." *NATO Review* 27 (December 1979): 6-11.

Structure of the Alliance

Kidd, Isaac. "NATO's Double Dependence on the Atlantic." *NATO Review* 5 (October 1978): 3-8.

Kruger-Sprengel, Friedhelm. *The Role of NATO in the Use of the Sea and the Seabed*. Washington, D.C.: Woodrow Wilson International Center for Scholars, October 1972.

Leach, Henry. "How Vulnerable Is the West to a Warsaw Pact Mining Campaign?" *Navy International* 84 (March 1979): 5-11.

Lehman, John F., Jr. "Rebirth of a U.S. Naval Strategy." *Strategic Review* 9 (Summer 1981): 9-15.

Mansfield, (Vice Adm.) E.G.N. "Shifting Strategic Balance in the Atlantic." *Strategic Review* 2 (Summer 1974): 16-21.

Marriott, John. "Naval Missiles." *International Defense Review* 3 (1969): 245-248.

Martin, Laurence W. *The Sea in Modern Strategy*. New York: Praeger, 1967.

Moore, J.E. "Sea Power in the Eastern Mediterranean." *NATO's Fifteen Nations* 24 (June-July 1979): 38-40.

Muller, Felix. "Maestrale Class Frigates to Set New Standards." *Armada International* 3 (1979): 6-10.

Nailor, Peter. *The Roles of Maritime Forces in the Security of Western Europe*. Southampton: Department of Extra-Mural Studies, University of Southampton, 1972.

Naugle, (Comdr.) J.O. "The Allied Command Atlantic--Submarine Challenge." *NATO's Fifteen Nations* 17 (February-March 1972): 62-68.

"Naval Challenge in the Mediterranean." *NATO's Fifteen Nations* 18 (August-September 1973): 58-62.

Nitze, Paul H. "Securing the Seas: Soviet Naval Challenge and Western Alliance Options." *Atlantic Community Quarterly* 16 (Winter 1978-79): 473-499.

──────. *Securing the Seas: The Soviet Naval Challenge and Western Alliance Options*. Boulder, CO: Westview Press, 1979.

Palmer, Joseph. "NATO Lives or Dies by the Sea: Unhampered Use Is Vital." *NATO's Fifteen Nations* 19 (October-November 1974): 20-23.

"Polaris Successor." *RUSI Journal for Defense Studies* 125 (September 1980): 16-25.

The Security of North Sea Oil and the Overall Soviet Naval Threat. Paris, France: Atlantic Treaty Association, 1976.

Smeeton, (Vice-Adm.) M.R. "Oceans to Defend." *Survival* 5 (May/June 1963): 131-134.

Sokol, Anthony. *Sea Powers in the Nuclear Age.* Washington, D.C.: Public Affairs Press, 1961.

Swartztrauber, Sayre A. "The Potential Battle of the Atlantic." *U.S. Naval Institute Proceedings* 105 (May 1979): 108-125.

Train, Harry D. "The Growing Soviet Naval Menace." *Atlantic Community Quarterly* 19 (Spring 1981): 50-62.

―――. "NATO's Maritime Increased Challenges." *Studia Diplomatica* (Brussels) 36 (No. 6, 1980): 647-662.

Underwood, (LCDR.) G.L. "Soviet Threat to the Atlantic Sea Lines of Communication: Lessons Learned from the German Capture of Norway in 1940." *Naval War College Review* 34 (May-June 1981): 43-47.

van Dem, (Capt., Ret.) Nico. "Joint Surveillance of Northern Coastline." *Interavia* 35 (January 1980): 38-39.

Wall, Patrick. "A Maritime or Continental Strategy?" *Sea Power* 22 (April 1979): 17-21.

Wegener, Edward. "A Baltic Squadron for NATO?" *U.S. Naval Institute Proceedings* (January 1974): 63-70.

Wettern, Desmond. "Replenishment at Sea and Fleet Support." *Navy International* 84 (January 1979): 29-35.

Wood, Derek. "Control of the Eastern Seaways." *Interavia* 35 (January 1980): 44-46.

NUCLEAR TACTICS, STRATEGY AND DOCTRINE

Allen, Lew. "The Strategic Nuclear Scene." *Vital Speeches of the Day* (1 Jan. 1979): 185-188.

Armstrong, (Lt. Col.) Alan P. "Nuclear Weapons and NATO." *Military Review* 40 (May 1980): 11-17.

Aron, Raymond. "The American Atomic Monopoly and Europe." *Atlantic Community Quarterly* 1 (March 1963): 42-44.

―――. *The Great Debate: Theories of Nuclear Strategy.* Garden City: Doubleday, 1965.

Ball, George W. "The Nuclear Deterrent and the Atlantic Alliance." *Atlantic Community Quarterly* 1 (Summer 1963): 199-204.

Beaufre, (Gen.) Andre. "The Sharing of Nuclear Responsibilities--A Problem in Need of Solution." *International Affairs* 41 (July 1965): 411-419.

Bennett, W.S.; Sandoval, R.R.; and Shreffler, R.G. "A Credible Nuclear-Emphasis Defense for NATO." *Orbis* 17 (Summer 1973): 463-479.

Beres, Louis Rene. "Tilting Toward Thanatos: America's 'Countervailing' Nuclear Strategy." *World Politics* (Princeton) 34 (October 1981): 25-46.

Berry, F. Clifton, Jr. "Pershing II: First Step in NATO Theatre Nuclear Force Modernization?" *International Defense Review* 12 (No. 8, 1979): 1303-1308.

Bertram, Christoph. "The Implications of Theater Nuclear Weapons in Europe." *Foreign Affairs* 60 (Winter 1981/1982): 305-326.

Blackett, P.M.S. *Atomic Weapons and East-West Relations.* Cambridge University Press, 1956.

———. "Nuclear Weapons and Defense: Comments on Kissinger, Kennan and King-Hall." *International Affairs* 34 (October 1958): 421-434.

Bonnert, Frederick. "Eurostrategy-Theatre Nuclear Weapons." *NATO's Fifteen Nations* 25 (April-May 1980): 48-49+.

Brenner, Michael J. "Tactical Nuclear Strategy and European Defence: A Critical Reappraisal." *International Affairs* (London) 51 (January 1975): 23-42.

Brodie, Bernard. "The Atom Bomb as Policy Maker." *Foreign Affairs* 27 (October 1948): 17-33.

———. "Nuclear Weapons: Strategic or Tactical." *Foreign Affairs* 32 (January 1954): 217-229.

———. *Escalation and the Nuclear Option.* Princeton, NJ: Princeton University Press, 1966.

Brooks, (Capt.) Linton F. "Tactical Nuclear Weapons: The Forgotten Facet of Naval Warfare." *U.S. Naval Institute Proceedings* 106 (January 1980): 28-33.

Brown, Harold. "Strategic Military Balance." *Asian Defense Journal* 5 (September-October 1980): 131+.

Brown, Neville. *Nuclear War: The Impending Strategic Deadlock.* New York: Praeger, 1965.

———. "Towards the Super-Power Deadlock." *The World Today* 22 (September 1966): 366-374.

―――. "Towards the Super-Power Deadlock." *The World Today* 22 (September 1966): 366-374.

Brown, (Maj.) William D. "Whatever Happened to ... Tactical Nuclear Warfare." *Military Review* 60 (January 1980): 46-53.

Buchan, Alastair. "The Multilateral Force--A Study in Alliance Politics." *International Affairs* 40 (October 1964): 619-637.

Bull, Hedley. "Limited and Nuclear War." *Survival* 5 (March/April 1963): 54-57.

Bundy, McGeorge; Kennan, George F.; McNamara, Robert S.; and Smith, Gerard. "Nuclear Weapons and the Atlantic Alliance." *Foreign Affairs* 60 (Summer 1982): 753-768.

Burns, Arthur Lee. *Ethics and Deterrence: A Nuclear Balance Without Hostage Cities?* (Adelphi Paper No. 69). London: The International Institute for Strategic Studies, 1970.

Burt, Richard R. "The Alliance of a Crossroad [Emphasis on the Nuclear Debate in Europe and the Position of the North Atlantic Treaty Organization]." *Department of State Bulletin* 82 (February 1982): 42-45.

Buteux, Paul. "Theatre Nuclear Weapons and European Security." *Canadian Journal of Political Science (Ont.)* 10 (December 1977): 781-808.

Buzzard, (Rear Adm.) Anthony; Slessor, John; and Lowenthal, Richard. "The H-Bomb: Massive Retaliation or Graduated Deterrence?" *International Affairs* 32 (April 1956): 148-165.

Buzzell, (Maj.) Calvin A., and Rose, John P. (Maj.). "New Concept for Battlefield Employment of Nuclear Weapons." *Military Review* 61 (August 1981): 64-73.

Chandler, (Lt. Col.) Robert W. "Political Sufficiency of Nuclear Forces." *Air University Review* 31 (September-October 1980): 61-69.

Coffey, J.I. "A NATO Nuclear Deterrent?" *Orbis* 8 (Summer 1965): 584-594.

Cohen, Samuel T. "Tactical Nuclear Weapons and U.S. Military Strategy." *Orbis* 15 (Spring 1971): 178-193.

―――, and Lyons, W.C. "A Comparison of U.S.-Allied and Soviet Tactical Nuclear Force Capabilities and Policies." *Orbis* 19 (Spring 1975): 72-92.

―――. "Whither the Neutron Bomb? A Moral Defense of Nuclear Radiation Weapons." *Parameters* 11 (June 1981): 19-27.

"Collective Use of Nuclear Weapons--A Symposium." *Atlantic Community Quarterly* 4 (Spring 1966): 66-72.

Cordesman, Anthony H. "NATO's Long-range Theater Nuclear Forces: Europe's Quiet Profile in Courage." *Armed Forces Journal International* 118 (June 1981): 38-47.

Cotter, Donald R. "NATO Theater Nuclear Forces: An Enveloping Military Concept." *Strategic Review* 9 (Spring 1981): 44-53.

Cottrell, Alvin J., and Dougherty, James E. "Nuclear Weapons, Policy and Strategy." *Orbis* 1 (Summer 1957): 138-160.

"Currie Says Excessive Duplication Harms NATO; 100 Tactical Missiles in NATO Cited." *Defense Space Business Daily* (23 April 1975): 25.

Davidson, Charles N. "Tactical Nuclear Defense--The West German View." *Parameters* 4 (No. 1, 1974): 47-57.

Davis, Lynn Etheridge. *Limited Nuclear Options: Deterrence and the New American Doctrine*. (Adelphi Paper No. 121). London: The International Institute of Strategic Studies, 1975-1976.

Davis, Paul C. "A European Nuclear Force: Utility and Prospects." *Orbis* 17 (Spring 1973): 110-131.

de Rose, Francois. "Atlantic Relationships and Nuclear Problems." *Foreign Affairs* 41 (April 1963): 479-490.

De Vries, Klass G. "Responding to the SS-20: An Alternative Approach." *Survival* 21 (November/December 1979): 251-255.

Douglass, Joseph D. "NATO Theater Nuclear Modernization." *International Security Review* 5 (Spring 1980): 57-71.

Dupuy, T.N. "Can America Fight a Limited Nuclear War?" *Orbis* 5 (Spring 1961): 31-42.

Dyer, (Lt. Col.) Philip W. "Will Tactical Nuclear Weapons Ever Be Used?" *Political Science Quarterly* (June 1973): 214-229.

----------. "The Moral Dimensions of Tactical Nuclear Weapons in Europe." *Parameters* 10 (June 1980): 44-50.

Emmet, Christopher. "The U.S. Plan for a NATO Nuclear Deterrent." *Orbis* 7 (Summer 1963): 265-277.

Enthoven, Alain C. "American Deterrent Policy." *Survival* 5 (May/June 1963): 94-101.

Fair, (Col.) Stanley D. "A Tactical Nuclear Strategy for NATO." *NATO's Fifteen Nations* 19 (April-May 1974): 59-61.

"Final Communique of the Nuclear Planning Group." *NATO's Fifteen Nations* 24 (June-July 1979): 110-112.

Fortson, (Capt.) Thomas E. *Seaborne Multilateral Force: Mixed Manning.* (Professional Study No. 4336). Maxwell AFB, AL: Air War College, 1971.

———. "NATO's Theater Nuclear Dilemma: A New Set of Crucial Choices." *Armed Forces Journal International* (January 1979): 16-23.

Freedman, Lawrence. *The Evolution of Nuclear Strategy.* New York: St. Martin's, 1981.

Galen, Justin (pseud.). "Can NATO Meet Its Toughest Test? Strategic and Theater Nuclear Forces for the 1980s." *Armed Forces Journal* 117 (November 1979): 49-56+.

Gallois, (Gen.) Pierre. *The Balance of Terror: Strategy for the Nuclear Age.* Boston: Houghton Mifflin Co., 1961.

Gans, Daniel. "Neutron Weapons: Solution to a Surprise Attack?" *Military Review* 62 (Jan/Feb 1982): 19-37, 55-73.

Gareau, Frederick H. "Nuclear Deterrence: A Discussion of the Doctrine." *Orbis* 5 (Summer 1961): 182-197.

Garn, (Sen.) Jake. "Exploitable Strategic Nuclear Superiority." *International Security Review* 5 (Summer 1980): 173-192.

Geneste, (Lt. Col.) Marc E. "A Common Western Nuclear Doctrine." *Military Review* 51 (September 1971): 3-12.

Geritz, (RADM) E.P. "Theatre Nuclear Force Modernization." *RUSI Journal for Defense Studies* 125 (September 1980): 3-10.

Gladwyn, Lord. "Nuclear Weapons and Europe." *Survival* 16 (March/April 1974): 94-95.

Golden, James R.; Clark, Asa A.; and Arlinghaus, Bruce E. *Conventional Deterrence: Alternatives for European Defense.* Lexington, MA: Lexington Books, 1984.

Goodman, Elliot B. "Five Nuclear Options for the West." *Atlantic Community Quarterly* 2 (Winter 1964-65): 571-587.

Goodman, Elliot R. "The Duynstee Plan." *Atlantic Community Quarterly* 3 (Fall 1965): 340-346.

Gordon Walker, Patrick. "Voices in Opposition--to the MLF." *Survival* 6 (January/February 1964): 24-25.

Gormley, Dennis M. "NATO's Tactical Nuclear Option: Past, Present and Future." *Military Review* 53 (September 1973): 3-18.

Gray, Colin S. "Mini-Nukes and Strategy." *International Journal* 29 (Spring 1974): 216-241.

———. "Deterrence and Defense in Europe: Revising NATO Theater Nuclear Posture." *Strategic Review* 3 (Spring 1975): 58-69.

———. "Theater Nuclear Weapons: Doctrines and Postures." *World Politics* 28 (January 1976): 300-314.

———. "NATO Strategy and the 'Neutron Bomb.'" *Policy Review* (Winter 1979): 7-26.

———. "Targetting Problems for Central War." *Naval War College Review* 33 (January-February 1980): 3-21.

Green, Philip. *Deadly Logic: The Theory of Nuclear Deterrence.* Columbus: Ohio State University Press, 1966.

Greenwood, Ted, and Nacht, Michael L. "The New Nuclear Debate: Sense or Nonsense?" *Foreign Affairs* 52 (July 1974): 761-780.

Gromley, Dennis M. "NATO's Tactical Nuclear Option: Past, Present and Future." *Military Review* 53 (September 1973): 3-18.

Gueritz, (Rear Adm.) E.F. "Theatre Nuclear Force Modernization. (Report of a Seminar Held at RUSI, February 12, 1980)." *RUSI Journal for Defence Studies* 125 (September 1980): 3-10.

Guertner, Gary L. "Nuclear War in Suburbia [Soviet and North Atlantic Treaty Organization Strategies for a European War]." *Orbis* 26 (Spring 1982): 49-69.

Hahn, Walter F. "Nuclear Balance in Europe." *Foreign Affairs* 50 (April 1972): 501-516.

———. "Nuclear Mid-Range Systems and the NATO Confidence Gap." *Strategic Review* 7 (Spring 1979): 8-10.

———. "NATO and New Missiles." *Strategic Review* 8 (Winter 1980): 9-10.

Hannig, (Lt. Col., Ret.) Norbert. "NATO Theater Nuclear Force Modernization—A Military Necessity?" *Armada International* 5 (July-August 1981): 34-35+.

Heisenberg, Wolfgang. *The Alliance and Europe: Part I—Crisis Stability in Europe and Theatre Nuclear Weapons.* (Adelphi Paper No. 96). London: The International Institute for Strategic Studies, 1973.

Heymont, Irving. "The NATO Nuclear Bilateral Forces." *Orbis* 9 (Winter 1966): 1025-1041.

Hill, Andrew W. "Neutron Bomb Options." *National Defense* (Jan-Feb 1979): 34-37.

Hinterhoff, (Maj.) E. "NATO's Nuclear Strategy." *NATO's Fifteen Nations* 15 (October-November 1970): 42-48.

Hodgkinson, (Lt. Col.) Richard L. "USAF and Theater Nuclear Warfare: A Proposal." *Air University Review* 32 (September-October 1981): 89-97.

Holifield, Chet. "Nuclear Control in NATO." *Atlantic Community Quarterly* 3 (Winter 1965-66): 496-498.

Holst, Johan J., and Nerlich, Uwe. *Beyond Nuclear Deterrence: New Aims, New Arms.* New York: Crane, Russak, 1977.

Ikle, Fred Charles. "NATO's First Nuclear Use: A Deepening Trap?" *Strategic Review* 8 (Winter 1980): 18-23.

International Institute for Strategic Studies. "The Balance of Theatre Nuclear Forces in Europe." *Air Force Magazine* 63 (December 1980): 125-127.

Joshua, Wynfred. *Nuclear Weapons and the Atlantic Alliance.* New York: National Strategy Information Center, Inc., 1973.

―――, and Hahn, Walter F. *Nuclear Politics: America, France and Britain.* (The Washington Paper No. 9). Beverly Hills, CA: Sage Publications, 1973.

Kahn, Herman. *On Thermonuclear War.* Princeton, NJ: Princeton University Press, 1960.

―――; Fromm, Erich; and Maccoby, Michael. "A Debate on the Question of Civil Defense." *Survival* 4 (March/April 1962): 50-67.

Kaplan, Fred. "Warring over New Missiles for NATO." *New York Times Magazine* (December 9, 1979): 46ff.

Karber, Phillip A. "Nuclear Weapons and 'Flexible Response.'" *Orbis* 14 (Summer 1970): 284-297.

Keeny, Spurgeon M., Jr. and Panofsky, Wolfgang K.H. "MAD [Mutually Assured Destruction] Versus NUTS [Nuclear Utilization Target Selection]: Can Doctrine or Weaponry Remedy the Mutual Hostage Relationship of the Super Powers?" *Foreign Affairs* 60 (Winter 1981/1982): 287-304.

Kelleher, Catherine McArdle. "The Present as Prologue: Europe and Theater Nuclear Modernization." *International Security* 5 (Spring 1981): 150-168.

King, James E., Jr. "Nuclear Plenty and Limited War." *Foreign Affairs* 35 (January 1957): 238-256.

Kintner, William R. and Possony, Stefan T. "NATO's Nuclear Crisis." *Orbis* 6 (Summer 1962): 217-243.

Kissinger, Henry A. "Missiles and the Western Alliance." *Foreign Affairs* 36 (April 1958): 383-400.

Knorr, Klaus. *A NATO Nuclear Force: The Problem of Management.* (Policy Memorandum No. 26). Princeton, NJ: Center of International Studies, Woodrow Wilson School of Public and International Affairs, Princeton University, 1963.

―――. *NATO and the Nuclear Policy.* Washington, D.C.: Center for Strategic Studies, Georgetown University, 1964.

Kondracke, Morton. "Henry's Nuclear Agenda." *The New Republic* (15 September 1979): 16-18.

Korb, Lawrence J. "The Question of Deploying U.S. Theater Nuclear Weapons in Europe." *Naval War College Review* 33 (May-June 1980): 99-105.

Krehbel, (Capt.) Carl C. "Military Asymmetrics in the Soviet-American Strategic Balance." *RUSI Journal for Defense Studies* 125 (June 1980): 24-32.

La Roeque, Gene R. "Can We Avoid Nuclear War?" *Graduate Woman* 76 (May/June 1982): 18-20.

La Roeque, (Rear Adm.) Gene R. and others. "The Race to Nuclear War: Three Statements." *Defense Monitor* 9 (No. 6, 1980): entire issue.

Lautenschlager, Karl. "Theater Nuclear Forces and Grey Area Weapons." *Naval War College Review* 33 (September-October 1980): 13-22.

Lehman, John F. "The Soviet Strategic Advantage and How to Eliminate It." *International Security Review* 5 (Fall 1980): 271-285.

Leitenberg, Milton. "Presidential Directive (P.D.) 59: United States Nuclear Weapon Targeting Policy." *Journal of Peace Research* 18 (No. 4, 1981): 309-317.

Mandelbaum, Michael. "The Bomb, Dread and Eternity." *International Security* 5 (Fall 1980): 3-23.

Marriott, John. "The Development of NATO's Nuclear Potential 1949/74." *NATO's Fifteen Nations* 19 (February-March 1974): 39-44.

―――. "Tactical Nuclear Weapons." *Army Quarterly* 108 (April 1978): 142-148.

Martin, J.J. "Nuclear Weapons in NATO's Deterrent Strategy." *Orbis* 22 (Winter 1979): 875-895.

Martin, Laurence W. *Ballistic Missile Defense and the Alliance.* Paris: Atlantic Institute, 1969.

———. "Ballistic Missile Defense: The Great Debate." *Survival* 11 (August 1969).

Martin, Lawrence. "Theater Nuclear Weapons and Europe." *Survival* 16 (November/December 1974): 268-276.

McKinney, (Maj.) William R. "Tactical Nuclear Weapons: The Practical Side." *Military Review* 61 (October 1981): 60-65.

Menaul, (Air Vice-Marshal) S.W.B. "The Use of Nuclear Weapons in the European Theatre." *NATO's Fifteen Nations* (April-May 1975).

Miksche, (Lieut.-Col.) F.O. *Atomic Weapons and Armies.* New York: Praeger, 1955.

———. "The Case for Nuclear Sharing." *Orbis* 5 (Fall 1961): 292-305.

Millett, Stephen M. "The Moral Dilemma of Nuclear Deterrence." *Parameters* 10 (March 1980): 33-38.

Moore, Robert A. "Theatre Nuclear Forces--Thinking the Unthinkable." *International Defense Review* 14 (No. 4, 1981): 401-408.

Morgan, Michael. "NATO's Nuclear Debate." *Defense and Foreign Affairs* 8, Number 2 (1980): 15ff.

Mulley, Frederick W. "NATO's Nuclear Problems: Control or Consultation." *Orbis* 8 (Spring 1964): 21ff.

Nacht, Michael L. "The Delicate Balance of Error." *Foreign Policy* 19 (Summer 1975): 163-177.

"NATO Agrees to Deploy 572 New Long-Range Nucs." *Armed Forces Journal* 117 (January 1980): 38.

"NATO Nuclear Planning Group Communique, 25 April 1979." *NATO Review* 27 (June 1979): 31.

"NATO's Nuclear Missile Plans." *Flight International* 116 (November 10, 1979): 1553.

"NATO, Nuclear Weapons, and the Death of Detente." *Defense Monitor* 9 (March 1980): entire issue.

"NATO Strategic Counterforce." *Aviation Week* 111 (September 3, 1979): 66-67.

"NATO and Theater Nuclear Forces: Continued Tokenism, Inadequacy, and Indecision." *Armed Forces Journal* 116 (March 1979): 29.

Nerlich, Uwe. *The Alliance and Europe: Part V: Nuclear Weapons and East-West Negotiation.* (Adelphi Paper No. 120). London: International Institute for Strategic Studies, 1975-1976.

Neuman, H.J. *Nuclear Weapons for Western Europe.* The Hague: Netherlands Institute for Peace Questions, November 1974.

Nixon, Richard. "Ballistic Missile Defence." *Survival* 11 (May 1969): 146-149.

Norstad, (Gen.) Lauris. "NATO as the Fourth Atomic Power." *Survival* 2 (May/June 1960): 107.

———. "A Problem of the Alliance." *Atlantic Community Quarterly* 4 (Spring 1966): 57-65.

Norton, Augustus R. "NATO and Metaphors: The Nuclear Threshold." *Naval War College Review* (Fall 1977): 60-75.

"Nuclear Support for NATO: Commentary on the North Atlantic Council Meeting, Athens, May 1962." *Survival* 4 (July/August 1962): 184-185.

"Nuclear War in Europe: Causes, Combat, Consequences, and How to Avoid It." *Defense Monitor* 7 (1981): entire issue.

Nunn, (Maj.) Jack H. "Termination: The Myth of the Short, Decisive Nuclear War." *Parameters* 10 (December 1980): 36-41.

Osgood, Robert E. *The Case of the MLF.* Washington, D.C.: The Washington Center of Foreign Policy Research, 1964.

Otten, Alan L. "Europe and the U.S. 'Umbrella.'" *Wall Street Journal* 194 (August 1979): 18.

Payne, Keith B. *Nuclear Deterrence in U.S.-Soviet Relations.* Boulder, CO: Westview Press, 1982.

———. and Pickett. "Vulnerability Is Not an Adequate Strategy [Considers the Effect of Presidential Directive 59 on the Overall Strategic Defense Posture]." *Military Review* 61 (October 1981): 66-72.

Pierre, Andrew J. "Nuclear Diplomacy: Britain, France and America." *Foreign Affairs* 49 (January 1971): 283-301.

Polk, James H. "The Realities of Tactical Nuclear Warfare." *Orbis* 17 (Summer 1973): 439-447.

Possony, Stefan T. "Towards Nuclear Isolationism." *Orbis* 6 (Winter 1963): 623-644.

Powers, (Capt.) Robert C. "Flexible Response and External Force: A Contrast of U.S. and Soviet Strategies." *Strategic Review* 9 (Winter 1981): 52-60.

Ravenal, Earl C. "Counterforce and Alliance: The Ultimate Connection." *International Security* 6 (Spring 1982): 26-43.

Read, Thornton. "Nuclear Tactics for Defending a Border." *World Politics* 15 (April 1963): 390-402.

Record, Jeffrey. "To Nuke ot Not to Nuke: A Critique of Rationales for a Tactical Nuclear Defense of Europe." *Military Review* 54 (Octoner 1974): 3-13.

———. *U.S. Nuclear Weapons in Europe: Issues and Alternatives.* Washington, D.C.: Brookings Institution, 1974.

———. "U.S. Tactical Nuclear Weapons in Europe: 7,000 Warheads in Search of a Rationale." *Arms Control Today* 4 (1974): 1-2.

———. "Tactical Nuclear Weapons in Europe: Alternative Postures." *Survival* 17 (March/April 1975): 73-80.

———. "Theatre Nuclear Weapons: Begging the Soviet Union to Pre-empt." *Survival* 19 (September/October 1977): 208-211.

Reinhardt, (Col.) G.C. and Kintner, (Lt. Col.) W.R. *Atomic Weapons in Land Combat.* Harrisburg, PA: Military Service Publishing Co., 1953.

Richardson, (Brig. Gen.) Robert C., III, Ret. "Can NATO Fashion a New Strategy?" *Orbis* 17 (Summer 1973): 415-438.

———. "NATO Nuclear Strategy: A Look Back." *Strategic Review* 9 (Spring 1981): 35-43.

Rosecrance, Richard N. *The Dispersion of Nuclear Weapons: Strategy and Politics.* New York: Columbia University Press, 1964.

———. *Strategic Deterrence Reconsidered.* (Adelphi Paper No. 116). London: International Institute for Strategic Studies, 1975.

Rusk, Dean. "MLF." *Survival* 5 (November/December 1963): 251-252.

Sabrosky, Alan Ned. "America in NATO: The Conventional Delusion." *Orbis* 25 (Summer 1981): 293-306.

Santilli, (Lt. Col.) Joseph, Jr. "NATO Strategy Updated: A First Use Policy." *Military Review* 54 (March 1974): 3-20.

Schelling, Thomas C. "Nuclear Strategy in Europe." *World Politics* 14 (April 1962): 421-432; *Survival* 4 (September/October 1962): 206-211.

Schilling, Warner R. "U.S. Strategic Nuclear Concepts in the 1970's: The Search for Sufficiently Equivalent Countervailing Parity." *International Security* 6 (Fall 1981): 48-79.

Schlesinger, James R. "The Theatre Nuclear Force Posture in Europe: Report to Congress by Secretary of Defense Schlesinger, 1975." *Survival* 17 (September/October 1975): 235-241.

Schwartz, David N. "The Role of Deterrence in NATO Defense Strategy: Implications for Doctrine and Posture." *World Politics* 28 (October 1975): 118-133.

Scoville, Herbert, Jr. "Flexible Madness." *Foreign Policy* 14 (Spring 1974): 164-177.

Secclak, (Col.) William E. "Artillery Fired Atomic Projectiles--A Field Artillery-man's Viewpoint." *Field Artillery Journal* 48 (March-April 1980): 7-12.

Seim, Harvey B. "Nuclear Policy-Making in NATO." *NATO Review* 21 (No. 6, 1973): 11-13.

Shearer, Richard E. "Consulting in NATO on Nuclear Policy." *NATO Review* 27 (October 1979): 25-27.

Should the West Promise Never to Be the First to Use Nuclear Weapons? The Hague: Netherlands Institute for Peace Questions, 1974.

Shreffler, R.G. "The Neutron Bomb for NATO Defense: An Alternative." *Orbis* 21 (Winter 1978): 959-973.

Sinnreich, Richard H. "NATO's Doctrinal Dilemma." *Orbis* 19 (Summer 1975): 461-476.

Slessor, Sir John. "Control of Nuclear Strategy." *Foreign Affairs* 42 (October 1963): 96-106.

----------. "Multilateral or Multinational: An Alternative to the MLF." *Atlantic Community Quarterly* 2 (Summer 1964): 285-291.

----------. *NATO Nuclear Strategy--Some Lessons from History.* (Advanced Study Paper No. 1). Washington, D.C.: Center for Strategic Studies, Georgetown University, 1964.

----------. "Atlantic Nuclear Policy." *International Journal* 20 (Spring 1965): 143-157.

Spaak, Paul-Henri. "The Atom Bomb and NATO." *Foreign Affairs* 33 (April 1955): 353-359.

Stanley, Timothy W. "Decentralizing Nuclear Control in NATO." *Orbis* 7 (Spring 1963).

Steinhoff, Johannes. "The Nuclear Dilemma." *NATO's Fifteen Nations* 24 (1979): 110.

Struck, Myra. "Theater Nuclear Forces: Europe's New Maginot Line." *SAIS* (School of Advanced International Studies, Johns Hopkins University) *Review* (Summer 1981): 113-129.

Treverton, Gregory F. "Nuclear Weapons and the 'Gray Area.'" *Foreign Affairs* 57 (Summer 1979): 1075-1089.

Tucker, Robert C. *Proposal for No First Use of Nuclear Weapons: Pros and Cons.* Princeton, NJ: Center of International Studies, Woodrow Wilson School of Public & International Affairs, Princeton University, 1963.

"UK/NATO Nuclear Options for the 1980s." *International Defense Review* 12 (No. 9, 1979): 1487-1488.

Ullman, Richard H. "No First Use of Nuclear Weapons." *Foreign Affairs* 50 (July 1972): 669-683.

United States Congress. House Committee on Foreign Affairs. Subcommittee on Europe and the Middle East. *The Modernization of NATO's Long-range Theater Nuclear Forces: Report, December 31, 1980.* 96th Congress, 2nd Session, 1980.

United States Department of the Army. *Nuclear Weapons and NATO: Analytical Survey of Literature.* Washington, D.C.: Government Printing Office, 1975.

United States. Department of State. "The Alliance at a Crossroad [Emphasis on the Nuclear Debate in Europe and the Position of the North Atlantic Treaty Organization]." *Department of State Bulletin* 82 (Fall 1982): 42-45.

Utgoff, Victor. "In Defense of Counterforce." *International Security* 6 (Spring 1982): 44-60.

Van Veen, E. "Theatre Air Forces and Tactical Nuclear Weapons." *NATO's Fifteen Nations* 17 (August-September 1972): 34-39.

Williams, Alan Lee. "Is a European Nuclear Force Desirable?" *Atlantic Community Quarterly* 10 (Summer 1972): 185-187.

Wohlstetter, Albert. "The Delicate Balance of Terror." *Foreign Affairs* 37 (January 1959): 211-234.

Worner, Manfred. "NATO Defenses and Tactical Nuclear Weapons." *Strategic Review* 5 (Fall 1977): 11-18.

ALLIANCE POLITICS

ALLIANCES IN WORLD POLITICS

Atkeson, (Maj. Gen.) Edward B. "When Turfs Overlap: A Study of Organizations in Collision." *Army* 30 (November 1980): 38-43.

Beer, Francis A., ed. *Alliances: Latent War Communities in the Contemporary World.* New York: Holt, Rinehart and Winston, 1970.

———. *The Political Economy of Alliances: Benefits, Costs and Institutions in NATO.* Beverly Hills, CA: Sage Publications, 1972.

Deutsch, Karl W., et al. *Political Community and the North Atlantic Area: International Organization in the Light of Historical Experience.* Westport, CT: Greenwood Press, reprint of 1957 ed.

Fromkin, David. "Entangling Alliances." *Foreign Affairs* 48 (July 1970): 688-700.

Gasteyger, Curt. "End or Reform of the Alliances?" *Survival* 8 (August 1966): 251-255.

Hahn, Walter F. "Does NATO Have a Future?" *International Security Review* 5 (Summer 1980): 151-172.

Hoffman, Stanley. "The Western Alliance: Drift or Harmony?" *International Security* 6 (Fall 1981): 105-125.

Lippmann, Walter. *Isolation and Alliances: An American Speaks to the British.* Boston: Atlantic (Little, Brown), 1952.

Liska, George. *Nations in Alliance: The Limits of Interdependence.* Baltimore: Johns Hopkins Press, 1962.

———. *Europe Ascendant: The International Politics of Unification.* Baltimore: Johns Hopkins Press, 1964.

Munk, Frank. *Atlantic Dilemma, Partnership or Community.* Dobbs Ferry, NY: Oceana Publications, 1964.

Neustadt, Richard E. *Alliance Politics.* New York: Columbia University Press, 1970.

O'Leary, James P. "Can NATO Survive Eurocommunism?" *International Security Review* 5 (Spring 1980): 73-90.

Osgood, Robert E. *Alliances and American Foreign Policy.* Baltimore: Johns Hopkins Press, 1968.

Perazic, Professor Gavro. "The International Legal Implications of Membership in Military Alliance." *Review of International Affairs* (20 Dec. 1978): 24.

Rosecrance, Richard, ed. *The Future of the International Strategic System.* London and San Francisco: Chandler Publishing Co., 1972.

Sandler, Todd, and Cauley, Jon. "On the Economic Theory of Alliances." *Journal of Conflict Resolution* 19 (June 1975): 330-348.

Train, (Adm.) Harry D., II. "Preserving the Atlantic Alliance." *U.S. Naval Institute Proceedings* 107 (January 1981): 24-28.

Treires, James J. "Making Sense Out of National Defense." *Graduate Woman* 76 (May/June 1982): 12-17.

Treverton, Gregory F. "Global Threats and Trans-Atlantic Allies." *International Security* 5 (Fall 1980): 142-158.

Wolfers, Arnold, ed. *Alliance Policy in the Cold War.* Baltimore: Johns Hopkins Press, 1959.

INTERNATIONAL RELATIONS OF NATO

Allen, Richard V. "The Atlantic Alliance at a Crossroad." *Strategic Review* 9 (Fall 1981): 9-14.

Atlantic Council of the U.S. *The Common Security Interests of Japan, the United States, and NATO.* Cambridge, MA: Ballinger Publishers, Inc., 1981.

"Austria and the Berlin Conference." *The World Today* 10 (April 1954): 149-157.

"Austria: East or West?" *The World Today* 4 (August 1948): 346-353.

Ball, M. Margaret. *NATO and the European Union Movement.* Westport, CT: Greenwood Press, 1974.

Barlow, Jeffrey G. "Western Europe and the NATO Alliance." *Journal of Social and Political Studies* 4 (Spring 1979): 3-15.

Barman, Thomas. "Britain, France and West Germany: The Changing Pattern of Their Relationship in West Germany." *International Affairs* 46 (April 1970).

Belfiglio, V.J. "The Strategic Importance of the Cape Sea Route." *International Problems* (Tel Aviv) 19 (Fall 1980): 32-39.

Birnbaum, Karl E. "The Nordic Countries and European Security." *Co-operation and Conflict* 3 (1968): 1-17.

Bolton, David. "European Defense: The Underlying Trends." *RUSI Journal* 119 (June 1974): 63-66.

Brosio, Manlio. "Will NATO Survive Detente?" *Atlantic Community Quarterly* 9 (Summer 1971): 143-155.

Cicco, John A., Jr. "The Atlantic Alliance and the Arab Challenge: The European Perspective." *World Affairs* 137 (Spring 1975): 303-325.

Coughran, Joe F. "Middle East Oil: Achilles' Heel of NATO." (Research Study). Maxwell AFB, AL: Air Command and Staff College, 1974.

Critchley, Julian. *The North Atlantic Alliance and the Soviet Union in the 1980's*. London: Macmillan, 1982.

"Cyprus and the NATO Intervention." *The World Today* 14 (July 1958): 277-279.

"Cyprus: Conflict and Reconciliation." *The World Today* 15 (April 1959): 137-146.

Ellsworth, Robert F. "Reagan and NATO." *Armed Forces Journal International* 118 (January 1981): 29-30.

Fernsworth, Lawrence. "Spain in Western Defense." *Foreign Affairs* 31 (July 1953): 648-662.

Foster, Charles R. "Political-Military Factors in the Atlantic Relationships: Outlook Under Reagan." *Atlantic Community Quarterly* 19 (Fall 1981): 304-311.

Freymond, Jacques. "The European Neutrals and the Atlantic Community." *International Organisation* 17 (Summer 1963): 592-609.

Galen, Justin (pseud.). "NATO's National Opportunities: France and the Iberian Peninsula." *Armed Forces Journal International* 116 (April 1979): 37-45.

Gaustad, Peter J. "Swedish Neutrality: Its Impact on NATO." *Military Review* 54 (April 1974): 46-53.

Gervase, Sean. "Under the NATO Umbrella." *Africa Report* 21 (September-October 1976): 12-16.

Griffith, William E. *The Superpowers and Regional Tensions: The USSR, The United States and Europe.* Lexington, MA: Lexington Books, 1982.

Grosser, Alfred. "France and Germany: Less Divergent Outlooks?" *Foreign Affairs* 48 (January 1970): 235-244.

Hartman, Arthur A., and Davis, Rodger P. "The Impact of the Middle East Crisis on the Atlantic Alliance." *The Department of State Bulletin* 70 (18 March 1974): 279-284.

Hinterhoff, (Maj.) E. "NATO and Spain." *NATO's Fifteen Nations* 15 (April-May 1970): 66-70.

Hyland, William G. "The USSR and the Western Alliance." *Atlantic Community Quarterly* 19 (Fall 1981): 312-330.

Kane, Pamela, and Dulin, (1st Lt.) Carol. "Joined Hands Across the Sea." *National Guard* 34 (October 1980): 20-27.

Kaplan, Lawrence S. "NATO and Adenauer's Germany: Uneasy Partnership." *International Organisation* 15 (Autumn 1961): 618-629.

Keatinge, Patrick. "Odd Man Out? Irish Neutrality and European Security." *International Affairs* 48 (July 1972): 438-449.

Lambropoulos, P. "Cyprus, NATO and the Greek Future." *The Nation* 219 (28 September 1974): 267-269.

Latour, Charles. "South Africa: NATO's Unwelcome Ally." *Military Review* 57 (February 1977): 84-93.

Luns, J.M. "NATO in the Present World Situations." *Studia Diplomatica* (Brussels) 33 (No. 6, 1980): 637-646.

MacDonald, Hugh. "The Western Alliance and the Polish Crisis." *World Today* (London) 38 (February 1982): 42-50.

Manderson-Jones, R.B. *The Special Relationship: Anglo-American Relations and Western European Unity 1947-1956.* New York: Crane, Russak, 1972.

Marriott, John. "MALTA and NATO." *NATO's Fifteen Nations* 15 (October-November 1970): 34-40.

Murray, A.H. "Should NATO Worry About the Scramble for Africa?" *NATO's Fifteen Nations* 17 (April-May 1972): 16-22.

Pauls, Rolf Friedemann. "The Widening Focus: Security Problems of the Eighties." *NATO's Fifteen Nations* 25 (October-November 1980): 18-20.

Price, Harry Bayard. *The Marshall Plan and Its Meaning.* Ithaca: Cornell University Press, 1955.

Rostow, Eugene V. "America, Europe, and the Middle East." *Commentary* 57 (February 1974): 40-55.

Rostow, Walt W. "Politico-Economic World Developments as They Affect NATO Nations in the 1970's." *Naval War College Review* 23 (April 1971): 4-13.

Salter, Sir Arthur. *The Meaning of the Marshall Plan Now.* London: Benn, 1948.

Sanchez-Gijon, Antonio. "Spain and the Atlantic Alliance." *Survival* 18 (November/December 1976): 248-253.

Schemmer, Benjamin F. "NATO's Challenge in the Persian Gulf and Middle East." *Armed Forces Journal International* 119 (November 1981): 34-35+.

Schumann, Maurice. "France and Germany in the New Europe." *Foreign Affairs* 41 (October 1962): 66-77.

Simes, Dimitri K. "The Death of Detente? [Some Effects of Russia's Intervention in Afghanistan]." *International Security* 5 (Summer 1980): 3-25.

Sorensen, Theodore C. "Why We Should Trade with the Soviets." *Foreign Affairs* 46 (April 1968): 575-583.

Stern, Geoffrey. "The Soviet Union, Afghanistan and East-West Relations." *Millenium* 9 (Autumn 1980): 135-146.

Stevens, (Col.) F.R. "Spain and NATO: Problems and Prospects." *Air University Review* 31 (March-April 1980): 2-14.

Sutton, Anthony C. *Western Technology and Soviet Economic Development, 1945-1965.* Stanford, CA: Hoover Institution Press, 1968.

Teicher, Howard. "The Soviet Union in Afghanistan: The Political-Military Costs." *Levicthen* (Boston) 3 (Fall 1980): 28-32.

Tower, (Sen.) John. "Challenges Facing the Atlantic Alliance." *RUSI Journal for Defense Studies* 126 (September 1981): 15-17.

Treverton, Gregory F. "Global Threats and Trans-Atlantic Allies." *International Security* 5 (Fall 1980): 142-158.

U.S. Congress. *East-West Relations in the Aftermath of Soviet Invasion of Afghanistan. The Western European Response: United States-Soviet Relations. Hearings Before the Committee on Foreign Affairs and Its Subcommittee on Europe and* the Middle East, House of Representatives, 96th Congress, 2nd Session, January 24 and 30. Washington, D.C.: U.S. Government Printing Office, 1980.

U.S. Congress. NATO After Afghanistan. Report to the Committee on Foreign Affairs and Subcommittee on Europe and the Middle East Prepared by Foreign Affairs and National Defense Division, Congressional Research Service, Library of Congress, 96th Congress, 2nd Session, 27 October 1980. Washington, D.C.: U.S. Government Printing Office, 1980.

U.S. Congress. Cyprus--1974. Hearings Before the Committee on Foreign Affairs and Its Subcommittee on Europe, House of Representatives, Ninety-Third Congress, Second Session, August 19 and 20th, 1974. Washington, D.C.: U.S. Government Printing Office, 1974.

U.S. Department of Defense, War College. Effects of the Middle East War and the Energy Crisis on the Future of the Atlantic Alliance. Proceedings, National Security Affairs Conference, July 1974 Panel VII. Washington, D.C.: National War College, February 1975.

U.S. Senate. Committee on Armed Services. Europe and the Middle East: Strains on Key Elements of America's Vital Interests: Report, April 23, 1982. 97th Congress, 2nd Session. Washington, D.C.: U.S. Government Printing Office, 1982.

van der Beugel, Ernst H. From Marshall Aid to Atlantic Partnership: European Integration as a Concern of American Foreign Policy. New York: Elsevier, 1966.

Vego, Milan. "Balkan Strategic Trends." Defense & Foreign Affairs Digest (December 1978): 8.

Wall, Patrick. "Is Europe Becoming Neutral?" Government Executive 13 (August 1981): 22-23.

Weiss, Seymour, and Adelman, Kenneth. "A Critical Phase in Trans-Atlantic Relations." Strategic Review 9 (Spring 1981): 24-31.

West, F.J., Jr. "NATO II: Common Boundaries for Common Interests." Naval War College Review 34 (January-February 1981): 59-67.

Whetten, Lawrence L. "Turkey and NATO's Second Front." Strategic Review 9 (Summer 1981): 57-64.

Whitaker, Arthur P. Spain and Defence of the West. New York: Harper for the Council on Foreign Relations, 1961.

———. "Spain and the Atlantic Alliance." *Orbis* 10 (Spring 1966): 42-78.

Wigforss, Harold. "Sweden and the Atlantic Pact." *International Organisation* 3 (August 1949): 434-443.

Windsor, Philip. "NATO and the Cyprus Crisis." (Adelphi Paper No. 14). London: I.S.S., 1964.

Wyllie, T.H. "Atlantic Relations: An Appreciation of the Crisis of 1980." *RUSI Journal for Defense Studies* 126 (September 1981): 17-21.

Zea, (Lt. Cmdr.) Antonio. "Should Spain Join NATO?" *Naval War College Review* 32 (November-December 1979): 78-87.

WARSAW PACT

GENERAL

Adomeit, Hannes. *Soviet Risk-Taking and Crisis Behavior: From Confrontation to Co-Existence?* (Adelphi Paper No. 101). London: International Institute for Strategic Studies, 1973.

―――. *Soviet Risk-Taking and Crisis Behavior: A Theoretical and Environmental Analysis.* London: Allen & Unwin, 1982.

Anderson, Alvin T. "The Soviets and Northern Europe." *World Politics* 4 (July 1952): 468-487.

Arbatov, G.A. "A Step Serving the Interests of Peace." *Survival* 14 (January/February 1972): 16-19.

―――. "On Soviet-American Relations." *Survival* 15 (May/June 1973): 124-130.

―――. "The American Strategic Debate: A Soviet View." *Survival* 16 (May/June 1974): 133-134.

Ascherson, Neal. "Poland's Place in Europe." *The World Today* 25 (December 1969): 520-529.

Aspaturian, Vernon V. "Moscow's Foreign Policy." *Survey* 65 (October 1967): 35-60.

―――. "Soviet Foreign Policy at the Crossroads: Conflict and/or Collaboration?" *International Organisation* 23 (Autumn 1969): 589-620.

Barghoorn, Frederick C. "The Soviet View of America." *Orbis* 2 (Spring 1958): 96-107.

Barnet, Richard J. "Initiative and Response in Soviet Foreign Policy." *World Politics* 16 (October 1963): 173-187.

Barrett, Raymond. "Geography and Soviet Strategic Thinking." *Military Review* (January 1970): 17-25.

Bender, Peter. "Inside the Warsaw Pact." *Survey* 74/75 (Winter/Spring 1970): 253-268.

―――. *East Europe in Search of Security*. Translated by S.F. Young. London: Cletto and Windus, 1972.

Berdal, Bivind. "The Projection of Soviet Military Power in the North; Margins of Western Safety in the Norwegian Sea and the North Atlantic Are Wearing Thin." *NATO's Fifteen Nations* 19 (February-March 1974): 58-64.

Bilen, I. "The Purposes of NATO." *World Marxist Review* 22 (June 1979): 45-50.

Billington, James H. "Force and Counterforce in Eastern Europe." *Foreign Affairs* 47 (October 1968): 26-35.

Birnbaum, Karl E. "Soviet Policy in Northern Europe." *Survival* 12 (July 1970): 227-232.

―――. "The Member States of the Warsaw Treaty Organisation and CSCE: Current Preoccupations and Expectations." *Co-operation and Conflict* 9 (1974): 29-34.

Bjol, Erling. "A Soviet View of Northern Europe." *Co-operation and Conflict* 2 (1967): 112-115.

Bloemer, Klaus. "East European Politics and Reunification." *Atlantic Community Quarterly* 5 (Summer 1967): 219-222.

Boychuck, Peter. "NATO Against Detente." *World Marxist Review* 20 (May 1977): 54-62.

Bregman, Alexander. "The Cold War in Retrospect: The Polish Question." *Survey* 58 (January 1966): 159-167.

Brezhnev, Leonid. "European Security: Soviet View." *Survival* 9 (June 1967): 174-176.

―――. *The Soviet View of NATO*. Washington, D.C.: U.S. Government Printing Office, 1967.

―――. *On the Policy of the Soviet Union and the International Situation*. Garden City, NY: Doubleday, 1973.

Bromke, Adam. "Ideology and National Interest in Soviet Foreign Policy." *International Journal* 22 (Autumn 1967): 547-562.

―――, and Rakowska-Harmstone, Teresa, eds. *The Communist States in Disarray, 1965-1971*. Minneapolis, MN: The University of Minnesota Press, 1972.

Brosio, Manlio. "Soviet Policy: Weakness, Yes, But Danger Too." *Atlantic Community Quarterly* 6 (Winter 1968/1969): 493-500.

General

Brown, Aurel. "The Evolution of the Warsaw Pact." *Canadian Defence Quarterly* 3 (Winter 1973/74): 27-36.

Brzezinski, Zbigniew K. "The Organization of the Communist Camp." *World Politics* 13 (January 1961): 175-209.

———. *The Soviet Bloc: Unity and Conflict*. Cambridge, MA: Harvard University Press, 1967.

Burt, (Lt. Col.) Donald L. *The Warsaw Treaty Organization: An Appraisal*. (Professional Study No. 4087). Maxwell AFB, AL: Air War College, 1971.

Bykov, Vladimir L. "The USSR and Security in Europe." *The Annals of the American Academy of Political and Social Science* (July 1974): 96-104.

Byrnes, Robert F. "Russia in Eastern Europe: Hegemony Without Security." *Foreign Affairs* 49 (July 1971): 682-697.

Caldwell, Lawrence T. *Soviet Attitude to SALT*. (Adelphi Paper No. 750). London: International Institute for Strategic Studies, 1971.

———. *Soviet-American Relations: One-Half Decade of Detente Problems and Issues*. (Atlantic Papers 1975, No. 5). Paris, France: Atlantic Institute for International Affairs, 1975.

———. "The Warsaw Pact: Directions of Change." *Problems of Communism* 24 (September/October 1975): 1-19.

———. *Soviet Security Interests in Europe and MFR*. (Research Paper No. 72). Santa Monica, CA: California Seminar on Arms Control and Foreign Policy, April 1976.

———, ed. *Soviet-American Relations in the 1980's: Superpower Politics and East-West Trade*. New York: McGraw-Hill, 1981.

"Call for a European Conference, March 1969." *Survival* 11 (May 1969): 159-161.

Campbell, John C. "Soviet Strategy in the Balkans." *Problems of Communism* 23 (July/August 1974): 1-16.

Caputo, (Maj.) Robert P. *The Future Effect of Nationalism on the Warsaw Pact: A Rumanian Case Study*. (Research Study). Maxwell AFB, AL: Air Command and Staff College, 1973.

Clemens, Walter C., Jr. "The Future of the Warsaw Pact." *Orbis* 11 (Winter 1968): 996-1033.

"Communique and Annexe." *Survival* 10 (February 1968): 62-64.

Conquest, Robert. *Russia After Khruschev*. New York: Praeger, 1965.

――――. "Stalin's Successors." *Foreign Affairs* 48 (April 1970): 509-524.

――――. "A New Russia? A New World?" *Foreign Affairs* 53 (April 1975): 482-497.

Constraints on European Security: The Soviet Factor. McLean, VA: Research Analysis Corp., May 1970.

Corry, J.A. *Soviet Russia and the Western Alliance.* Toronto: Canadian Institute of International Affairs, 1958.

Cottrell, Alvin J. "Soviet Views of U.S. Overseas Bases." *Orbis* 7 (Spring 1963): 77-95.

Crozier, Brian, ed. *European Security and the Soviet Problem.* London: Institute for the Study of Conflict, 1971.

"Czechoslovakia." *Survival* 10 (November 1968): 350-377.

Czerwinski, E.J., and Piekalkiewicz, J., eds. *The Soviet Invasion of Czechoslovakia: Its Effects on Eastern Europe.* New York: Praeger, 1972.

Dale, Reginald. "The Brezhnev Initiative: NATO Ponders the Kremlin's Surprise Proposal." *Atlas World Press Review* 26 (December 1979): 44.

Dallin, Alexander. *The Soviet Union, Arms Control and Disarmament.* New York: School of International Affairs, Columbia University, 1964.

――――, and Larson, Thomas B., eds. *Soviet Politics Since Khruschev.* Englewood Cliffs, NJ: Prentice-Hall, 1968.

Dallin, David J. *Soviet Foreign Policy After Stalin.* Philadelphia: Lippincott, 1961.

Daniels, Robert V. "Doctrine and Foreign Policy." *Survey* 57 (October 1965): 3-11.

"Declaration of Ministers of Foreign Affairs of Warsaw Pact." *Survival* 11 (December 1969): 394-395.

"Declaration of Strengthening Peace and Security in Europe." *Survival* 8 (September 1966): 289-293.

Degras, Jane. "The Communist Camp Ten Years After Stalin." *The World Today* 19 (March 1963): 108-115.

de Staercke, Andre. "Where Does the Atlantic Alliance Stand Today?" *Atlantic Community Quarterly* 11 (Winter 1973-74): 448-455.

"Detente and Peaceful Coexistence." *NATO Review* 19 (July/August 1971): 14-16.

General

Dodd, Thomas J. "If Co-Existence Fails: The Khruschev Visit Evaluated." *Orbis* 3 (Winter 1960): 393-423.

Douglas-Home, Charles. "Russians on the Move." *Survival* 11 (February 1969): 63-65.

Druks, Herbert. *Harry S. Truman and the Russians.* New York: Speller, 1966.

Duchacek, Ivo. "The Strategy of Communist Infiltration, Czechoslovakia, 1944-48." *World Politics* 2 (April 1950): 345-372.

──────. "The February Coup in Czechoslovakia." *World Politics* 2 (July 1950): 511-532.

Dunn, Keith A. "Power Projection or Influence: Soviet Capabilities for the 1980's." *Naval War College Review* 33 (September-October 1980): 31-47.

Dzirkals, Lilita, and Johnson, A. Ross, eds. *Soviet and Eastern European Forecasts of European Security: Papers from the 1972 Varna Conference.* Santa Monica, CA: Rand, June 1973.

Easterly, James. *Soviet Interests in Scandinavia: An Analysis of Soviet Foreign Policy Toward the Nordic States.* Norfolk: The Naval War College, 1974.

Edmonds, Robin. *Soviet Foreign Policy 1962-1973.* London: Oxford University Press, 1975.

Erickson, John. "Detente, Deterrence and Military 'Superiority': A Soviet Dilemma." *The World Today* 21 (August 1965): 337-346.

"European Security: An East German View." *Survival* 11 (November 1969): 357-358.

European Security and the Menace of West German Militarism. Prague: *Orbis* for the Institute for International Politics and Economics, 1962.

Fackenthall, (Maj.) James B. *The Warsaw Pact--A Two-Edged Sword.* (Research Study No. 0458-70). Maxwell AFB, AL: Air Command and Staff College, 1970.

Finlayson, Jack and Marantz, Paul. "Interdependence and East-West Relations." *Orbis* 26 (Spring 1982): 173-194.

Fischer-Galati, Stephen, ed. *Eastern Europe in the Sixties.* New York: Praeger, 1964.

Floyd, David. *Rumania: Russia's Dissident Ally.* New York: Praeger, 1965.

Gabelic, Andro. "New Accent in Soviet Strategy." *Survival* 10 (February 1968): 45-47.

Gallois, Pierre M. "The Soviet Global Threat and the West." *Orbis* 25 (Fall 1981): 649-662.

Garthoff, Raymond L. "The Concept of the Balance of Power in Soviet Policy Making." *World Politics* 4 (October 1951): 85-111.

Gasteyger, Curt. "Moscow and the Mediterranean." *Foreign Affairs* 46 (July 1968): 676-687.

Gehlen, Michael P. *The Politics of Co-Existence: Soviet Methods and Motives.* Bloomington, IN: Indiana University Press, 1967.

Goldman, Marshall I. "Economic Revolution in the Soviet Union." *Foreign Affairs* 45 (January 1967): 319-331.

Gomulka, Wladyslaw. "The Policy of the Polish People's Republic." *Foreign Affairs* 38 (April 1960): 402-418.

Goodman, Elliot R. "Detente: The Soviet View." *Survey* 70/71 (Winter/Spring 1969): 121-148.

Goure, Leon. "The U.S. 'Countervailing Strategy' in Soviet Perception [Effort to Emphasize the Nuclear War Aspects of United States Strategy]." *Strategic Review* 9 (Fall 1981): 51-64.

Griffith, William E. *The Superpowers and Regional Tensions: The USSR, the United States and Europe.* Lexington, MA: Lexington Books, 1982.

Griswold, Lawrence. "Warsaw Pact: The Brood of the Bear." *Sea Power* (April 1975): 27-32.

Gromyko, Anatolii A. *The International Situation and Soviet Foreign Policy.* Moscow: Novosti Press Agency, 1969.

―――. *Through Russian Eyes: President Kennedy's 1,036 Days.* Washington, D.C.: International Library, 1973.

Guk, S. "The 'Chinese Card' in NATO's Deck." *Soviet Military Review*, Number 11 (November 1980): 48-49.

Gundersen, H.F. Zeiner. "Soviet Power Build-up Decisive for U.S." *Atlantic Community Quarterly* 3 (Fall 1977): 337-338.

Haigh, Patricia. "Reflections on the Warsaw Pact." *The World Today* 24 (April 1968): 166-172.

Haines, C. Grove, ed. *The Threat of Soviet Imperialism.* Baltimore, MD: Johns Hopkins Press, 1954.

General

Hanak, H., ed. *Soviet Foreign Policy Since the Death of Stalin*. London: Routledge and Kegan Paul, 1972.

Hangen, Welles. *The Muted Revolution: East Germany's Challenge to Russia and the West*. New York: Knopf, 1966.

Harriman, W. Averell. *America and Russia in a Changing World*. Garden City, NY: Doubleday, 1971.

Hartman, Arthur A. "U.S.-Soviet Detente: Perceptions and Purposes." *Atlantic Community Quarterly* 12 (Fall 1974): 300-307.

Haselkorn, Avigdor. "The Soviet Collective Security System." *Orbis* 19 (Spring 1975): 231-254.

Hayter, William. *Russia and the World: A Study of Soviet Foreign Policy*. London: Secker and Warburg, 1970.

Hoffman, Stanley. "The Geopolitical Strategy of the East and the American Will and Capacity to Respond to It." *Studia Diplomatica* (Brussels) 33 (No. 3, 1980): 267-280.

Holloway, David. "The Warsaw Pact in the Era of Negotiation." *Military Review* 53 (July 1973): 49-55; and *Survival* 14 (November/December 1972): 275-279.

──────. *The Soviet Approach to MBFR*. Edinburgh: The University of Edinburgh, March 1975.

Holst, Johan Jorgen. "The Soviet Build-Up in the Northeast Atlantic." *NATO Review* 19 (September/October 1971): 21-23; and *Survival* 14 (January/February 1972): 25-28.

Hottelet, Richard C. "Khruschev's German Gambit." *Orbis* 3 (Spring 1959): 13-25.

How Did the Satellites Happen? A Study of the Soviet Seizure of Eastern Europe. London: Batchworth Press, 1952.

Humphrey, Hubert H. "The Course of Soviet Foreign Policy and Soviet-American Relations in the 1970's." *Orbis* 15 (Spring 1971): 65-71.

Hyland, William G. "The Soviet Union and the United States." *Current History* 80 (October 1981): 309-312.

──────. "U.S.-Soviet Relations: The Long Road Back." *Foreign Affairs* 60 (No. 3, 1982): 525-550.

"In the Front Line of Soviet Propaganda Offensive." *NATO's Fifteen Nations* 1 (Feb.-Mar. 1980): 79.

Ionescu, Ghita. "Action and Reaction in the Soviet Bloc." *The World Today* 24 (May 1968): 179-188.

James, Robert Rhodes, ed. *The Czechoslovak Crisis 1968.* London: Weidenfeld & Nicholson, 1969.

Jaster, Robert S. "The Defeat of Khruschev's Plan to Integrate Eastern Europe." *The World Today* 19 (December 1963): 514-522.

Jespersen, Knud. "U.S. Imperialism and the Destinies of Western Europe." *World Marxist Review* 18 (June 1975): 13-22.

Jones, Christopher D. "Soviet Hegemony in Eastern Europe: The Dynamics of Political Autonomy and Military Intervention." *World Politics* 29 (January 1977): 216-241.

―――. *Soviet Influence in Eastern Europe: Political Autonomy and the Warsaw Pact.* New York: Praeger Publishers, Inc., 1981.

Jones, W. Treharne. "East Germany Under Honecker." *The World Today* 32 (September 1976): 339-346.

Jordan, Zbigniew. *Oder-Neisse Line: A Study of the Political, Economic and European Significance of Poland's Western Frontier.* London: Polish Freedom Movement, 1952.

Kaiser, Karl. "Europe and America: A Critical Phase." *Foreign Affairs* 52 (July 1974): 725-741.

"The Karlovy Vary Conference." *Survival* 9 (July 1967): 208-213.

Katerinich, (Col.) V. "Militarist Fumes in NATO." *Soviet Military Review*, Number 9 (September 1980): 50-52.

Kertesz, Stephen D., ed. *The Fate of East-Central Europe.* Notre Dame, Ind.: University of Notre Dame Press, 1956.

Khrushchev, Nikita S. "On Peaceful Coexistence." *Foreign Affairs* 38 (October 1959): 1-18.

―――. *Soviet Policy on Germany.* London: Souret Booklets, 1961.

King, Robert R., and Dean, Robert W., eds. *East European Perspectives on European Security and Cooperation.* New York: Praeger Publishers, 1975.

Kleb, Geoffrey H. "NATO: A View from the East." *Military Review* 56 (November 1976): 3-10.

Kohler, Roy D. *Understanding the Russians: A Citizen's Primer.* New York: Harper and Row, 1970.

―――. "The Communist Objective." *Ordnance* (September-October 1971): 118-120.

―――. *Soviet Strategy for the Seventies: From Cold War to Peaceful Co-Existence.* Coral Gables, FL: Center for Advanced International Studies, University of Miami, 1973.

General

Kolkowicz, Roman, ed. *The Warsaw Pact*. Arlington, VA: Institute for Defense Analysis, 1969.

Korbel, Josef. *Detente in Europe: Real or Imaginary?* Princeton, NJ: Princeton University Press, 1972.

Korbonski, Andrzej. *The Warsaw Pact*. New York: Carnegie Endowment for International Peace, 1969.

―――――. "Detente, East-West Trade, and the Future of Economic Integration in Eastern Europe." *World Politics* 28 (July 1976): 568-589.

Kostko, Y. "Mutual Force Reductions in Europe." *Survival* 14 (September/October 1972): 236-239.

Kosygin, Alexei. "Soviet Foreign Policy Reviewed." *Survival* 8 (October 1966): 320-326.

Kristensen, (Col.) K.A. "The Threat to the North European Command." *NATO's Fifteen Nations* 18 (February/March 1973): 32-39.

Kudriavtsev, Vladimir. *Peace Programme for Europe*. Moscow: Novosti Press Agency, 1972.

Kulski, W.W. *The Soviet Union in World Affairs: A Documented Analysis 1964-1972*. Syracuse, N.Y.: Syracuse University Press, 1973.

Lachs, Manfred. "Poland's Quest for European Security." *International Affairs* 35 (July 1959): 305-309.

Larionov, (Lt. Col.) V. "The Doctrine of Aggression in Doses." *Survival* 1 (September/October 1959): 135-136.

Leebaert, Derek, ed. *Soviet Military Thinking*. Winchester, MA: Allen and Unwin, 1981.

Leighton, Marian. *The Soviet Threat to NATO's Northern Flank*. New York: National Strategy Information Center, Inc., 1979.

Lendvai, Paul. "Soviet Hegemony and Detente with the West." *Survey* 77 (Autumn 1970): 75-92.

Leonhard, Wolfgang. "The Domestic Politics of the New Soviet Foreign Policy." *Foreign Affairs* 52 (October 1973): 59-74.

Linden, Carl A. *Khrushchev and the Soviet Leadership 1957-1964*. Baltimore, MD: Johns Hopkins University Press, 1966.

Lippmann, Walter. "Interview with Khrushchev." *Survival* 3 (July/August 1961): 154-158.

Liska, George. "Russia and the West: The Next to Last Phase." *SAIS (School of Advanced International Studies) Review* (Summer 1981): 141-153.

Littell, Robert, ed. *The Czech. Black Book.* New York: Praeger, 1969.

Livingston, Robert Gerald. "East Germany Between Moscow and Bonn." *Foreign Affairs* 50 (January 1972): 297-309.

Lockhart, Robert Bruce. "The Czechoslovak Revolution." *Foreign Affairs* 26 (July 1948): 632-644.

Lukaszewski, Jerzy. "Western Integration and the People's Democracies." *Foreign Affairs* 46 (January 1968): 377-387.

―――. *The People's Democracies After Prague: Soviet Hegemony, Nationalism, Regional Integration?* Bruges, Belgium: De Tempel, for the College of Europe, 1970.

Lyon, Peyton V. "A Case for the Recognition of East Germany." *International Journal* 15 (Autumn 1960): 337-345.

MacCracken, John. "The Future of the Warsaw Pact." *NATO Review* 19 (May/June 1971): 11-13.

Mackintosh, J.M. *Strategy and Tactics of Soviet Foreign Policy.* London: Oxford University Press, 1962.

Mackintosh, Malcolm. "Soviet Strategy Postures." *Survival* 4 (May/June 1962): 116-119.

―――. "Soviet Motives in Cuba." *Survival* 5 (January/February 1963): 16-18.

―――. "Soviet Foreign Policy." *The World Today* 24 (April 1968): 145-150.

―――. *The Evolution of the Warsaw Pact.* (Adelphi Paper No. 58). London: International Institute for Strategic Studies, June 1969.

―――. "Era of Negotiation? Clues to Soviet Policy." *Survival* 13 (January 1971): 25-29.

―――. "The Warsaw Pact Today." *Survival* 16 (May/June 1974): 122-126.

Malinovsky, Marshal R.Y. "The 'New Look' in Moscow." *Survival* 2 (March/April 1960): 43-46.

―――. "Warning to the West." *Survival* 4 (January/February 1962): 32-33.

Marantz, Paul. "Prelude to Detente: Doctrinal Change Under Khrushchev." *International Studies Quarterly* 19 (December 1975): 501-528.

Mazza, Ugo. "The Eastern Alliance." *Armies and Weapons* 3 (15 July-15 September 1974): 48-52.

General

McGuire, Michael. *The Soviet Union in Europe and the Near East: Her Capabilities and Intentions.* London: R.U.S.I., 1971.

Meissner, Boris. *The Brezhnev Doctrine.* (East European Monograph No. 2). Kansas City: Goverment Research Bureau, Park College, December 1970.

Mellor, Roy E.H. *East Europe: A Geography of the Comecon Countries.* New York: Columbia University Press, 1975.

Mikhailov, M. "Concerning Exchanges and Contacts." *International Affairs* (Moscow) 5 (May 1973): 64-68.

Mikoyan, Sergo. "NATO, the Soviet Union and European Security." *Atlantic Community Quarterly* 7 (Fall 1969): 342-350.

Millar, T.B. *The East-West Strategic Balance.* London: George Allen and Unwin Ltd., 1981.

Miller, Margaret. "Poland and Khrushchev's Russia." *The World Today* 19 (October 1963): 422-430.

Millett, Stephen M. "Soviet Perceptions of the Theater Nuclear Balance in Europe and Reactions to American LRTNFs (Long-Range Theater Nuclear Forces)." *Naval War College Review* 34 (March-April 1981): 3-17.

Modrzhinskaya, Y. "Quiet Anti-Communism." *Survival* 10 (November 1967): 363-370.

Montias, John Michael. "Communist Rule in Eastern Europe." *Foreign Affairs* 43 (January 1965): 331-348.

Moreton, N. Edwina. *East Germany and the Warsaw Alliance: The Politics of Detente.* Boulder, CO: Westview Press, 1978.

Moseley, Philip E. "The Kremlin's Foreign Policy Since Stalin." *Foreign Affairs* 32 (October 1953): 20-33.

Moskowitz, Harry, and Roberts, Jack. *Communist Eastern Europe: Analytical Survey of Literature.* Washington, D.C.: Department of the Army, 1971.

Murarka, D. "Russian Realpolitik." *Survival* 8 (October 1966): 318-319.

Myer, (Lt. Col.) Allan A. "The Balance in Central Europe: Reflections Through the Soviet Prism." *Naval War College Review* 33 (November-December 1980): 15-43.

Nalin, Y. "NATO--Weapon of Aggression." *Survival* 1 (May/June 1959): 42-43.

"NATO Decision on New Missiles Slammed." (Seven Articles). *Current Digest of Soviet Press* 31 (January 9, 1980): 1-5. Translated and condensed from Pravda, December 11-16, and Pzvestia, December 13, 1979.

Nelson, Daniel N. "The Early Success of Ostpolitik: An Eastern European Perspective." *World Affairs* 138 (Summer 1975): 32-50.

Nygren, Bertl. *Cooperation Between the Soviet Union and Three Western Great Powers 1950-1975.* Stockholm: Swedish Institute of International Affairs, 1981.

Olenicoff, S.M. *Territorial Waters in the Arctic: The Soviet Position.* Santa Monica, CA: Rand Corp., July 1972, pp. 44-52.

On Events in Czechoslovakia: Facts, Documents, Press Reports and Eye Witness Accounts. Moscow: Press Group of Soviet Journalists, 1968.

Orvik, Nils. *Europe's Northern Cape and the Soviet Union.* Cambridge, MA: Center for International Affairs, Harvard University, 1963.

The Peacetime Strategy of the Soviet Union. London: Institute for the Study of Conflict, 1973.

Pethybridge, Roger W. *A History of Post-War Russia.* New York: New American Library, 1966.

Petrov, Vladimir. *U.S.-Soviet Detente: Past and Future.* Washington, D.C.: American Enterprise Institute for Public Policy Research, 1975.

Pick, Otto. "Reacting to Reagan: Soviet Fears and Opportunities." *World Today* (London) 37 (July/August 1981): 262-269.

─────, and Wiseman, A. "The USSR and Her Northern Neighbours." *The World Today* 15 (October 1959): 387-393.

Pipes, Richard. "Soviet Foreign Policy: Background and Prospects." *Survey* 17 (Autumn 1971): 1-9.

─────, ed. *Soviet Strategy in Europe.* New York: Crane, Russak, 1976.

Polyanov, N. "Europe at the Turn of the Decade." *International Affairs* (Moscow) (April 1980): 88-96.

Porzgen, Hermann. "Why Moscow Wanted the Treaty." *Survival* 12 (October 1970): 324-325.

Possony, Stefan T. "The USSR: Beyond Its Zenith?" *Orbis* 15 (Spring 1971): 87-103.

Prina, Edgar L. "Defense Dilemma: Inflation and the Soviet Threat." *The National Guardsman* (February 1975): 2-9.

Radvanyi, Janos. *Hungary and the Superpowers: The 1956 Revolution and Realpolitik.* Stanford: Hoover Institution Press, 1972.

"Reaching for the Moon: The Soviet Seven-Year Plan." *The World Today* 15 (February 1959): 47-58.

Remington, Robin Alison. *The Warsaw Pact: Case Studies in Communist Conflict Resolution.* Cambridge, Mass.: M.I.T. Press, 1971.

Ripka, Hubert. *Eastern Europe in the Post-War World.* London: Methuen; New York: Praeger, 1961.

Roberts, Henry L. *Eastern Europe: Politics, Revolution and Diplomacy.* New York: Knopf, 1970.

Rubenstein, Alvin Z. "The Soviet Union and the Eastern Mediterranean: 1968-1978." *Orbis* (Summer 1979): 299.

Rzhevsky, Yuri. *West Berlin: A Special Political Entity.* Moscow: Novisti Press Agency, n.d.

Salisbury, Harrison E. "Characteristics of Soviet Foreign Policy." *International Journal* 11 (Autumn 1956): 243-250.

Schopflin, George, ed. *The Soviet Union and Eastern Europe: A Handbook.* New York: Praeger, 1970.

Schwartz, Harry. *The Soviet Economy Since Stalin.* Philadelphia: Lippincott, 1965.

Seton-Watson, Hugh. "Soviet Foreign Policy on the Eve of the Summit." *International Affairs* 36 (July 1960): 287-298.

Shtemenko, (Gen.) Sergei. "The Warsaw Pact System." *Survival* 18 (July/August 1976): 168-170.

Shub, Anatole. "Lessons of Czechoslovakia." *Foreign Affairs* 47 (January 1969): 266-280.

Shulman, Marshall D. *Stalin's Foreign Policy Reappraised.* Cambridge, MA: Harvard University Press, 1963.

On the Situation in Berlin 1948. London: Soviet News, 1948.

"Six Months After: The East European Response to Helsinki." *Atlantic Community Quarterly* 14 (Spring 1976): 59-65.

"Soviets' Buildup in North Exceeds Protection Level." *Aviation Week and Space Technology*, Vol. 114 (15 June 1981): 101-107.

"The Soviet Union, 1981." *Current History* 80 (October 1981): 305-346.

"The Soviet Union, 1974." *Current History*, Vol. 67 (October 1974): 145-192.

"The Spectrum of Impotence: Statements on the Czechoslovakia Crisis 1968." *Survival* 10 (October 1968): 314-315.

Starr, Richard F. *The Communist Regimes in Eastern Europe: An Introduction*. Stanford, CA: Hoover Institution, 1977.

―――. "Soviet Policies in East Europe." *Current History* 80 (October 1981): 317-320.

Storm, Walter. *The Crisis in Czechoslovakia*. Prague: Orbis, 1948.

Strauss-Hupe, Robert. "Protracted Conflict: A New Look at Communist Strategy." *Orbis* 2 (Spring 1958): 13-38.

Stueck, William. "The Soviet Union and the Origins of the Korean War." *World Politics* 28 (July 1976): 622-635.

Sugar, Peter F., and Ivo, T. Lederer. *Nationalism in Eastern Europe*. Seattle, WA: University of Washington Press, 1969.

Sullivan, Eugene P. "The Adriatic: Soviet Seaway Someday?" *U.S. Naval Institute Proceedings* 98 (August 1972): 27-31.

Synhorst, (Capt.) Gerald E. "Soviet Strategic Interest in the Maritime Arctic." *United States Naval Institute Proceedings* 99 (May 1973): 88-111.

Szulc, Tad. *Czechoslovakia Since World War II*. New York: The Viking Press, 1971.

Talbott, Strobe, ed. *Khruschev Remembers: The Last Testament*. Boston, MA: Little, Brown, 1974.

Thrush, Aaron D. "Behind the Iron Curtain." *Air Force Magazine* 53 (September 1970): 116-120.

Treml, Vladimir G., and Hardt, John P., eds. *Soviet Economic Statistics*. Durham, NC: Duke University Press, 1972.

Triska, Jan F., and Finley, David D. *Soviet Foreign Policy*. New York: Macmillan, 1968.

Ulam, Adam B. "Soviet Ideology and Soviet Foreign Policy." *World Politics* 11 (January 1959): 153-172.

―――. *Expansion and Co-Existence: The History of Soviet Foreign Policy, 1917-1967*. New York: Praeger, 1968.

―――. *The Rivals: America and Russia Since World War II*. New York: The Viking Press, 1971.

General

―――, and Windsor, Philip. "Moscow Plays the Balance ... But Europe Shouldn't." *Foreign Policy* 8 (Fall 1972): 86-91.

United States. National Defense University. *Soviet Perceptions of War and Peace*. Washington, D.C.: Superintendent of Documents, 1982.

van der Beugel, Ernst H., and Kohnstamm, Max. "Western Europe and America in the Seventies." *The Atlantic Community Quarterly* 10 (Fall 1972): 295-311.

Vigor, P.H. *The Soviet View of War, Peace and Neutrality*. London: Routledge and Kegan Paul, 1975.

Vukadinovic, Radovan. "The Warsaw Pact and European Security and Cooperation." *Review of International Affairs* 25 (20 May 1974): 23-25.

Wall, Patrick. "Russia's Arctic Might Keeps NATO on the Hop." *To the Point* 8 (April 13, 1979): 12.

Weeks, Albert L. *The Other Side of Co-Existence*. New York: Pitman, 1970.

Werth, Alexander. *The Khrushchev Phase*. London: Robert Hale, 1961.

―――. *Russia: Hopes and Fears*. New York: Simon and Schuster, 1969.

―――. *Russia: The Post-War Years*. New York: Taplinger, 1971.

Wettig, Gerhard. *Community and Conflict in the Socialist Camp: The Soviet Union, East Germany and the German Problem 1965-1972*. New York: St. Martin's Press, 1975.

"What Finlandization Means." *The Economist* 248 (August 1973) 15-16.

"What Is It Russia Wants--Detente or a New Arms Race?" *U.S. News & World Report* 76 (25 March 1974): 40-41.

Whetten, Lawrence, ed. "Recent Changes in East European Approaches to European Security." *The World Today* 26 (July 1970): 277-288.

―――. "Soviet Strategy--The Mediterranean Threat." *Survival* 12 (August 1970): 252-258.

―――. "The Warsaw Pact Threat in the 1970's." *NATO's Fifteen Nations* 15 (October-November 1970): 20-28.

―――. *The Political Implications of Soviet Military Power*. New York: Crane, Russak, 1977.

Whitney, Thomas P., ed. *Khrushchev Speaks*. Ann Arbor, MI: University of Michigan Press, 1963.

Wiewiona, Boleslaw. *The Polish-German Frontier from the Standpoint of International Law.* Pozvan, Warsaw: Wydawnictwo Zachodnie, 1959.

Willetts, H.T. "Pavlov or Khrushchev? Soviet Methods in Political Warfare." *The World Today* 16 (October 1960): 426-435.

Wilson, (Col.) Minter L., Jr. "Bears in the Med." *NATO's Fifteen Nations* 17 (April-May 1972): 50-56.

Windsor, Philip. *Western Europe in Soviet Strategy.* (Adelphi Paper No. 8). London: Institute of Strategic Studies, 1964.

――――, and Roberts, Adam. *Czechoslovakia, 1968.* London: Chatto and Windus, 1969.

Wolfe, Bertram D. "Communist Ideology and Soviet Foreign Policy." *Foreign Affairs* 41 (October 1962): 152-170.

Wolfe, Thomas W. *Soviet Strategy at the Crossroads.* Cambridge, MA: Harvard University Press, 1964.

――――. "The Warsaw Pact in Evolution." *Survival* 8 (July 1966): 217-221.

――――. *Soviet Power and Europe, 1945-1970.* Baltimore, MD: Johns Hopkins Press, 1970.

――――. "The Soviet Union's Strategic Stake in the GDR." *The World Today* 27 (August 1971): 340-349.

――――. *Soviet Attitudes Towards MBFR and the USSR's Military Presence in Europe.* Santa Monica, CA: Rand Corp., 1972.

――――. *The Global Strategic Perspective from Moscow.* Santa Monica, CA: Rand Corp., 1973.

――――. *Role of the Warsaw Pact in Soviet Policy.* Santa Monica, CA: Rand Corporation, 1975.

Woods, William H. *Poland: Eagle in the East.* New York: Hill and Wang Books, 1968.

Yefremov, V. "Lasting Peace and Reliable Security for Europe." *Soviet Military Review*, Number 7 (July 1980): 52-53.

Yeremenko, Marshal A. "Arguments Against Foreign Bases." *Survival* 3 (March/April 1961): 62-66.

Zimmerman, William. *Soviet Perspectives on International Relations 1956-1967.* Princeton, NJ: Princeton University Press, 1969.

Zinner, Paul E. "Marxism in Action: The Seizure of Power in Czechoslovakia." *Foreign Affairs* 28 (July 1950): 644-658.

――――. "The Ideological Bases of Soviet Foreign Policy." *World Politics* 4 (July 1952): 488-511.

MILITARY

Abellara, James W. and Clark, Rolf. "Forces of Habit: Budgeting for Tomorrow's Fleets [Trends in United States and Russian Naval Developments and Forces, Balance of Seapower and Naval Spending]." *Foreign Policy and Defense Review* 3 (Nos. 2/3, 1981): 1-55.

"Air Forces of the World--Part 3: Soviet Union and the Warsaw Pact Nations." *Interavia* 28 (November 1973): 1232-33.

Baldwin, Hanson W. "The Soviet Navy." *Foreign Affairs* 33 (July 1955): 587-604.

———. "Soviet Submarines." *Survival* 7 (January/February 1965): 41-45.

Barnett, Frank R. "Moscow's Grand Strategy Unfolds, Part II." *American Legion* (February 1979): 12.

Baz, (Col.) I. "The Characteristics of Modern War." *Survival* 1 (November/December 1959): 180-184.

Berdal, Bivind. "The Projection of Soviet Military Power in the North: Margins of Western Safety in the Norwegian Sea on the North Atlantic Are Wearing Thin." *NATO's Fifteen Nations* 19 (February/March 1974): 58-64.

Bergson, Abram. "Russian Defense Expenditures." *Foreign Affairs* 26 (January 1948): 373-376.

Betit, Eugene D. "Soviet Tactical Doctrine and Capabilities and NATO's Strategic Defense." *Strategic Review* 4 (Fall 1976): 95-107.

Biryuzov, Marshal S. "Training the Soviet Forces." *Survival* 6 (July/August 1964): 188-192.

Buchan, Alastair. *The Soviet Threat to Europe: An Analysis of Soviet Intentions and Potentials.* London: Foreign Affairs Publishing Co., 1969.

Dinerstein, Herbert S. *War and the Soviet Union.* London: Atlantic Books; New York: Praeger, 1962.

———. "Current Soviet Strategic Ideas." *Survey*, No. 34 (October/December 1960): 74-79.

———. "Soviet Goals and Military Force." *Orbis* 5 (Winter 1962): 425-436.

Donnelly, C.N. "Tactical Problems Facing the Soviet Army's Recent Debates in the Soviet Military, Part II." *Military Review* (July 1979): 60-68.

Dziak, John J. *Soviet Perceptions of Military Power: The Interaction of Theory and Practice;* Foreword by Gerald L. Steibel. New York: Crane, Russak and Company, Inc., 1981.

Eller, Ernest McNeill. *The Soviet Sea Challenge: The Struggle for Control of the World's Oceans.* Chicago: Cowles Book Co., Inc., 1971.

Ely, (Col.) Louis B. *The Red Army Today.* Harrisburg: Military Service Publishing Co., 1953.

Epstein, Joshua M. "On Conventional Deterrence in Europe: Questions of Soviet Confidence." *Orbis* 26 (Spring 1982): 71-86.

Erickson, John. "The 'Military Factor' in Soviet Policy." *International Affairs* 39 (April 1963): 214-226.

———. "The Northern Theater: Soviet Capabilities and Concepts." *Strategic Review* 3 (Summer 1976): 67-82.

———. "The Soviet Air Programme." *NATO's Fifteen Nations* 25 (August-September 1980): 28-32.

Fairhall, David. *Russia Looks to the Sea: A Study of the Expansion of Soviet Maritime Power.* London: Andre Deutsch, 1971.

Forster, Thomas M. *The East German Army: The Second Power in the Warsaw Pact.* London: Allen and Unwin, 1980.

Gallagher, Matthew P., and Spielmann, Karl F. *Soviet Decision-Making for Defence: A Critique of U.S. Perspectives on the Arms Race.* New York: Praeger, 1972.

Garthoff, Raymond L. *Soviet Military Doctrine.* Glencoe, IL: The Free Press, 1953.

———. *Soviet Military Policy: A Historical Analysis.* New York: Praeger, 1966.

Goldhammer, Herbert. *The Soviet Soldier.* New York: Crane Russak, 1975.

Gorshkov, (Adm.) Sergi C. *Red Star Rising at Sea.* Annapolis, MD: United States Naval Institute, 1974.

Goure, Leon. *Civil Defence in the Soviet Union.* Berkeley, Los Angeles: University of California Press, 1962.

Grechko, Andrei. *The Armed Forces of the Soviet State.* Washington, D.C.: U.S. Air Force, 1975.

Green, William, and Swanborough, Gordon. *The Observer's Soviet Aircraft Directory.* London: Frederick Warne & Co., 1975.

Military

Griswold, Lawrence. "The Cork in the Baltic Bottle." *Sea Power* 15 (January 1972): 9-13.

Harvey, David. "Is Cuba's Build-up Aimed Against NATO Reinforcement?" *Defense & Foreign Affairs Digest* 7 (June 1979): 36-37.

Herrick, (Cmdr.) Robert Waring. *Soviet Naval Strategy: Fifty Years of Theory and Practice.* Annapolis, MD: U.S. Naval Institute, 1968.

Holloway, David. *Technology, Management and the Soviet Military Establishment.* (Adelphi Paper No. 76). April 1971.

Horelick, Arnold L., and Rush, Myron. *Strategic Power and Soviet Foreign Policy.* Chicago, IL: University of Chicago Press, 1966.

Hudson, George E. "Soviet Naval Doctrine and Soviet Politics, 1953-1975." *World Politics* 29 (October 1976): 90-113.

Iovlev, (Col.) A.M. "The Value of Numbers in the Nuclear Age: A Soviet View." *Survival* 3 (September/October 1961): 233-234.

Jacobsen, C.G. *Soviet Strategy--Soviet Foreign Policy: Military Considerations Affecting Soviet Policy-Making.* Glasgow: The University Press, Robert Maclehose & Co., Ltd., 1972.

------. "The Soviet Military Reappraised." *Current History* 80 (October 1981): 305-308.

Johnson, Michael W. "Debunking the 'Window of Vulnerability': A Comparison of Soviet and American Military Forces." *Technology Review* 85 (January 1982): 58-65.

Jones, Ellen. "Soviet Military Manpower: Prospects in the 1980's." *Strategic Review* 9 (Fall 1981): 65-75.

Jukes, Geoffrey. *The Development of Soviet Strategic Thinking Since 1945.* Canberra: Australian National University Press, 1972.

Kane, Francis X. "Anti-Satellite Systems [of the Soviet Union] and U.S. Options." *Strategic Review* 10 (Winter 1982): 56-63.

Kolkowicz, Roman. *The Soviet Military and the Communist Party.* Princeton, NJ: Princeton University Press, 1967.

------. "U.S. and Soviet Approaches to Military Strategy: Theory Vs. Experience." *Orbis* 25 (Summer 1981): 307-329.

Kozlov, (Col.) S. "Modern War--A Russian View." *Survival* 3 (July/August 1961): 159-160.

Kurasov, (Army Gen.) V.V. "On the Question of a Forestalling Blow." *Survival* 1 (March/April 1959): 3-5.

Kurochkin, (Army Gen.) P. "Conventional Forces in the Nuclear Age." *Survival* 3 (November/December 1961): 282-283.

Lambeth, Benjamin S. "The Evolving Soviet Strategic Threat." *Current History* 69 (October 1975): 121-125ff.

Liddell Hart, B.H., ed. *The Red Army*. New York: Harcourt Brace, 1956.

──────. *Deterrent or Defence*. London: Stevens and Sons; New York: Frederick A. Praeger, Inc., 1960.

Lilov, (Lt. Col.) L. "The Soviet Missile Programme." *Survival* 4 (March/April 1962): 86-91.

Lomov, (Col.-Gen.) N.A., ed. *Scientific-Technical Progress and the Revolution in Military Affairs*. Moscow: Soviet Ministry of Defence Publishing House, 1973 (Washington, D.C.: U.S. Government Printing Office, 1974).

Mackintosh, Malcolm. "Soviet Strategy in World War II." *Survival* 2 (July/August 1960).

──────. *Juggernaut: A History of Soviet Armed Forces*. London: Secker & Warburg, 1967.

──────. "Soviet Strategic Policy." *The World Today* 26 (July 1970): 269-276.

──────. "Moscow's View of the Balance of Power." *The World Today* 29 (March 1973): 108-118.

Malinovsky, Marshal R.Y. "Soviet Strategy." *Survival* 4 (September/October 1962): 229-232.

──────. "Soviet Defense Policy." (Speech by the Minister of Defence to the 23rd Party Congress). *Survival* 8 (July 1966): 232-235.

McGuire, Michael. "The Mediterranean and Soviet Naval Interests." *International Journal* 27 (Autumn 1972): 511-527.

──────, ed. *Soviet Naval Developments: Capability and Context*. New York: Praeger, 1973.

──────. "Soviet Naval Programmes." *Survival* 15 (September/October 1973): 218-227.

────── and others. *Soviet Naval Policy: Objectives and Constraints*. New York: Praeger, 1975.

──────, and McDonnell, John, eds. *Soviet Naval Influence: Domestic and Foreign Dimensions*. New York: Praeger, 1977.

Military

Mumford, Jay C. "Geographic Constraints on the Soviet Navy." *Military Review* 61 (August 1981): 39-48.

"NATO Strategy--Soviet View." *Survival* 10 (August 1968): 256-259.

Odom, William E. "The Soviet Military and Foreign Policy." *Survival* 17 (November/December 1975): 276-281.

Orvik, Nils. "Soviet Approaches on NATO's Northern Flank." *International Journal* 20 (Winter 1964): 54-67.

Peck, Edward. "Soviet Military Power and Political Influence." *NATO Review* 27 (April 1979): 14-17.

Pick, Otto. "Armies in Eastern Europe." *The World Today* 16 (December 1960): 540-548.

Polmar, Norman. "Alarmist Versus Realist." *Atlantic Community Quarterly* 10 (Fall 1972): 368-378.

──────. *Soviet Naval Power: Challenge for the 1970's*. New York: National Strategy Center, 1974.

Possony, Stefan T. *Soviet Military Doctrine on the Eve of Salt*. (Monograph No. 16). Philadelphia: Foreign Policy Research Institute, University of Pennsylvania, 1974.

Proektor, Dimitry. "Military Detente: A Soviet View." *Survival* 18 (November/December 1976): 261-265.

Record, Jeffrey. *Sizing Up the Soviet Army*. Washington, D.C.: The Brookings Institution, 1975.

Rybkin, (Lt.-Col.) E. "War and Policy." *Survival* 8 (January 1966): 12-16.

Saunders, (Comm.) Malcom G., ed. *The Soviet Navy*. New York: Praeger, 1958.

Schneider, William, Jr. "Changes in the Soviet Defense Posture in Europe." *Journal of Social and Political Studies* 2 (Summer 1977): 67-71.

Shtemenko, (Col.-Gen.) S.M. "Soviet Ground Forces in Modern War." *Survival* 5 (July/August 1963): 180-183.

Smirnov, (Vice-Adm.). "Soviet Navy in the Mediterranean." *Survival* 11 (February 1969): 65-66.

Smith, R.G. "The Soviet Armoured Threat and NATO Anti-armour Capabilities." *Army Quarterly* 109 (April 1979): 153-61.

Sokolovsky, (Marshal) V.D., ed. *Military Strategy: Soviet Doctrine and Concepts*. New York: Praeger, 1963.

———. *Soviet Military Strategy.* Englewood Cliffs, NJ: Prentice-Hall, Inc., 1963.

———. "The Military Revolution." *Survival* 6 (November/December 1964): 280-283.

———. "Soviet Military Structure." *Survival* 7 (July 1965): 236-241.

———, and Cherednichenko, (Maj.-Gen.) M.I. "Current Military Strategy." *Survival* 8 (August 1966): 266-270.

Sokolsky, Joel. "Soviet Naval Aviation and the Northern Flank: Its Military and Political Implications." *Naval War College Review* 1 (Jan/Feb 1981): 34-45.

Sosnovy, Timothy. "Soviet Military Budgets." *Foreign Affairs* 42 (April 1964): 487-496; *Survival* 6 (July/August 1964): 182-187.

"The Soviet General Staff Takes Stock: Changes in Military Doctrine." *The World Today* 11 (November 1955): 492-502.

Soviet Sea-Power. (Special Report Series No. 10. Center for Strategic and International Studies). Washington, D.C.: Georgetown University, 1969.

Talensky, (Maj.-Gen.) N. "On the Character of Modern Warfare." *Survival* 3 (January/February 1961): 16-21.

Theberge, James, ed. *Soviet Seapower in the Caribbean: Political and Strategic Implications.* New York: Praeger, 1972.

Thomas, John R. "Soviet Foreign Policy and the Military." *Survey* 17 (1971): 129-156.

Timofeyev, K. "Navies in Imperialist Policy." *Survival* 12 (March 1970): 101-104.

"Trends in Warsaw Pact Military Developments." *NATO Review* 21 (No. 4, 1973): 8-11.

Uhlig, Frank, Jr. "The Threat of the Soviet Navy." *Foreign Affairs* 30 (April 1952): 444-454.

United States. Department of Defense. *Soviet Military Power.* Washington, D.C.: Superintendent of Documents, 1981.

Vernon, (Col.) Graham D. "Soviet Options for War in Europe: Nuclear or Conventional?" *Strategic Review* (Winter 1979): 56-66.

"Warsaw Pact Military Power." *NATO Review* 20 (July/August 1972): 13-16.

"Warsaw Pact Military Status." *NATO Review* 22 (August 1974): 21-22.

"Warsaw Pact's Buildup Includes Nuclear Missiles." *Aviation Week & Space Technology* 110 (21 May 1979): 18-19.

Weinland, Robert G. "The Changing Mission of the Soviet Navy." *Survival* 14 (May/June 1972): 129-133.

———. "Admiral Gorshkov's 'Navies in the War and Peace.'" *Survival* 17 (March/April 1975): 54-63.

Whetten, Lawrence L., ed. "Military Aspects of the Soviet Occupation of Czechoslovakia." *The World Today* 25 (February 1969): 60-67.

———. *The Future of Soviet Military Power*. London: Macdonald and Jane's, 1976.

Whittier, (Capt.) Henry S., Jr. "Soviet Special Operations/Partisan Warfare: Implications for Today." *Military Review* (January 1979): 48-57.

Wolfe, Thomas W. "Shifts in Soviet Strategic Thought." *Foreign Affairs* 42 (April 1964): 475-486.

———. "Some New Developments in the Soviet Military Debate." *Orbis* 8 (Fall 1964): 550-562.

———. "Soviet Military Policy." *Survival* 10 (January 1968): 2-9.

———. "The Projection of Soviet Power." *Survival* 10 (May 1968): 159-165.

———. *Soviet Power and Europe, 1945-1970*. Baltimore: Johns Hopkins Press, 1970.

Wooldridge, E.T., Jr. "The Groshkov Papers: Soviet Naval Doctrine for the Nuclear Age." *Orbis* 18 (Winter 1975): 1153-1175.

Yakubovsky, I.I. "Soviet Ground Forces." *Survival* 9 (October 1967): 327-328.

Zakharov, Marshal M. "Science and Military Leadership." *Survival* 7 (March/April 1965): 85-89.

NUCLEAR

Barber, (Col.) Ransom E. "The Myth of Soviet Nuclear War Strategy." *Army* 25 (June 1975): 10-17.

Barlow, William J. "Soviet Damage Denial: Strategy, Systems, SALT, and Solution [Defensive Nature of Russian Nuclear

Strategy]." *Air University Review* 32 (September/October 1980): 2-20.

Beglov, Spartak. *International Relations in the Nuclear Age.* Moscow: Novosti Press Agency Publishing House, 1968.

Borawski, John. "Mutual Force Reduction in Europe from a Soviet Perspective." *Orbis* (Winter 1979): 845.

Chuikov, Marshal. "Soviet Land Forces in Nuclear War." *Survival* 6 (March/April 1964): 86-89.

Donnelly, C.N. "Winning the NBC (Nuclear, Biological and Chemical) War: Soviet Army Theory and Practice." *International Defense Review* 14 (No. 8, 1981): 989-996.

Douglass, Joseph D., Jr. *The Soviet Theater Nuclear Offensive.* (Research Note 201). Arlington, VA: System Planning Corp., 6 February 1975, 88pp. Washington, D.C.: U.S. Government Printing Office, 1976.

———. "Soviet Nuclear Strategy in Europe: A Selective Targeting Doctrine?" *Strategic Review* (Fall 1977): 19-32.

Garthoff, Raymond L. *Soviet Strategy in the Nuclear Age.* New York: Praeger, 1958.

———. *The Soviet Image of Future War.* Washington: Public Affairs Press, 1959.

Goure, Leon; Kohler, Roy; and Harvey, Mose L. *The Role of Nuclear Forces in Current Soviet Strategy.* Washington, D.C.: Center for Advanced International Studies, University of Miami, 1974.

Gromely, Dennis M. "Understanding Soviet Motivations for Deploying Long-range Theater Nuclear Forces." *Military Review* 61 (September 1981): 20-34.

Hoffman, Hubertus. "SS-20 Multiples USSRs Superiority." *NATO's Fifteen Nations* 23 (Dec. 1978-Jan. 1979): 42-48.

Houn, Franklin W. "Nuclear Deterrence: The Soviet Position." *Orbis* 8 (Winter 1965): 922-936.

Jackson, William D. "Soviet Images of the U.S. as Nuclear Adversary, 1969-1979." *World Politics* (Princeton) 33 (July 1981): 370-398.

Kaplan, Fred M. *Dubious Specter: A Skeptical Look at the Soviet Nuclear Threat, 2nd Edition.* Washington, D.C.: Institute for Policy Studies, 1980.

Kennedy, Robert. "Soviet Theater-Nuclear Forces: Implications for NATO Defense." *Orbis* 25 (Summer 1981): 331-350.

――――. "Soviet Theater Nuclear Forces." *Air Force Magazine* 4 (March 1981): 78-83.

Kintner, William R., and Scott, Harriet Fast, eds. *The Nuclear Revolution in Soviet Military Affairs.* Norman, OK: University of Oklahoma Press, 1968.

McCormick, Gordon H. and Miller, Mark E. "American Seapower at Risk: Nuclear Weapons in Soviet Naval Planning." *Orbis* 25 (Summer 1981): 351-367.

Mercer, (Maj.) Donald L. "The Warsaw Pact Shortwarning Nuclear Attack: How Viable an Option?" *Military Review* Pt. 1, 60 (October 1980): 23-32; Pt. 2, 60 (November 1980): 28-36.

Miller, Martin J., Jr. "Soviet Nuclear Tactics." *Ordnance* (May-June 1970): 624-627.

Millett, Stephen M. "Soviet Perceptions of the Theater Nuclear Balance in Europe and Reactions to American LRTNFs (Long Range Theater Nuclear Forces). *Naval War College Review* 34 (March-April 1981): 3-17.

Myerson, Michael. "The Nuclear Balance: Myths and Reality." *Political Affairs* 61 (February 1982): 26-30.

Petersen, Phillip A. "Flexibility: A Driving Force in Soviet Strategy." *Air Force Magazine* 63 (March 1980): 94-98.

Portugalov, Nikolei. "European Nuclear Balance--A Soviet View." *NATO's Fifteen Nations* 26 (October-November 1981): 40-43.

Rickelson, Jeffrey T. "Soviet Responses to MX." *Political Science Quarterly* 96 (Fall 1981): 401-410.

Sobik, (Col.) Erich. "Command and Control in the Soviet Ground Forces." *NATO's Fifteen Nations* 24 (October-November 1979): 96-98+.

Soll, Richard S. "The Soviet Union and Protected Nuclear War." *Strategic Review* (Fall 1980): 15-28.

Zavilov, I. "Nuclear Weapons and War." *Survival* 13 (March 1971): 90-93.

AUTHOR INDEX

Aaron, David, 124
Abellara, James W., 217
Abs, Hermann J., 102
Acheson, Dean, 8, 13, 23, 38
Adelman, Kenneth, 73, 198
Adeneauer, Konrad, 172
Adomeit, Hannes, 201
Ailleret, (Gen.) C., 23, 80, 135
Ailleret, (Gen.) Charles, 141
Akmandor, Neset, 100
Albert, E.H., 102
Alberts, (Maj.) Donald J., 173
Albrecht-Carrie, Rene, 141
Alder-Karlsson, Gunnar, 115
Alexander, Fred, 75
Alexander, (Lt. Col.) Joseph H., 178
Aliano, Richard A., 60
Aliboni, Roberto, 97
Allais, Maurice, 13
Allemann, F.R., 102, 113
Allen, H.C., 13
Allen, Lew, 180
Allen (Gen.) Lew, Jr., 173
Allen, Raymond W., 177
Allen, Richard V. 69, 194
Allison, (Wing Comdr.) Duncan, 87
Allison, Graham, 38
Almond, Gabriel A., 102
Alperovitz, Gar, 38

Alphand, Herve, 80
Alves, Dora, 102, 177
Amaduzzi, (Comdr.) Francesco, 156
Amason, Robert, 94
Amery, Julian, 87
Amme, Carl H., 141
Amme, Carl H., Jr., 23, 87, 102, 128
Anatolyev, G., 87
Andersen, K.B., 79
Anderson, Alvin T., 201
Anderson, David K., 141
Anderson, Evelyn, 102
Anderson, Frederic M., 156
Anderson, John, 156
Andren, Nils, 60, 98, 141
Andreyev, N., 23
Anghelatos, A.G., 93
Anon., 113
Apel, Hans, 102
Aptheker, Herbert, 13
Albatov, G.A., 201
Are, Giusseppe, 96
Arlinghaus, Bruce E., 184
Armitage, (Air Vice Marshal) M.J., 180
Armstrong, (Lt. Col.) Alan P., 180
Armstrong, Hamilton Fish, 3, 4
Aron, Raymond, 5, 14, 38, 60, 80, 84, 180
Aronson, James, 38
Art, Robert J., 115
Ascherson, Neal, 201
Ashcroft, Geoffrey, 156

Aspaturian, Vernon V., 201
Aspin, Les, 115
Atkenson, (Maj. Gen.) Edward B., 164, 193
Attlee, Clement R., 87
Augstein, Rudolf, 113

Bader, W.B., 135
Bader, William B., 24
Bagley, Worth H., 177
Bahr, Egon, 102
Bailey, George, 102
Bailey, (Maj.) Jerry T., 38
Bailey, Thomas A., 60
Bailly-Cowell, G.M., 156
Baker, Steven, 135
Baldwin, Hanson W., 3, 5, 217
Ball, George W., 14, 24, 38, 181
Ball, M. Margaret, 8, 194
Ball, Robert, 39
Ball, Robert A., 141
Balniel, Lord, 39
Bambini, (Maj.) Adrian P., 156
Bambini, Adrian P., Jr., 141
Barber, (Comdr.) James A., Jr., 39
Barber, (Col.) Ransom E., 223
Barclay, (Brig.) C.N., 39
Bare, C. Gordon, 115
Barghoorn, Frederick C., 201
Barham, (Lt. Col.) Thomas J., 164, 175
Bark, Dennis L., 113
Barker, Elisabeth, 113
Barkway, Michael, 8, 75
Bar-Levov, Doron, 128
Barlow, Jeffrey G., 195
Barman, Thomas, 195
Barnes, (Capt.) Dwight H., 178

Barnet, Richard J., 24, 39, 201
Barnett, Frank R., 117
Barnett, Roger W., 155
Barnhart, (Maj.) William C., 103
Barrett, Jane R., 75
Barrett, Raymond, 201
Bartlett, (Sen.) Dewey F., 52
Barton, John H. 128
Barzaghi, Antonio, 173
Basagni, Fabio, 96
Basevi, Giorgio, 107
Basiuk, Victor, 156
Bathurst, M.E., 103
Baudissin, Count Wolf, 103
Baylis, John, 87, 135, 141
Baz, (Col.), I., 217
Beal, John Robinson, 8
Beaton, Leonard, 14, 24, 75, 135, 141
Beaufre, Andre, 60
Beaufre, (Gen.) Andre, 14, 24, 142, 181
Beaumont, Jane, 75
Beavers, (Comdr.) Roy L., Jr., 124
Bechhoeffer, Bernhard G., 128
Beckett, (Sir) Eric W., 5
Beer, Francis A., 24, 193
Beetham (ACM) Michael, 87
Beglov, Spartak, 224
Behr, Robert M., 148
Belfiglio, V.J., 195
Bell, Carol, 39, 128
Bellini, James, 80, 87
Beloff, Max, 3, 87
Bender, Peter, 103, 202
Bennecke, (Gen.) J., 164
Bennecke, (Gen.) Jurgen., 175
Benediktsson, Bjarni, 94
Bennett, (Vice Adm.) Fred G., 177
Bennett, W.S., 181
Berdal, Bivind, 202, 217
Beres, Louis Rene, 181

Author Index

Berg, John, 94
Bergquist, Mats, 116
Bergson, Abram, 217
Bergsten, C. Fred, 60
Bernard, S., 5
Bernard, Stephen,]28
Bernos, Roger, 81
Berry, F. Clifton, Jr., 184
Bertram, Christoph, 39, 60, 98, 103, 128, 142, 181
Bethe, Hans A., 128
Betit, Eugene D., 217
Betts, Richard K., 142, 156
Bevan, Aneurin, 87
Biden, Joseph R., Jr., 124
Bieri, Ernst, 8, 14
Bilen, I., 202
Billington, James J., 202
Binkin, Martin, 116
Birgi, Nuri, 39, 100
Birnbaum, Immanuel, 103
Birnbaum, Karl, 60, 103
Birnbaum, Karl E., 24, 39, 195, 202
Birrenbach, Kurt, 14, 39, 103, 164
Biryuzov, Marshal S., 217
Bittner, Donald, 94
Bjamason, Bjorn, 95
Bjol, Erling, 79, 202
Blackaby, F.T., 87
Blackett, P.M.S., 8, 14, 135, 181
Blackette, Patrick M., 3
Blades, (Cdr.) Todd, Ret., 142
Blaisdell, (Maj.) Allan C., 128
Blanchard, George S., 156
Blaney, Harry C., 39
Blechman, Barry M., 116, 128, 151
Bleek, Wilhelm, 103
Bletz, Donald F., 39
Bloemer, Klaus, 202
Bloomfield, Lincoln P., 24, 39

Bluhm, Georg R., 103
Boel, Baron Rene, 75
Bohlen, Charles E., 24, 39
Boll, Michael M., 93, 100
Bolling, Klaus, 103
Bolton, David, 164, 195
Bolton, (Comdr.) David, 87
Bonnart, Frederick, 60, 75, 100, 164, 181
Booth, Ken, 60, 177
Booth, Kenneth, 124
Borawski, John, 128, 224,
Borcier, Paul, 142
Borden, Donald F., 142
Borklund, C.W., 156
Bothwell, Robert, 75
Bowie, Robert R., 14
Bowman, (Brig. Gen.) Richard C., 60
Boy, Siegfried, 156
Boychuck, Peter, 202
Boyd, (Maj.) Alfred A., 128
Boyd, Andrew, 3
Boyd, (Maj.) Darwin D., 142, 164
Boyle, Dan, 157, 164, 173
Bracken, Paul, 142, 157, 164
Brady, Linda P., 129
Braeman, J., 40
Bragmann, (Brig. Gen.) G., 175
Brandon, Donald, 24
Brandon, Henry, 40
Brandt, Willy, 14, 24, 40, 103, 104, 204
Bray, Caroline, 114
Bregman, Alexander, 202
Brennan, Donald G., 129
Brenner, Michael J., 135, 181
Brentano, Heinrich von, 14
Brett, (Lt. Gen.) Devol, 173
Brewin, Andres, 75, 76
Brezhnev, Leonid, 202
Bridge, T.D., 87, 88, 135
Briefs, H.W., 25
Brinton, Crane, 24
Brodie, Bernard, 24, 88, 142, 164, 173, 181

Broga de Macedo, Jorge, 99
Bromke, Adam, 202
Bronska-Pampuch, Wanda, 104
Brooks, (Capt.) Linton F., 181
Brooks, Tony, 173
Brosio, Manlio, 24, 25, 40, 195, 202
Brown, Aurel, 203
Brown, David A., 173
Brown, George, 88
Brown, (Gen.) George, 60
Brown, George W., 8
Brown, Harold, 25, 181
Brown, James, 175
Brown, (Dr.) James, 69
Brown, Neville, 15, 40, 88, 135, 173, 181, 182
Brown, Peter V., 157
Brown, Seyom, 25
Brown, (Maj.) William D., 182
Bruber, Frederic J., 164
Brzezinski, Zbiginew K., 15, 25, 40, 65, 129, 203
Buchan, Alastair, 8, 15, 25, 40, 41, 88, 142, 177, 182, 217
Buchanan, Keith C., 164
Bull, Hedley, 15, 25, 124, 129, 182
Bundy, McGeorge, 3, 5, 15, 25, 41, 129, 182
Bundy, William P., 41
Buntinx, Henry M.V., 129
Burbank, Lyman B., 143, 164
Burgess, Philip M., 98
Burgess, W. Randolph, 41
Burgin, Don, 164
Burnham, T., 116
Burns, Arthur Lee, 182
Burrell, R.M., 116
Burrows, Bernard, 143
Burrows, Sir Bernard, 41
Burt, (Lt. Col.) Donald L., 203
Burt, Richard, 41, 124, 129, 157

Burt, Richard R., 182
Bussmann, Bernard, 41
Buteux, Paul, 182
Butler, Francis P., 100
Butler, Sir Harold, 3
Buzzard, (Rear Adm.) Anthony, 143, 182
Buzzell, (Maj.) Calvin A., 182
Byers, R.B., 76
Bykov, Vladimir L., 203
Byrnes, James Francis, 3
Byrnes, Robert F., 203

Caldwell, Lawrence T., 124, 129, 203
Callaghan, Thomas A., Jr., 126, 157, 176
Callahan, James, 88
Calleo, David, 25, 41
Calleo, David P., 88
Calogero, Francesco, 124
Calvocoressi, Peter, 15
Cameron, Air Vice Marshal Robert, 143, 165
Campaigne, Jameson C., 15
Campbell, (Lt. Cmdr.) Craig S., 95
Campbell, John C., 25, 60, 203
Camps, Miriam, 41
Canby, Steven, 143
Canby, Steven L., 41, 60, 165, 173
Cancian, Mark F., 177
Caputo, (Maj.) Robert P., 203
Carey, Roger, 135
Carleton, William Graves, 5, 9
Carleton, William Graves, 5
Carothers, Thomas, 100
Carrington, William M., 165
Carruthers, James F., 157
Carter, Barry, 143
Carter, Jimmy, 60
Carter, Luther J., 124
Case, (Col.) Frank B., 177
Catlin, George, 9, 25

Author Index

Cauley, Jon, 94
Celac, Sergia, 43
Cerami, Charles A., 15
Cerny, K.H., 25
Chace, James, 41, 61
Chalfont, Alun, 88
Challener, Richard D., 3, 9
Chamberlin, Waldo, 9
Chamberlin, William Henry, 15
Chambost, G., 81
Chandler, (Lt. Col.) Robert W., 182
Chaplin, Dennis, 61
Chester, Conrad V., 129
Chilcote, Robert H., 99
Chirac, Jacques, 135
Chopping, Douglas, 173, 177
Christopher, Warren, 100, 157
Cubbuck, (Maj.) R.M., 173
Chuikov, Marshal, 224
Church, (Sen.) Frank C., 15
Church, Frank G., 26
Cicco, John A., Jr., 195
Cipra, (Lt. Col.) Donald J., 104
Clark, Asa A., 184
Clark, John J., 61, 165
Clark, (Adm.) Joseph J., 178
Clark, Rolf, 217
Clark, Wilson, 116
Clarke, Bruce C., 143
Clarke, John L., 157
Clarke, Nick, 93
Clarkson, Stephen, 76
Clawson, Robert W., 70
Clay, (General) Lucius D., 104, 113
Clayton, James L., 116
Clemens, Diane Shaver, 41
Clemens, Walter, C., Jr., 41, 129, 143, 203,
Cleveland, Harlan, 26, 41, 61, 143, 165
Cleveland, Harold van B., 5, 26
Cleveland, Joan B., 26
Cliffe, Trevor, 157
Clokie, H.M., 76
Coates, W.P., 88
Cobb, (Maj.) Tyrus W., 41
Cobban, Alfred, 81
Coblenz, Constance G., 12
Coffey, J.I., 61, 124, 125, 129, 143, 182
Coffey, Joseph I., 15, 26
Coffey, Kenneth J., 143
Coggi, Igino, 143, 165
Cohen, Samuel T., 182, 183
Cohen, Stephen D., 116
Cohen, Stuart D., 116
Colbert, (Adm.) Richard G., 143, 165, 178
Coleman, David W., 161
Coleman, Herbert J., 129
Coles, Harry L., 15
Collier, David S., 26, 113
Collins, (V. Adm.) D.A., 116
Collins, John M., 42, 69
Colonna, Guido, 96
Combeaux, (Gen.) Edmund, 26, 42
Conant, Melvin, 76
Conant, Melvin A., 116
Connell (Maj.) George M., 143
Connery, Robert H., 26
Conquest, Robert, 26, 203, 204
Conwell, (Lt. Col.) Leslie C., 173
Cook, Don, 129
Cooper, Caroline C., 133
Cooper, Richard N., 116
Copley, Gregory, 176
Cordesman, Anthony H., 183
Cordier, Sherwood, 69
Cordier, Sherwood S., 88
Cornell, Alexander H., 157
Cornides, Wilhelm, 104
Corry, J.A., 4, 204
Cotter, Donald R., 183
Cottrell, Alvin J., 15, 42, 116, 183, 204
Coughran, Joe F., 95
Coulmas, Peter, 16

Couloumbis, Theodore, 94
Courtade, Pierre, 81
Couve de Murville, Maurice, 81
Cox, (Capt.) G.W., 42
Crabb, Cecil V., Jr., 81
Craig, Gordon A., 104
Crane, Peggy, 89
Crane, Robert Dickson, 26, 27
Crankshaw, Edward, 42
Critchley, Julian, 26, 144, 157, 195
Croan, Melvin, 104
Croker, F.P.U., 95
Crollen, Luc, 99
Cromwell, William C., 26, 165
Crowther, Geoffrey, 9
Crozier, Brian, 81, 204
Curl, Richard L., 144
Currie, Malcolm R., 116
Cuthbertson, B.C., 165
Cutler, (Capt.) Katie, 144
Cutler, Lloyd N., 125
Czempiel, Ernst-Otto, 69
Czerwinski, E.J., 204

Dabezies, Pierre, 81
Dahrendorf, Ralf, 104
Dale, Reginald, 204
Dallin, David J., 204
Daniels, Robert V., 204
Davidow, Mike, 42
Davidson, Charles N., 183
Davidson, Eugene, 104
Davis, Lynn Etheridge, 42, 183
Davis, Paul C., 183
Davis, Rodger P., 196
Davison, Michael S., 165
Davison, (Gen.) Michael S., 42, 176
Davison, W. Phillips, 110, 113
Davydov, Y., 42
Dawson, Raymond, 27
Dawson, Raymond H., 166
Day, A.C.L., 117

Day, Bonner, 173
Dean, Robert W., 104, 157, 208
Dean, Vera M., 3, 5
De Borchgrave, Arnaud, 27
Debre, Michel, 42, 81
de Carmoy, Guy, 81, 135
Deerin, James B., 176
Defourneaux, Marc, 81
de Freitas, Geoffrey, 11
de Gara, John P., 42
de Gaulle, Charles, 81, 82, 135
Degras, Jane, 204
de Kadt, Emanuel J., 89
Delarue, Maurice, 82
del la Malene, Christian, 84
de Marchi, Antonio, 166
Demetracopoulos, Elias P., 94
Dennett, Raymond, 5
Dennison (Adm.) Robert Lee, 178
de Poix, Vincent Paul, 166
DePort, Anton W., 61
Dernberg, H.J., 104
de Rose, Francois, 183
de Smedt (Lt. Gen.) M., 75
Desmond, P., 173
De Staercke, Andre, 27, 42, 204
Dethleffsen, Erich, 104
Deutsch, Harold C., 113
Deutsch, Karl W., 27, 104, 129, 193
Deutsch, Karl Wolfgang, 9
Deutscher, Isaac, 27
De Vries, Klass G., 183
DeWeerd, H.A., 89, 117
Dewey, Arthur E., 144, 166
Dewey, (Lt. Col.) Arthur E., 129
Diebold, William, Jr., 117
Dietrich, E. Handt, 153
Digby, James F., 158
Dinerstein, Herbert S., 217
Dobell, Peter C., 76
Dobell, W.M., 94
Dobney, Frederick J., 42

Author Index

Dodd, (Col.) Norman, 42
Dodd, Norman L., 144, 166
Dodd, Thomas J., 32, 205
Donelan, Michael, 16
Donhoff, Marion, 104
Donnelly, C.N., 117, 224
Donovan, Robert J., 9
Doty, Laurence, 173
Dougherty, James E., 15, 16, 61, 129, 130, 183
Douglas-Home, Charles, 117, 205
Douglass, Joseph D., 183
Douglass, Joseph D., Jr., 224
Drischler, Alvin Paul, 178
Druks, Herbert, 27, 205
Drummond, Dennis M., 117
Drummond, (Maj.) Dennis M., 61
Dube, F.P., 166
Duchacek, Ivo, 205
Duchene, Francois, 27, 43
Duffield, E.S., 6
Dulin, (1st Lt.) Carol, 196
Dulles, Eleanor Lansing, 27, 104, 105, 113
Dulles, John Foster, 5, 9, 27
Duncan, Charles K., 166
Dunn, Keith A., 205
Dupuy, T.N., 183
Dupuy, (Col.) T.N., Ret., 144
Duroselle, J.B., 27
Dyer, (Lt. Col.) Philip W., 183
Dziak, John J., 218
Dzirkals, Lilita, 205

Eaker, (Lt. Gen., Ret.) Ira C., 69
Earl, C., 61
Earle, Edward Mead, 5
East, Maurice A., 98
East, W. Gordon, 5
Easterly, James, 205
Eayrs, James, 76, 136
Ecobescu, Nicolae, 43
Eden, Anthony, Earl of Avon, 16, 89

Edinger, Lewis J., 104
Edmonds, Martin, 117, 158
Edmonds, Robin, 205
Eekelen, W.F., 158
Eggertsson, T., 95
Eisenhammer, J.S., 82
Eisenhower, Dwight D., 27
Eliot, Christian, 166
Eliot, George Fielding, 3, 166
Eliou, Chris G., 94
Eller, Ernest McNeill, 218
Ellsworth, Robert, 27, 43
Ellsworth, Robert F., 69, 195
Elwood, (Lt. Col.) Niles T., 43
Ely, (Col.) Louis B., 218
Emerson, Rupert, 16
Emmet, Christopher, 183
Engle, Kenneth W., 130
Engleberdt, Stanley L., 144
Enthoven, Alain C., 61, 144, 183
Eppstein, John, 9
Epstein, Joshua M., 218
Epstein, Leon D., 89
Erhard, Ludwig, 105
Erhardt, Carl A., 43
Erickson, John, 61, 130, 205, 218
Eriksen, Bjarne, 166
Erler, Fritz,
Etzioni, Amitai, 16
Evans, (ACM) David, 89
Even-Tov, Ori, 144

Facer, Roger, 158
Facey, David A., 174
Fackenthall, (Maj.) James B., 205
Fair, (Col.) Stanley D., 184
Fairhall, David, 218
Fairlamb, John, 71, 95
Fallows, James, 144
Fama, Joseph, 178
Farran, Charles d'Oliver, 9
Fay, James R., 100
Fedder, R.H., 27

Feis, Herbert, 43
Feld, Werner J., 65, 105
Felder, Wilson N., 158
Ferguson, George, 76
Fernsworth, Lawrence, 195
Ferraira, (Lt. Gen.) Jose Lemos, 99
Ferreira, Jose Medeiros, 99
Fiddler, (Maj.) John F., 174
Fieleke, Norman S., 117
Finger, Seymour Maxwell, 61
Finlay, Patrick, 158
Finlayson, Jack, 205
Finletter, Thomas K., 5, 16
Finley, Daivd D., 214
Fischer, Robert Lucas, 176
Fischer-Galati, Stephen, 205
Fisher, (Lt. Comdr.) M.J., 178
Fleming, D.F., 16
Fliegel (LCDR) Robert A., 95
Floyd, David, 205
Flynn, Gregory, 69
Flynn, Gregory A., 96
Fontaine, Andre, 27, 43, 82
Fontaine, Francois, 82
Forster, Thomas M., 218
Fortson, (Capt.) Thomas E., 184
Fosdick, Dorothy, 9
Foster, Charles R., 69, 195
Foster, Richard B., 43, 49
Foster, William C., 9, 130
Fostervoll, Alv Jakob, 117
Fouquet, David, 62
Fowler, (Col.) Delbert M., 144, 176
Fowles, John S., 89
Fox, (Maj.) Charles L., 174
Fox, Annette Baker, 28
Fox, William T., 43
Fox, William T.R., 28, 166
Francois-Poncet, Andre, 82
Frankel, Joseph, 89, 98
Frankland, Noble, 89
Franklin, William M., 114
Franks, H. George, 62, 158

Franks, Lord, 117
Fraser, Blair, 28
Fredholm, (Capt.) Christer, 178
Freedman, Lawrence, 89, 125, 136, 184
Freedman, Max, 5
Freeland, Richard M., 43
Frei, Otto, 114
Freund, Gerald, 105
Freymond, Jacques, 16, 28, 62, 195
Fried, Anne, 43
Friederich, J.S., 158
Friedland, Edward, 62, 117
Friedmann, Wolfgang, 9
Friedrich, P.J., 82
Frisbee, John L., 62
Fromkin, David, 193
Fromm, Erich, 186
Fromm, Ernst Ulrich, 82
Fulbright, (Sen.) J.W., 16, 17
Fullerton, John, 144
Furlong, R.D.M., 97, 117, 144
Furniss, E.S., 11
Furniss, Edgar S., 9, 82
Furniss, Edgar S., Jr., 28
Fusi Aizpurva, Juan Pablo, 100

Gabelic, Andro, 206
Gaddis, John Lewis, 44
Gail, Bridget, 117, 144
Gaitskell, Hugh, 5, 9
Galen, Justin (pseud.), 184, 195
Gallagher, Matthew P., 218
Gallois, Pierre M., 17, 82, 206
Gallois, (Gen.) Pierre M., 17, 136, 144, 184
Galtung, Johan, 44, 62
Gamson, William A., 44
Gangler, Jacques S., 158
Gans, Daniel, 184
Gans, (Col.) Daniel, 176

Author Index

Gans, (Col. Ret.) Daniel, 144
Gardner, Lloyd C., 44
Gareau, Frederick H., 184
Garn, (Sen.) Jake, 184
Garnett, John, 28
Garnett, John C., 145, 176
Garthoff, Raymond L., 206, 218, 224
Gasteyger, Curt, 28, 44, 62, 145, 166, 193, 206
Gati, Charles, 44
Gaustad, Peter J., 195
Gebel, Wolfgang R., 167
Gehlen, Michael P., 206
Geiger, Theodore, 5, 28, 44
Gelb, Leslie H., 44, 58
Gelber, Lionel, 17, 28, 62, 89
Gellner, John, 76, 158
Geneste, Marc, 82
Geneste, (Lt. Col.) Marc E., 184
Genscher, Hans-Deitrich, 69, 105
Geoffrey, Pattie, 87
George, Alexander L., 145
Geritz, (RADM) E.P., 184
Gervase, Sean, 196
Gesienheyner, Stefan, 145
Gessert, Robert A., 62
Gibson, James A., 76
Giffin, S.F., 17
Gijzen, (Air Cmdr.) Johannes A., 174
Gilmour, I.H.J., 44
Gilpatric, Roswell L., 17
Ginsburgh, (Col.) Robert N., 145
Giscard d'Estaing, President Valery, 82
Gittings, John, 130
Gladwyn, Lord, 17, 28, 44, 62, 184
Glaser, Kurt, 26, 113
Glass, George A., 62
Glazov, (Col.) V., 145
Godson, Joseph, 44, 62

Goldberg, Alfred, 89, 136
Goldberg, Edward D., 117
Golden, James R., 117, 118, 120, 184
Goldhammer, Herbert, 82, 218
Goldman, Eric F., 9
Goldman, Marshall I., 206
Goldman, Nancy L., 167
Goldmann, Kjell, 44, 45, 145, 148
Goldsborough, James O., 82
Goldsborough, James Oliver, 70
Goldstein, Walter, 70, 90,
Goldwater, Barry, 45
Goldwin, Robert A., 28
Gole, (Lt. Col.) Henry G., 145
Gollancz, Victor, 130
Gomulka, Wladyslaw, 206
Gooch, G.P., 83
Goodfellow, Robin, 90
Goodman, Elliot B., 184
Goodman, Elliot R., 62, 83, 105, 184, 206
Goodpaster, Andrew J., 45
Goodpaster (Colonel) Andrew J., 167
Goodpaster, (Gen.) Andrew J., 145, 167
Goodwin, Roger, 90
Goold-Adams, Richard, 17, 90
Goormaghtigh, John, 83
Gorden, Morton, 32
Gordenker, Leon, 28
Gorden Walker, Patrick, 184
Gordon, Colin, 62, 118
Gordon, Lincoln, 9, 10, 118
Corgey, Lazslo, 105
Gorshkov, (Adm.) Sergei C., 218
Gott, Richard, 130, 136
Goure, Leon, 206, 218, 224
Graebner, Norman A., 17, 28
Graham, Daniel O., 62
Grammuller, Harald, 167
Graubard, Stephen R., 45
Gray, Colin S., 78, 125, 130, 145, 184, 185

Gray, Norman, 145
Gray, Robert C., 62
Grayson, George W., 99
Grechko, Andrei, 218
Green, Philip, 185
Green, William, 218
Greenhill, Denis, 45
Greenwood, David, 90
Greenwood, Ted, 130, 185
Gregg, (Lt. Col.) William R., 158
Gregg, Robert W., 45
Gregory, Frank, 162
Gretton, (Vice-Adm.) Sir Peter, 178
Greve, Tim, 98
Grey, Collin S., 45
Griffin, (Maj.) Donald K., 145
Griffith, William E., 28, 45, 106, 196, 206
Griffiths, Franklyn, 28, 45, 63, 106, 196, 206
Griffiths, Richard T., 97
Grigoryev, K., 100
Grindrod, Muriel, 96
Griswold, Lawrence, 83, 99, 118, 206, 219
Gromley, Dennis M., 185, 234
Gromyko, Anatoli A., 206
Grondal, Benedikt, 95
Grosser, Alfred, 9, 83, 106, 145, 146, 196
Grover, Major General J., 176
Gueritz, (Rear Adm.) E.F., 185
Guertner, Gary L., 185
Guk, S., 206
Gundersen, H.F. Zeiner, 118, 206
Gunderson, (Gen.) H.F., 174
Gutteridge, William, 28, 130
Gwyn, William B., 90

Haagerup, Niels J., 79, 151

Haas, Ernst, B., 6, 9, 167
Hackel, Erwin, 146
Hackett, (Gen.) Sir John, 29
Haddock, (Lt. Col.) Clovis C., 158
Hadik, Laszlo, 45
Hadley, Guy, 45
Haekkerup, Per, 79, 80
Haffner, Sebastian, 17, 114
Hahn, Walter F., 48, 63, 70, 106, 146, 185, 186, 190, 193
Haig, Alexander, 146
Haig, Alexander M., Jr., 63, 70, 118, 125, 130
Haigh, Patricia, 206
Haines, C. Grove, 206
Hainl, (Col.) Robert D., Jr., 95
Hall, David K., 118
Halle, Louis J., 10, 17, 29
Hallgrimsson, Geir, 95
Hallstein, Walter, 17, 106
Halperin, Morton J., 44, 46, 136
Hammond, Paul Y., 29, 46
Hanak, H., 207
Handwork, Bertrand, 63
Hangen, Welles, 207
Hannig, (Lt. Col., Ret.) Norbert, 185
Hanreider, Wolfram, 46
Hanreider, Wolfram F., 106
Hansen, Guttorm, 98
Hansen, Peter, 80
Hardt, John P., 118, 214
Harlech, Lord, 90
Harned, Joseph, 167
Harnig (Lt. Col., Ret.) Norbert, 146
Harnwell, Gaylord P., 118
Haroche, C., 29
Harriman, W. Averell, 207
Harris, George S., 100
Harrison, Eric, 77
Harrison, Michael M., 83
Harrison, Dr. S.L.R., 29

Author Index

Harrison, Stanley L., 130
Harrison, Stanley R., 46
Harrison, W.E.C., 77
Harrod, Roy, 6
Hartig, C. Hans-Chr., 146
Hartley, Anthony, 46, 63, 136
Hartley, Livingston, 17, 29, 167
Hartman, Arthur A., 46, 196, 207
Hartman, Richard, 159
Hartmann, Frederick H., 106
Harvey, David, 118, 219
Harvey, Mose L., 118, 224
Haselkorn, Avigdor, 207
Hassner, Pierre, 29, 46, 63, 106
Hastings, Paul, 29
Haviland, H., Jr., 23
Haviland, H. Field, Jr., 9, 17
Hawtrey, R.G., 90
Hayter, William, 207
Hayter, Sir William, 6
Hazan, Joseph, 83
Head, (Brig.) A.H., 146
Head, Richard G., 46
Healey, Denis, 9, 17, 19, 130, 146
Heath, Edward, 90
Heathcote, Nina, 106
Heck, Robert, 178
Heilbrunn, Otto, 146
Heisenberg, Wolfgang, 185
Heldring, J.L., 29
Herbert, (Wing Cmdr.) Clive A., 146
Herlofson, Ch. O., 98
Herrick, (Cmdr.) Robert Waring, 219
Herter, Christian A., 18
Herz, John H., 106
Hessman, James D., 146, 178
Heusinger, Adolf Ernst, 29
Hewish, Mark, 63
Heyerdahl, (Col.) L.R., 146
Heyhoe, D.C.R., 63

Heymont, Irving, 185
Hildebrand, George H., 96
Hilgers, (Lt. Col.) J.J.W., 167
Hill, Andrew W., 186
Hill, R.J., 46, 83, 130, 167
Hillenbrand, Martin L., 114
Hill-Norton, Peter, 63
Hinterhoff, (Maj.) E., 146, 167, 186, 196
Hinterhoff, Eugene, 9, 18
Hirsch, Mario, 63
Hiscocks, Richard, 106
Hitch, Charles, J., 118
Hoag, Malcolm W., 9, 18, 118, 136, 167
Hodgkinson, (Lt. Col.) Richard L., 186
Hodson, H.V., 18
Hoeberg, (Brig.) Kjell T., 159
Hoeffding, Oleg, 118
Hoffman, Fred S., 178
Hoffman, Hubertus, 125, 234
Hoffman, Stanley, 18, 29, 46, 47, 63, 70, 83, 136, 193, 207
Hogg, Quintin, 90
Hogglund, (Maj.) Gustav, 47
Holborn, Hago, 6
Holifield, Chet, 29, 186
Hollander, Paul, 47
Holloway, David, 207, 219
Holmes, John W., 17, 167
Holst, Johan, 60, 98
Holst, Johan J., 98, 146, 167, 180, 186
Holst, Johan Jorgen, 63, 131, 142, 217
Holstsorensen (Maj. Gen.) Neils, 80
Holtzel, Michael, 63
Holzman, Franklyn D., 118
Hoopes, Townsend, 146
Hooson, Emlyn, 30, 168
Horelick, Arnold L., 219
Horowitz, David, 30
Horowitz, S., 159

Horton, Frank B., 47
Horwer, D.M., 150
Hoskins, Halford L., 4
Hottelet, Richard C., 18, 207
Houn, Franklin W., 224
Hovey, J. Allan, 168
Howard, (Col.) G.B., 75
Howard, (Major-Gen.) G.B., 159
Howard, Michael, 10, 47, 63, 90, 178
Howe, Quincy, 47
Howell, (Cpt.) Phillip D., 147
Hudson, G.F., 30
Hudson, George E., 219
Huebner, (Lt. Col.) Gerhard, 174
Hughes, Emmet John, 18
Hugo, Grant, 90
Huizinga, J.H., 30
Humphrey, Hubert H., 30, 207
Hunt, (Cmdr.) Herman L., 147
Hunt, Kenneth, 83, 168
Hunter, Robert, 18, 30, 47
Hunter, Robert E., 147
Huntington, S.P., 18, 47
Huntington, Samuel P., 64
Huntley, James R., 30
Huntley, James Robert, 41, 47
Hussain, Farooq, 64
Huyser, Robert E., 174
Hyland, William G., 196, 207

Ignatieff, George, 136
Ikle, Fred Charles, 147, 186
Ingram, Kenneth, 9
Ionescu, Ghita, 207
Iovlev, (Col.) A.M., 219
Ireland, Timothy P., 4, 70
Irwin, Christopher, 41, 47, 143
Ismay, Lord, 6
Israelyan, V., 131
Ivo, T. Lederer, 114

Jablonsky, David, 70, 147
Jackson, Henry M., 30, 125
Jackson, James, 158
Jackson, William D., 224
Jacobi, Claus, 116
Jacobsen, C.G., 219
Jacoviello, Alberto, 96
James, Robert Rhodes, 218
Janczeswki, George H., 64
Janosik, Edward G., 136
Janowitz, Morris, 47
Janquet, L.G.M., 30, 48
Jaroch, (Maj.) Roger M., 70
Jaspers, Karl, 106
Jaster, Robert S., 208
Javits, Jacob K., 30, 32
Jefferies, (Maj.) Chris L., 70
Jenner, Peter, 48, 118, 178
Jennings, (Col.) Richard M., 48
Jespersen, Knud, 208
Jockel, Joseph T., 77
Johansen, (Capt.) Erik B., 147
Johns, Claude J., 35
Johnson, A. Ross, 205
Johnson, Christopher, 136
Johnson, Lyndon B., 30
Johnson, Michael W., 219
Johnson, U. Alexis, 131
Johnston, Ernest B., Jr., 118
Jones, (Lt. Col.) L.M. 147
Jones, Christopher D., 208
Jones, David C., 48
Jones, Ellen, 219
Jones, Stephen B., 6
Jones, Thomas P., Jr., 148
Jones, W. Treharne, 6, 208
Jordan, Amos A., 119
Jordan, R.S., 168
Jordan, Robert S., 48, 64, 168
Jordan, Zbigwiew, 208
Joshua, Wynfred, 48, 186
Joyce, J.A., 30
Jukes, Geoffrey, 219
Jungius, James, 178

Author Index

Kahan, J.H., 147
Kahn, Herman, 30, 119, 186
Kaiser, Karl, 48, 90, 106, 208
Kaiser, Robert G., 48
Kaltefleiter, Werner, 48, 106
Kane, Francis X., 219
Kane, Pamela, 196
Kanter, Hershel, 119
Kaplan, Fred, 186, 224
Kaplan, Lawrence S., 4, 6, 70, 196
Kaplan, Morton A., 12, 30, 31, 48, 125, 147
Karas, Thomas H., 159
Karber, Philip A., 159, 178, 186
Katerinich (Col.) V., 208
Kaufmann, William W., 10, 18, 147
Kaysen, Carl, 6, 147
Keane, (Maj.) John J., Jr., 163
Keatinge, Patrick, 196
Keeny, Spurgean M., Jr., 186
Kegley, Charles W., Jr., 45, 71
Keliher, John G., 131
Kelleher, Catherine McArdle, 186
Kelly, George A, 136
Kelly, Robert C., 120
Kemp, Geoffrey, 41, 136, 137
Kennan, George F., 6, 9, 18, 31, 48, 182
Kennedy, Floyd D., Jr., 77
Kennedy, Gavin, 119
Kennedy, John F., 9, 18, 19
Kennedy, Robert, 159, 224, 225
Kennedy, William, 147
Kent, Tom, 77
Kerry, Richard J., 199
Kertesz, Stephen, D., 208
Keyserling, Leon H., 119
Khlestov, O., 131
Khruschev, Nikita S., 208

Kidd, Isaac, 181
Kielmansegg, (Gen.) J.A. Graf, 107, 147
Kiep, Walther L., 48
Kiep, Walther Leisler, 101
Kieval, Hillel J., 83
Killick, Sir John, 70
Kim, Young Hum, 31
Kindleberger, Charles P., 31
King, James E., Jr., 186
King, Robert R., 208
King, Wilfred, 119
King-Hall, Stephen, 148
Kingston-McCloughry, (Air Vice-Marshal) E.J., 148
Kintner, (Lt. Col.) W.R., 49, 125, 187, 225
Kirby, Stephen, 70, 119
Kirgis, Frederic I., Jr., 168
Kirk, Grayson, 4
Kissinger, Henry A., 9, 19, 30, 49, 64, 70, 125, 148
Klaiber, Wolfgang, 49, 131
Kleb, Geoffrey H., 208
Kleiman, R., 19
Klenberg, Jan, 148, 168
Klepacki, Zbigniew M., 168
Klippenberg, Eirk, 159
Knapp, Wilfred, 31
Knorr, Klaus, 8, 31, 64, 78, 137, 148, 168, 187
Knorr, Klaus E., 49
Knowlton, William A., 168
Kochenour, Robert W., 64
Kogan, Norman, 96
Kohl, Wilfrid L., 49, 64, 107, 137
Kohler, Roy D., 208, 224
Kohn, Hans, 11, 19, 31
Kohnstamm, Max, 57
Kolko, Gabriel, 49
Kolko, Joyce, 49
Kolkowicz, Roman, 209, 219
Kolodziej, Edward A., 31, 83, 137
Komer, R.W., 148

Komer, Robert, 49, 64
Kondracke, Morton, 187
Korb, Lawrence J., 119, 187
Korbel, Josef, 49, 107, 209
Korbonski, Andrzej, 209
Korkegi, Robert H., 64, 168
Kostko, Y., 209
Kosygin, Alexei, 209
Kovrig, Bennett, 32
Kozicharow, Eugene, 64, 119, 125, 131, 148
Kozlov, (Col.) S., 219
Kraft, Joseph, 19
Krause, Lawrence B., 119
Krehbrel, (Capt.) Carl C., 187
Krell, Gert, 119
Kressler, Diane A., 107
Krippendorff, Ekkehart, 107
Kristensen, (Col.) K.A., 209
Kristol, Irving, 64, 148
Krivinyi, Nikolaus, 159
Kroesen, (Gen.) Frederic J., 176
Kronenberg, 57
Kronenberg, Vernon J., 77
Krosby, H. Peter, 99
Kruger-Sprengel, Friedhelm, 179
Kruls, (Gen.) H.J., 6, 49
Kruzel, Joseph, 126
Kudriavtsev, Vladimir, 209
Kuhlman, James A., 57
Kuklick, Bruce, 49
Kulski, W.W., 84, 209
Kupperman, Robert H. Behr, 148
Kurasov, (Army Gen.) V.V., 220
Kurochkin, (Army Gen.) P., 220
Kurth, James R., 159
Kuzmack, Arnold M., 116
Kyle, Deborah, M., 159, 168, 174

La Feber, Walter, 32, 49

Lachs, Manfred, 131, 209
Lacqueur, Walter, 49
Laham, Donald C., 149
Laird, Melvin R., 64
Laloy, Jean, 32, 49
Lambert, Mark, 174
Lambeth, Benjamin S., 220
Lambropoulos, P., 196
Landau, David, 49
Landauer, Carl, 107
Landes, David, 64
Lane, (Maj. -Gen.) Thomas A., 64
Lange, Christian, 148
Lange, Halvard, 19
La Roeque, (Rear Adm.) Gene R., 187
Larionov, (Lt. Col.) V., 7, 209
Larson, Thomas B., 131, 204
Latour, Charles, 159, 160, 174, 196
Lauder, John A., 148
Lautenschlager, Karl, 187
Lawrence, R.D., 168
Lawson, Ruth C., 11
Layton, (Lord) C.H., 90
Leach, Henry, 179
Le Bailly, Louis, 65
Leebaert, Derek, 209
Legault, Albert, 137
Legere, Lawrence J., 119
Legien, R., 114
Legters, Lyman, 107
Legvold, Robert, 50, 218
Lehman, John F., 126, 187
Lehman, John F., Jr., 179
Lei, Helge Salomonsen, 98
Leifer, Michael, 50
Leighton, Marian, 209
Leitenberg, Milton, 120, 137, 187
Leites, Nathan, 84
Lemnitzer, (Gen.) Lyman L., 32, 65, 148
Lendvai, Paul, 209
Lentner, Howard H., 77
Leonhard, Wolfgang, 209

Author Index

Lerche, Charles O., Jr., 32
Lerner, Daniel, 32, 84
Lettau, (Maj.) Ulrich H., 169
Lettau, Ulrich H., 120
Levin, Viktor A., 148
Lewis, Flora, 107
Lewis, Geoffrey, 101
Libby, Ruthven, E., 99
Lichtheim, G.A., 19
Liddell Hart, B.H., 6, 176, 220
Lider, Julian, 149
Lieber, Robert J., 137
Lilov, (Lt. Col.) L., 220
Linden, Carl A., 209
Link, Werner, 65
Lippmann, Heinz, 107
Lippmann, Walter, 4, 19, 120, 193, 209
Liska, George, 19, 193, 209
Lisle, Alan G., Jr., 174
Littell, Robert, 210
Livingston, Robert Gerald, 210
Lloyd, Trevor, 131
Lochen, Einar, 99
Lockhart, Robert Bruce, 210
Lockley, Lt. Col. Stanton G., 169
Lodge, John Davis, 32
Loob, Larry M., 160
Lomov, (Col.-Gen.) N.A., 220
Lorell, Mark A., 160
Lorenzini, (Lt. Col.) Dino A., 174
Lovins, Amory B., 137
Lowenstein, Hubertus Prince zu, 19
Lowenthal, Richard, 107
Lower, Arthur, 107
Loy, (Maj.) Noah E., 174
Luard, Evan, 19, 32
Luciolli, Mario, 65
Ludz, Peter Christian, 65, 107
Lukacs, John, 20
Lukaszewski, Jerzy, 210

Luns, J.M., 196
Luns, Dr. J.M.A.H., 20
Luns, Joseph, 50, 65, 131
Luthy, Herbert, 84
Lyon, Peyton V., 50, 210
Lyons, W.C., 182

MacCaskill, (Lt. Col.) Douglas C., 199
MacCloskey, (Brig.-Gen.) Monro, 169
Maccoby, Michael, 186
MacCracken, John, 210
Macdonald, H.I., 11
Macdonald, Hugh, 131, 196
Macdonald, R. St. J., 78
Mackenzie (Lt. Gen.), G.A., 78
MacKenzie, Kenneth, 101
Mackintosh, J.M., 210
Mackintosh, Malcolm, 210, 220
MacLaren, (Col.) William G., Jr., 50
Maclean, Donald, 90, 91
Macmillan, Harold, 32, 91
MacNeil, Robert, 65
Maconochie, Alexander K., 149
Macridis, Roy C., 84
Maddison, Angus, 120
Maddox, Robert James, 50
Madzojewski, A., 91
Magathan, Wallace C., Jr., 107
Mahncke, Dieter, 114
Majonica, Ernst, 107
Major, (Wing Comdr.) Douglas H., 131
Major, John, 20
Makins, Christopher J., 70
Makins, Sir Roger, 6
Malinovsky, Marshal R.Y., 210, 220
Mallorie, (AVM) Paul R., Ret., 160
Mally, Gerhard, 32, 51, 65
Malmgren, H.B., 149

Malone, (Col.) Daniel K., 149
Mancini, Angelo N., Jr., 160
Mandelbaum, Michael, 187
Mander, John, 114
Manderson-Jones, R.B., 196
Manor, F.S., 65
Mansfield, Mike, 32
Mansfield, (Sen.) Mike, 149
Mansfield, (Vice Adm.) E.G.N., 179
Manshall, Warren D., 47
Marantz, Paul, 205, 210
Marriott, John, 91, 120, 160, 174, 176, 179, 187, 196
Marshall, Andrew, 199
Marshall, Charles Burton, 6
Marshall, D. Bruce, 84, 137
Martin, J.J., 187
Martin, Kingsley, 91
Martin, Laurence W., 149, 179, 188
Martin, Michael L., 84
Martin, Michael L., 84
Martin, Paul, 78
Martin, Thomas L., 149
Mason, Edwards, 4
Mason, Roy, 91
Mathias, (Sen.) Charles McC., Jr., 51
Matteson, Robert E., 131
Matthews, Roy A., 78
Maudling, Reginald, 32
Maurischat, G., 120
Maxwell, Stephen, 149
May, Ernest, 38
Mayhew, Christopher, 91
Mayo, H.B., 6, 11
Mazza, Ugo, 210
McCartney, (Lt. Cmdr.) R. Scott, 95
McCloy, John J., 32
McCormick, Gordon H., 225
McDonnell, John, 220
McGee, (Sen.) Gale, 50, 169
McGeehan, Robert, 50, 70
McGhee, George C., 101
McGlasson, W.D., 176
McGowan, Pat, 71

McGuire, Michael, 211, 220
McInnis, Edgar, 11, 107
McKean, Roland N., 118
McKean, Roland N., 118
McKenney, (Lt.) Edward A., 131
McKinney, (Maj.) William R., 188
McKitterick, T.E.M., 11
McLachlan, Donald, 5, 11
McLin, John B., 78
McNamara, Robert S., 11, 20, 33, 149, 182
McQuade, Lawrence C., 149
Meany, George, 65
Medearis, Joseph, 169
Meehan, (Maj.) John F., 169
Meeker, Thomas A., 120
Meissner, Boris, 211
Melander, Karen Alette, 131
Meller, R., 160
Mellor, Roy E.H., 211
Melton, T.R., 149
Menaul, (Air Vice-Marshall) S.W.B., 188
Menaul, Stewart, 126
Menaul, Stewart W.B., 46, 65, 91
Menaul, (ADM.) Stewart W.B., Ret., 137
Mendershausen, H., 120, 149
Mendershausen, Horst, 51, 65
Mendl, Wolf, 84, 137
Mensonides, Louis J., 51
Mercer, (Maj.) Donald L., 225
Merchant, Livingston T., 20
Merkl, Peter H., 107, 167
Merlini, Cesare, 97
Merritt, Jack N., 175
Mery, (Gen.) Guy, 84
Messmer, Pierre, 84, 137, 169
Metcalf, Arthur G.B., 126
Mets, David R., 71
Metson, William, 3
Mettiamano (Gen.) Alessandro, 97

Author Index

Mettler, Erich, 107
Middleton, Drew, 6, 33, 91, 149
Mikhailov, M., 211
Mikoyan, Sergo, 211
Miksche, (Lieut.-Col.) F.O., 188
Millar, T.B., 211
Miller, (Lt. Col.) D.M.O., 149
Miller, Lynn H., 51, 149
Miller, Margaret, 211
Miller, Mark E., 225
Miller, Martin J., Jr., 225
Millett, Stephen M., 188, 211, 225
Millis, Walter, 6
Milton, T.R., 51, 174
Milton, (Gen.) T.R., 65, 149
Milton, Theodore Ross, 101
Minich, Cecil M., 150
Minter, (Vice Adm.) Charles S., Jr., 132
Modar, Daniel, 78
Modigliani, Andre, 44
Mordzhinskaya, Y., 211
Mogensen, (Capt.) Ebbe, 51
Moisi, Dominique, 84
Molander, Roger C., 125
Mollet, Guy, 84
Mondale, Walter F., 51, 64
Montias, John Michael, 211
Moore, Ben T., 11
Moore, J.E., 179
Moore, Robert A., 188
Moreton, N. Edwina, 211
Morgan, Carlyle, 33
Morgan, Michael, 188
Morgan, Roger, 51, 84, 108, 114
Morgenstern, John, 160
Morgenstern, Oskar, 120
Morgenthau, Hans J., 7, 44, 51, 108
Morgenthau, Hanson, 33
Morris, Eric, 114
Morris, Joe A., 8

Morse, Edward L., 51, 85
Morse, John H., 65, 160
Mosely, Philip E., 20, 211
Moskowitz, Harry, 66, 211
Moulin, Leo, 11
Moulton, Harland B., 51, 150
Moulton, J.L., 20
Moulton, (Maj. Gen.) J.L. 150
Moynihan, Daniel P., 33
Moyse, Robert, 7
Muhlen, Norbert, 108
Muller, Felix, 179
Mulley, F.W., 20
Mulley, Frederick W., 137, 188
Multan, W., 132
Mumford, Jay C., 221
Mumford, (Lt. Col.) Jay C., 137
Munk, Frank, 20, 193
Munro, Dana G., 7
Murarka, D., 211
Murovchik, Joshua, 126
Murphy, Patrick, 94
Murray, A.H., 196
Murray, John Middleton, 4
Murray-Rochard, Alan, 167
Murville, Couve de, 11
Myer, (Lt. Col.) Allan A., 8, 211
Myers, Kenneth, 66
Myers, Kenneth A., 71
Myers, William, 100
Myerson, Michael, 225

Nacht, Michael L., 185, 188
Nagel, (Lt. Col.) Richard A., Jr., 91
Nailor, Peter, 179
Nalin, Y., 211
Narvhus (Maj. Gen.) Ingar T., 99
Nash, Henry T., 52
Nathan, James A., 66
Nau, Henry R., 161
Naugle, (Comdr.) J.O., 179
Neal, Alfred C., 161
Neal, Fred Warner, 108
Neff, John C., 146

Author Index

Neff, Richard, 169
Neild, Robert, 91
Nelson, Daniel N., 212
Nelson, Harold I., 108
Nerlich, Uwe, 63, 66, 85, 186, 188
Nesbitt, (Maj.) Robert L., 80
Nettl, J.P., 108
Neuchterlein, Donald E., 96
Neuman, H.J., 97, 89
Neustadt, Richard E., 194
Newhouse, John, 29, 52, 85, 126, 150, 169
Newing, Anthony, 161
Newman, (Wing Comdr.) Anthony T., 91
Newman, Parley W., Jr., 168
Nicholas, Herbert, 91
Nicholls, Anthony, 58
Nicholls, Daivd, 150
Nicholls, (Air Marshall) John, 174
Nicholson, George E., Jr., 166
Niemeyer, Gerhard, 11
Nitze, Paul H., 66, 126, 132, 150, 179
Nixon, Richard M., 33, 52, 189
Noble, G. Bernard, 52
Norman, Floyd, 161
Norstad, Lauris, 20, 132
Norstad, (Gen.) Lauris, 85, 150, 169, 189
Northedge, F.S., 33, 52, 66
Norton, Augustus R., 189
Nott, John, 91
Nouel, Elise, 161
Novoseltsev, Y., 108
Nuechterlein, Donald E., 52
Nunn, (Maj.) Jack H., 189
Nunn, (Sen.) Sam, 52, 150, 169
Nunnerly, David, 92
Nutting, Anthony, 132

Nygren, Bertl, 212

Oakeshott, Robert, 120
Obleser, (Lt. Gen.), F., 108
O'Connor, Neil, 96
Odom, William E., 221
Okyar, Osman, 101
O'Leary, James P., 71, 194
Olenicoff, S.M., 212
Oliphant, M.L., 150
Olvey, Lee D., 120
O'Neil, Robert, 150
Onslow, C.G.D., 108
Oppenheimer, J. Robert, 174
Oppermann, Thomas, 108
O'Rourke, (Maj.) Robert J., 174
Orvik, Nils, 33, 52, 71, 78, 151, 169, 170, 212, 221
Osgood, Robert E., 7, 20, 52, 71, 151, 189, 194
Ostendorf, Col T.H., 170
Ott, George, 120
Otten, Alan L., 189
Ottoman, (Col.), Raymond H., 52
Owen, David, 53
Owen, Henry, 170
Owen, J.I., 151, 161
Ozarne, (Maj.) E.H., 151, 170
Ozdas, Nimet, 120

Page, Jack, 116
Paice, Anthony, 92
Paige, D.C., 87
Palit, (Maj. Gen.) D.K., 151
Palmer, Joseph, 179
Palmer, Michael, 53, 132
Panofsky, Wolfgang K.H., 151, 186
Parker, (Lt. Col.) Glynn E., 121, 161
Parker, W.H., 53
Partlow, (Maj.) Frank A., 170
Pasternak, E., 33
Paterson, Thomas G., 53

Author Index

Paterson, W.E., 108
Patijn, C.L., 33
Patterson, G., 11
Paul, Roland A., 53
Pauls, Rolf Friedemann, 196
Pauly, (Gen.) John W., 175
Pavid, Radovan, 94
Payne, Keith B., 189
Payne, Kenneth B., 125, 132
Pearson, Lester B., 12, 78
Peck, Edward, 221
Peeters, Paul, 151
Perazic, Professor Gavro, 194
Perla, Leo, 20
Perrett, Bryan, 161
Perry, William J., 121
Petersen, Nikolaj, 80
Petersen, Phillip A., 225
Pethybridge, Roger W., 212
Petrov, Vladimir, 212
Pfaff, William, 30
Pfaltzgraff, Diane, 61
Pfaltzgraff, Robert L., Jr., 33, 34, 53, 63, 71, 121, 125, 161
Philip, Andre, 34
Philipp, Udo, 175
Phillips, J., 170
Pick, Otto, 53, 85, 212, 221
Pickert, General, 108
Pickett, Neil, 189
Pickles, Dorothy, 85
Piekalkiewcz, J., 204
Piele, Otto, 85
Pierre, Andrew J., 34, 53, 121, 126, 132, 138, 189
Pigasse, Jean-Paul, 138
Pipes, Richard, 212
Pipinelis, Panayotis, 94
Pisar, Samuel, 121
Planck, Charles R., 108
Plants, (Maj.) Louis B., 132
Pleven, Rene, 85
Pocklington, (Lt. Col.) James H., 161
Polk, James H., 189

Polk, (Gen.) James H., 132
Polmar, Norman, 66, 221
Polyanov, N., 108, 212
Pompidou, Georges, 85
Port, A. Tyler, 161
Porth, Jacquelyn S., 170
Portugalov, Nikolei, 225
Porzgen, Hermann, 212
Possony, Stefan T., 175, 186, 189, 212, 221
Posvar, Wesley W., 34
Potter, (Maj.) G.A., 126
Pounds, Norman J.G., 114
Povolny, Mojmir, 132
Powell, Enoch, 92
Powers, (Capt.) J., 66
Pranger, Robert J., 66
Price, Harry Bayard, 197
Prina, Edgar L., 213
Prina, Edgar L., 66, 213
Pritt, D.N., 108
Prittie, Terence, 109
Proektor, Dimitry, 221
Pross, Harry, 109
Proxmire, (Sen.) William, 54
Pruessen, Ronald W., 51
Pugh, George E., 132
Pusey, Merlo J., 12
Pym, Francis, 138

Quanbeck, Alton J., 151
Quaroni, Pietro, 34
Quester, George H., 54

Radovanovic, Ljubomir, 54
Radvanyi, Janos, 213
Rakowska-Harmstone, Teresa, 202
Ranger, Robert, 34
Ranger, Robin, 78, 132
Rannestad, Andreas, 121
Rapoport, Anatol, 20, 54
Rashish, Myer, 121
Rasiulis, Andrew P., 151
Raskin, Marcus G., 24
Rasmussen, (Maj.) Kenneth H., 85
Rathjens, George W., Jr., 151, 170

Rattinger, Hans, 66
Ravenal, Earl C., 61, 121, 190
Read, (Brig.) Greg, 170
Read, Thornton, 168, 190
Reagan, Ronald, 133
Record, J., 168
Record, Jeffrey, 190, 221
Rees, David, 34, 170
Reid, Escott, 34
Reinhardt, (Col.) George C., 152, 190
Reitzel, William, 12
Remington, Robin Alison, 213
Rendel, Alexander, 66
Reppert, (Capt.) John C., 133
Resor, Stanley R., 126
Reynaud, Paul, 7
Reynolds, P.A., 92
Rhinelander, John B., 127
Richards, Ivor, 54
Richards, W.J., 161
Richardson, (Brig. Gen.) Robert C., III, Ret., 190
Richardson, Elliot, 54, 152
Richardson, J.L., 54
Richardson, James L., 109
Richardson, James L., 109
Richardson, R.C., 152
Rickelson, Jeffrey T., 225
Rienzi, Thomas M., 161
Ripka, Hubert, 213
Ritchie, Ronald S., 54, 78, 121
Roach, J.R., 34
Roberts, Adam, 66, 216
Roberts, Chalmers M., 54, 133
Roberts, Henry L., 12, 92, 213
Roberts, Jack, 66, 211
Robins, Yves, 161, 162
Robinson, Clarence A., Jr., 152, 175
Robinson, J.A., 27
Robison, David, 152, 170

Robson, Charles B., 114
Rocheron, Pierre, 85
Rock, Vincent P., 20
Rockefeller, Nelson A., 20, 21, 170
Rogers, (Gen.) Bernard W., 152
Rogers, Lindsay, 12
Rogers, William P., 54
Rokke, Erwin J., 46
Romaneski, (Col.) Albert Leo, 170
Rona, Thomas P., 70
Rorholt, Lars, 162
Rose, Eugene J., 54
Rose, Francois de, 85, 126, 152
Rose, (Maj.) John P., 182
Rose, Richard, 90
Rosecrance, R.N., 139
Rosecrance, Richard, 27, 54, 67, 190, 194
Rosen, Steven, 54
Rosenfeld, Stephen S., 54
Rosenthal, Benjamin S., 54, 133
Roskill, S.W., 7
Ross, Hugh, 21
Rostow, Eugene V., 21, 34, 54, 55, 133, 197
Rostow, Walt W., 28, 197
Rothstein, Robert L., 55
Rotvand, Georges, 85
Rowan, Sir Leslie, 121
Rubenstein, Alvin Z., 213
Rudnick, David, 162
Ruhl, Lothar, 55, 96, 138, 171
Ruhle, Hans, 109, 138
Ruhm von Oppen, Beate, 109
Rupp, Rainer W., 121
Rush, Kenneth, 55, 133
Rush, Myron, 219
Rusk, Dean, 24, 121, 190
Russett, Bruce M., 133, 152
Rustow, Dankwart A., 101
Rybkin, (Lt.-Col.) E., 221
Rzhevsky, Yuri, 213

Sabrosky, Alan Ned, 190
Sack, (Maj.) Thomas L., 175
Sadak, Necmiddin, 101
Saeter, Martin, 109
Sahinkaya, (Gen.) Tahsin, 101
Saint Brides, John Morrice Cairn Jones, Baron, 85
Salazar, Dr. Antonio de Oliveira, 99
Salisbury, Harrison E., 213
Salpeter, Eliahu, 67
Salter, Sir Arthur, 197
Salvadori, Massimo, 12
Samuel, (Lt. Col.) Wolfgang W.E., 152
Sanchez-Gijon, Antonio, 197
Sanders, John S., 71, 152
Sandler, Todd, 194
Sandoff, Lawrence R., 162
Sandoval, R.R., 181
Sandstron, Anders, 133
Sandwell, B.K., 7
Santilli, (Lt. Col.) Joseph, Jr., 152, 190
Sapin, Burton M., 7, 35
Sarkesian, Sam C., 55
Sassoon, Donald, 97
Sathyamurthy, T.V., 35
Sattler, James F., 133
Saulle, Maria R., 67
Saunders, (Comm.) Malcom G., 221
Schaetzel, J. Robert, 21, 35, 55, 67
Scheinman, Lawrence, 85, 138
Schelling, Thomas C., 152, 190
Schemmer, Benjamin F., 121, 159, 197
Schick, Jack M., 114, 115
Schilling, Warner R., 21, 43, 55, 166, 190
Schlamm, William S., 109
Schlesinger, Arthur, Jr., 21, 35, 44
Schlesinger, James R., 87, 152, 191
Schmid, Carlo, 109
Schmidt, Adolph W., 21
Schmidt, Helmut, 21, 35, 55, 109, 122
Schmuckle, Gerd, 152
Schneider, Andrew, 96
Schneider, Barry R., 162
Schneider, Ernest, 119
Schneider, Fred D., 78
Schneider, (Maj. Gen.) G., 171
Schneider, William, Jr., 221
Schoenthal, Klaus, 55
Schopflin, George, 152, 171, 213
Schroder, Gerhard, 109
Schuckburgh, (Sir) Evelyn, 55
Schultz, Heinz, 109
Schultze, Charles L., 122
Schulze, Franz-Joseph, 171
Schuman, Frederick L., 21
Schuman, Robert, 12, 85
Schumann, Maurice, 197
Schurkens, H., 162
Schutz, Klaus, 115
Schutz, Wilhelm Wolfgang, 12, 109, 110
Schwartz, David N., 191
Schwartz, Harry, 213
Schwarz, Hans Peter, 55
Schwarz, Urs, 21, 35, 152
Schweigler, Gebhard, 110
Schweitzer, Theodore, 96
Schwelien, Joachim, 55
Scott, Harriet Fast, 225
Scott, P.H., 67
Scoville, Herbert, Jr., 126, 191
Seabury, Paul, 35
Seagrave, Sterling, 152
Secclak, (Col.) William E., 191
Segni, Antonia, 21
Seim, Harvey G., 191
Serfaty, Simon, 55, 85, 99
Sestanovich, Stephan, 71
Seton-Watson, Hugh, 35, 213
Seybold, Calvin, 153

Sharp, Jane M.O., 126
Shearer, Richard E., 191
Shears, David, 110
Shell, Kurt L., 115
Shere, (Adm.) Harold E., 171
Sherman, Michael, 35
Sherman, Ronald, L., 171
Shisko, R., 159
Shohat, Murry, 162
Short, John, 92
Shreffler, R.G., 181, 191
Shtemenko, (Col.-Gen.) S.M., 221
Shtemenko, (Gen.) Sergei, 213
Shub, Anatole, 213
Shub, Joyce Lasky, 86
Shulman, Marshall D., 35, 56, 67, 213
Siegler, Heinrich von, 110
Silvestri, Stefano, 97
Simes, Dimitri K., 197
Simmons, Henry T., 162
Simpson, J.L., 103
Simpson, John, 162
Singer, J. David, 21
Sinnreich, Richard H., 191
Sjaastad, Anders C., 126
Skarlatos, Paul, 158
Skikker, Dirk, V., 67
Slambuk, George, 21
Sleiter (Adm. Ret.) Giovanni, 171
Slessor, Sir John, 12, 21, 92, 138, 153, 191
Slocombe, Walter, 153
Slominski, (Col.) Martin J., 126
Sloss, Leon, 67
Slusser, Robert M., 115
Smart, Ian, 66, 127, 133, 162
Smeeton, (Vice-Adm.) M.R., 180
Smirnov, (Vice-Adm.), 221
Smith, Gaddis, 56
Smith, Gerard, 182
Smith, Jean Edward, 56, 115

Smith, Mark E., 35
Smith, (Lt. Col.) Paul G., 56
Smith, R.G., 221
Smith, Sydney E., 153
Smith, (Gen.) W.Y., 153, 171
Smith, Walter Bedell, 7
Smoke, Richard, 145
Smyth, J.G., 153
Snow, Edward D., Jr., 138
Snyder, Glenn H., 21
Snyder, Jed, 79, 153
Snyder, Richard C., 7
Snyder, William P., 92
Sobik, (Col.) Erich, 225
Sokol, Anthony, 180
Sokolovsky, (Marshall), V.D., 221, 222
Sokolsky, Joel J., 77, 78, 222
Solberg, Carl, 56
Soll, Richard S., 224
Sommer, Theo, 22, 56, 110, 138
Sorensen, Theodore C., 56, 197
Sosnovy, Timothy, 222
Soustelle, Jacques, 86
Spaak, Paul-Henri, 12, 22, 35, 36, 191
Spanier, John W., 56
Sparring, Ashe, 96
Spaulding, Harry S., 122
Spiedel, (Gen.) Hans, 36
Speier, Hans, 110, 153
Speidel, (Gen.) Hans, 36
Spencer, Robert, 115
Spencer, Robert A., 79, 110
Speth, Gus, 122
Spielmann, Karl F., 218
Spinelli, Altiero, 22, 36
Spofford, Charles M., 7
Stacey, C.P., 79
Stahl, Walter, 110
Stambuk, George, 22
Stanger, Roland J., 115
Stanley, Timothy W., 12, 36, 56, 122, 133, 153, 191

Author Index

Stares, Paul, 86, 138
Starnes, John, 79
Starobin, Joseph R., 36
Starr, Richard F., 214
Staudenmaier, (Col.) William O., 153
Steel, Ronald, 22, 56
Steel, Sir Christopher, 92
Steeves, Thomas W., 153
Stefansson, Unnstein, 96
Stehle, Hansjakob, 110
Stehlin, Paul, 36
Stehlin, (Gen.) Paul, 153
Steibel, Gerard, L., 36
Stein, Arthur, 54
Steinbach, Udo, 101
Steinbrunner, John, 153
Steinbrunner, John D., 67
Steinhoff, (Gen.) Johannes, 67, 154, 191
Steinrucke, Rolf, 125
Stent, Angels E., 110, 122
Stenzl, Otto, 110
Stern, Frederick M., 12, 22
Stern, Geoffrey, 197
Stevens, (Col.) F.R., 197
Stevenson, Adlai Ewing, 7
Stewart, (Maj.) Leslie W., Jr., 57
Stewart, Michael, 92
Stewart-Smith, Geoffrey, 110
Stikker, Dirk U., 36, 86
Stoehrmann, (Lt.) Kenneth C., 162
Stoessel, Walter T., Jr., 71
Stone, Jeremy J., 127, 133
Stone, John, 162
Stone, Thomas R., 154
Storm, Walter, 214
Story, Jonathan, 99
Strachan, Hew, 92
Strachey, John, 22
Strang, Lord, 111
Strauss, Dr. Franz Josef, 36, 57, 111
Strausz-Hupe, Robert, 13, 22, 36, 86, 111, 214

Streit, Clarence K., 22
Struck, Myra, 191
Stueck, William, 214
Sugar, Peter F., 124
Sukovic, Olga, 133
Sullivan, Eugene P., 214
Sullivan, Leonard, Jr., 66, 122
Sulzberger, C.L., 94
Sundaram, Gowrie S., 162, 171
Sutherland, R.J., 79
Sutton, Anthony C., 197
Svetlov, B., 96
Swanborough, Gordon, 218
Swarztrauber, Sayre A., 180
Sweet, William, 122
Syed, Anwar, 22
Symms, Steven D., 138
Synhorst, (Capt.) Gerald E., 214
Szaz, A. Michael, 133
Szaz, Zoltan Michael, 111
Szent, Miklosy, Istvan, 36
Szulc, Tad, 127, 214

Talbott, Strobe, 214
Talensky, (Maj.-Gen.) N., 222
Tammen, Ronald L., 127, 154
Tatu, Michel, 57, 67, 86
Taubman, William, 49
Taylor, John W.R., 163
Taylor, Maxwell D., 22, 57
Taylor, (Gen.) Maxwell D., 67
Taylor, Paul, 97
Taylor, Phillip, 122
Taylor, William, 71
Teicher, Howard, 197
Terchek, Ronald J., 134
Theberg, James D., 42, 222
Thibault, (Capt.) George, 154
Thomas, David, 132
Thomas, John R., 222
Thompson, (Lt. Col.) James E., 111
Thompson, R.W., 79

Thompson, W.F.K., 171
Thompson, (Brig. Gen.) W.F.K., 134
Thorardson, Bruce, 79
Thrush, Aaron D., 214
Thumborg, Anders I., 138
Tighe, (Maj.) Earl E., 171
Tillema, Herbert K., 57, 92
Tilsen, Jonn C.F., IV., 154
Timbrell, Robert W., 122
Timbrell, (Rear Adm.) Robert W., 171
Timofeyev, K., 222
Tolmachov, P., 13
Tompkins, John S., 36
Tornudd, Klaus, 37
Towell, Pat, 122, 154
Tower, (Sen.) John, 197
Sowpik, A., 132
Toynbee, Philip, 138
Trager, Frank, 57
Train, Harry D., 180
Train, (ADM) Harry D., II, 72, 194
Treires, James J., 194
Treml, Vladimir G., 214
Treverton, Gregory F., 192, 194, 197
Trezise, Philip H., 68
Triemer, (Lt. Comdr.) William L., 95
Triska, Jan F., 214
Trotman, J.H., 57
Truman, Harry S., 13
Tsakalogannis, Panos, 94
Tsambiras, Sotirios, 122
Tucker, Gardiner, 122
Tucker, Gardiner L., 68, 163
Tucker, Robert C., 192
Turner, Arthur C., 7
Turner, Derek, 72
Turner, Stansfield (Adm.), 154
Tuthill, John W., 57, 123
Tuttle, Donald J., 57
Twining, (Gen.) Nathan F., 37
Twitchett, K.J., 57

Uhlig, Frank, Jr., 222
Ulam, Adam B., 57, 214, 215
Ullman, Marc, 86
Ullman, Richard H., 192
Ulsamer, Edgar, 154, 163
Ulstein, Egil, 154
Underwood, (LCDR) G.L., 154, 180
Unwin, Peter, 86, 92
Urban, B.R., 68, 98
Uri, Pierre, 22
Utgoff, Victor, 192

Vagts, Alfred, 4, 13
Valentine, (Col.) D.R., 163
Vali, Ferenc A., 101, 111
van Campen, S.I.P. 68, 97
Vance, Cyrus, 70, 127
van Dem, (Capt., Ret.) Nico, 180
Vandenberg, Arthur H., Jr., 8
van der Beugel, Ernst H., 37, 57, 198, 215
Vandevanter, E., Jr., 123
Van Hunn, (Lt. Col.), 86
van Lynden, (Rear Adm.) R.W., 172
Van Veen, E., 192
Van Wingen, John, 92
Vanicelli, Primo, 97
Vanscencelos, Alvaro, 154
Vatikiotis, P.J., 94
Vayrynen, Raimo, 58
Vego, Milan, 198
Vernant, Jacques, 86
Vernon, (Col.) Graham D., 222
Vernon, Raymond, 58, 123
Verrier, Anthony, 22, 92, 134
Vershinin, (Chief Air Marshal) K., 175
Vest, George S., 68, 73
Vidyasova, L., 134
Vigers, (colonel) T.W., 111
Vigor, P.H., 215
Vincent, R.J., 154

Author Index

Vlekke, B.H.M., 97
Volkov, Fyodor, 93
von Brentano, H., 111
von Cleave, William R., 155
von dem Bussche, Axel, 111
von Groll, Gotz, 58
von Hassel, Kai-Uwe, 22, 37
von Herwarth, Hans, 111
von Kielmansegg, (Gen.) J.A. Graf, 111
von Riekhoff, Harald, 37, 86
von Senger und Etterlin, (Gen.) F., 13
von Weizsacker, Carl-Fredrich, 155
von Zuhlsdorff, Volkmar, 19
Vukadinovic, Radovan, 215
Vuren, A.T. van, 97

Wagner, Wolfgang, 58, 111
Waites, Neville, 155
Walker, P.C. Gordon, 93
Walker, Rudolf F., 175
Walker, (Gen.) Walter, 155, 172
Wall, Patrick, 58, 68, 73, 155, 163, 172, 180, 198, 215
Wallace, William 68
Walsh, Bill, 163
Walton, Richard J., 58
Warburg, James, 37
Warburton, Anne, 123
Ward, Barbara, 4, 8
Ward, Chester C., 155
Warne, (Wing-Comm.) J.D., 8
Warnecke, Steven J., 50
Warner, Geoffrey, 22, 58, 86
Warnke, Paul C., 58, 68, 127, 155
Warnock, John W., 79
Warren, Jenny, 93
Warwick, Graham, 163
Waskow, Arthur I., 23
Wasserman, Sheri L., 70
Watson, Alan, 58

Watson, Hugh Seton, 23
Watt, Donald Cameron, 93
Watts, Anthony J., 111, 163
Webster, (Prof.) Sir Charles, 93
Weeks, Albert L., 125
Weers, (Col., Ret.) Mozes W.A., 97, 139
Wegener, Edward, 180
Weidenbaum, Murray L., 58
Weinland, Robert G., 223
Weinstein, Adalbert, 86, 155
Weintraub, Sydney, 123
Weiss, Seymour, 73, 126, 198
Wellershoff, (F. Adm.) Dieter, 124
Werth, Alexander, 225
Wertman, Douglas, 69
Wesche, (Rear-Adm.) H.H., 163
West, F.J., Jr., 73, 198
Wettern, Desmond, 180
Wettig, Gerhard,
Wetzel, (Maj. Gen.) Robert J., 163
Weymar, Paul, 111
Wheller, Barry C., 175
Wheeler, Tim, 134
Wheeler-Bennett, Sir John, 58
Shetten, Lawrence, 215
Whetten, Lawrence L., 58, 59, 112, 115, 172, 198, 223
Whitaker, Arthur P., 198, 199
White, Gilbert F., 4
White, William D., 175
Whitehead, Bill, 163
Whitely, Peter, 155
Whiteley, (Gen.) Peter, 172
Whitney, Thomas P., 215
Whitt, Darnell M., 56
Whittier, (Capt.) Henry S., Jr., 223
Wieck, Hans-Georg, 134
Wiegele, Thomas C., 172
Wiewiona, Boleslaw, 215

Wigforss, Harold, 199
Wighton, Charles, 112
Wigner, Eugene P., 129
Wilcox, Francis O., 23
Wilcox, John G., 124
Wildavsky, Aaron, 35
Wiles, P.J.D., 23
Wilkinson, Joe R., 80
Willetts, H.T., 216
Williams, Alan Lee, 59, 192
Williams, Francis, 93
Williams, Geoffrey Lee, 59
Williams, J. Emlyn, 59
Williams, John H., 8
Williams, Keith, 68
Williams, Phil, 127, 134
Williams, Roger, 93
Willis, F. Ray, 86
Willot, Albert, 134
Willrich, Mason, 127
Wilmot, Chester, 93, 155, 172
Wilson, (Col.) Minter L., Jr., 216
Wilson, Duncan, 93
Wilson, Paul A., 92
Wilson, Thomas W., Jr., 23
Wilson-Brown, (Maj.) M.S., 163
Windsor, Philip, 37, 59, 68, 112, 115, 199, 215, 216
Winkler, Theodor H., 139
Winne, (Col.) Clinton H., Jr., 127
Winton, John, 37
Winzer, Otto, 112
Wiseman, A., 212
Wiskemann, Elizabeth, 112, 115
Wohlstetter, Albert, 59, 139, 192
Wolf, Charles, Jr., 59, 124
Wolfe, Bertram D., 216
Wolfe, James H., 112
Wolfe, Thomas W., 216, 223
Wolfers, Arnold, 13, 23, 37, 194
Wood, Colonel Robert J., 172

Wood, Derek, 180
Wood, John, 123
Woodcock, Michael J., 163
Woodhouse, C.M., 13, 93
Woods, William H., 216
Wooldridge, E.T., 223
Woolsey, James, 155
Worner, Manfred, 112, 192
Worsthorne, Peregrine, 93
Wright, Quincy, 8
Wyle, Frederick S., 59, 127, 134
Wyllie, T.H., 199

Yakubovsky, I.I., 223
Yalcin, Aydin, 101
Yarmolinsky, Adam, 37, 38, 59
Yefremov, V., 216
Yeremenko, Marshal A., 216
Yochelson, John, 59, 134
Yochelson, John N., 73
Yost, Charles, 59, 73
Yost, David, 87
Yost, David S., 127, 134, 157, 172
Younger, Kenneth, 11, 93
Yudin, Y., 124
Yuriev, N., 134

Z, 59
Zakharov, Marshal M., 223
Zakheim, Dov S., 172
Zavilov, I., 225
Zea, (Lt. Cmdr.) Antonio, 199
Zelda, K., 88
Zellentin, Gerda, 59, 73
Zimmerman, Peter D., 134
Zimmerman, William, 216
Zinner, Paul E., 216
Zoppo, Ciro Elliott, 38
Zimwalt, Elmo R., 172